HISTORY
OF
ANCIENT LITERATURE

HISTORY OF ANCIENT LITERATURE

P. K. Sinha
Jagdish K. Ghosh

Commonwealth

History of Ancient Literature

Edition : 2020

ISBN 978-81-311-0320-3

Published by :
COMMONWEALTH PUBLISHERS PVT. LTD.
4831/24, Prahlad Street,
Ansari Road, Darya Ganj,
New Delhi - 110002
Ph. : 23275511, 23257835
e-mail : commonwealthbooks@gmail.com

Laser Typesetting by :
Arnav Computers
Delhi

Printed at :
Roshan Offset Printers
Delhi

Preface

The history of literature begins with the history of writing, in Bronze Age Mesopotamia and Ancient Egypt, although the oldest literary texts that have come down to us date to several centuries after the invention of writing; to the mid 3rd millennium BC. The earliest written literature dates from about 2600 BC, when the Sumerians started to write down their long epic poems. The earliest literary authors known by name are Shuruppak and Urukagina, dating to ca. the 27th and 24th centuries BC, respectively.

The present book *History of Ancient Literature* offers the general reader help of every kind in understanding of ancient literature. The main focus of this book remains the lives and works of the principal authors of ancient period. More than a book of authors and titles, this work illumines the faded images of mythological and historical figures.

This book is intended for advanced level students of literature, who are taking exams or modules in this field. It may also be suitable for teachers, researchers and the general reader who is interested in the history of literature. The breadth and accuracy of this volume will surely make it the standard reference book of its kind for years to come.

Authors

Contents

1

History of Literature

The history of literature begins with the history of writing, in Bronze Age Mesopotamia and Ancient Egypt, although the oldest literary texts that have come down to us date to a full millennium after the invention of writing, to the late 3rd millennium BC. The earliest literary authors known by name are Ptahhotep and Enheduanna, dating to ca. the 24th and 23rd centuries BC, respectively.

Texts handed down by oral tradition such as the Hindu Rigveda may predate their fixation in written form by several centuries, or, in extreme cases, even millennia. In ancient Iran, Avesta and Gahani poems and Gathas were written around 1000 BC. Classical Antiquity is usually considered to begin with Homer, in the 8th century BC. Many older literary texts are known, but often difficult to date. This includes the texts in the Hebrew Bible, the Pentateuch being traditionally dated to the 15th century BC, while modern scholars put it to the 10th century BC at the very earliest. An early example is the so called *Egyptian Book of the Dead* which was eventually written down in the *Papyrus of Ani* around 1240 BC, but other individuals' versions of the book probably date from about the 18th century BC.

Beginnings of Literature

Literature and writing, though obviously connected, are not synonymous. The very first writings from ancient Sumer by any reasonable definition do not constitute literature—the same is true of some of the early Egyptian hieroglyphics or the thousands of logs from ancient Chinese regimes. Scholars have always disagreed concerning when written record-keeping became more like "literature" than anything else; the definition is largely subjective.

Moreover, it must be borne in mind that, given the significance of distance as a cultural isolator in earlier centuries, the historical development of literature did not occur at an even pace across the world. The problems of creating a uniform global history of literature are compounded by the fact that many texts have been lost over the millennia, either deliberately, by accident, or by the total disappearance of the originating culture. Much has been written, for example, about the destruction of the Library of Alexandria in the 1st century BC, and the innumerable key texts which are believed to have been lost forever to the flames. The deliberate suppression of texts (and often their authors) by organisations of either a spiritual or a temporal nature further shrouds the subject.

Certain primary texts, however, may be isolated which have a qualifying role as literature's first stirrings. Very early examples are *Epic of Gilgamesh,* in its Sumerian version predating 2000 BC, and the *Egyptian Book of the Dead* written down in the *Papyrus of Ani* in approximately 250 BC but probably dates from about the 18th century BC. Ancient Egyptian literature was not included in early studies of the history of literature because the writings of Ancient Egypt were not translated into European languages until the 19th century when the Rosetta stone was deciphered.

Many texts handed down by oral tradition over several centuries before they were fixed in written form are difficult or impossible to date. The core of the Rigveda may date to the mid 2nd millennium BC. The Pentateuch is traditionally dated to the 15th century, although modern scholarship estimates its oldest part to date to the 10th century BC at the earliest.

Homer's *Iliad* and *Odyssey* date to the 8th century BC and mark the beginning of Classical Antiquity. They also stand in an oral tradition that stretches back to the late Bronze Age.

Indian œruti texts post-dating the Rigveda (such as the Yajurveda, the Atharvaveda and the Brahmanas), as well as the Hebrew Tanakh and the mystical collection of poems attributed to Lao Tze, the Tao te Ching, date to the Iron Age, but their dating is difficult and controversial. The great Hindu epics were also transmitted orally, likely predating the Maurya period. Other oral traditions were fixed in writing much later, such as the *Elder Edda,* written down in the 12th or 13th century.

Chinese Literature

China than in Europe prior to 1000, as multiple new forms developed in the Han, Tang, and Song dynasties: perhaps the greatest poets of this era in Chinese literature were Li Bai and Du Fu. Printing began in Tang Dynasty China. A copy of the *Diamond Sutra,* a key Buddhist text, found sealed in a cave in China in the early 20th century, is the oldest known dated printed book, with a printed date of 868. The method used was block printing.

The scientist, statesman, and general Shen Kuo (1031-1095 AD) was the author of the groundbreaking *Dream Pool Essays* (1088), a large book of scientific literature that included the oldest description of the magnetised compass. During the Song Dynasty, there was also the enormous historical work of the *Zizhi Tongjian*, compiled into 294 volumes of 3 million written Chinese characters by the year 1084 AD.

Some authors feel that China originated the novel form with the *Romance of the Three Kingdoms* by Luo Guanzhong (in the 14th century), although others feel that this epic is distinct from the novel in key ways.

Greek Literature

Ancient Greek society placed considerable emphasis upon literature. Many authors consider the western literary tradition to have begun with the epic poems *The Iliad* and *The Odyssey*, which remain giants in the literary canon for their skillful and vivid depictions of war and peace, honor and disgrace, love and hatred. Notable among later Greek poets was Sappho, who defined, in many ways, lyric poetry as a genre.

A playwright named Aeschylus changed Western literature forever when he introduced the ideas of dialogue and interacting characters to playwriting. In doing so, he essentially invented "drama": his *Oresteia* trilogy of plays is seen as his crowning achievement. Other refiners of playwriting were Sophocles and Euripides. Sophocles is credited with skillfully developing irony as a literary technique, most famously in his play *Oedipus the King*. Euripedes, conversely, used plays to challenge societal norms and mores—a hallmark of much of Western literature for the next 2,300 years and beyond—and his works such as *Medea, The Bacchae* and *The Trojan Women* are still notable for their ability to challenge our perceptions of propriety, gender, and war. Aristophanes, a comic playwright, defines and shapes the idea of comedy almost as Aeschylus had shaped tragedy as an art form—Aristophanes' most famous plays include the *Lysistrata* and *The Frogs.*

Philosophy entered literature in the dialogues of Plato, who converted the give and take of Socratic questioning into written form. Aristotle, Plato's student, wrote dozens of works on many scientific disciplines, but his greatest contribution to literature was likely his *Poetics,* which lays out his understanding of drama, and thereby establishes the first criteria for literary criticism.

The New Testament is an unusual collection of texts—Paul's epistles are the first collection of personal letters to be treated as literature, the Gospels arguably present the first realistic biographies in Western literature, and John's *Book of Revelation,* though not the first of its kind, essentially defines apocalypse as a literary genre.

Latin Literature

In many respects, the writers of the Roman Republic and the Roman Empire chose to avoid innovation in favor of imitating the great Greek authors. Virgil's *Aeneid,* in many respects, emulated Homer's *Iliad;* Plautus, a comic playwright, followed in the footsteps of Aristophanes; Tacitus' *Annals* and *Germania* follow essentially the same historical approaches that Thucydides devised (the Christian historian Eusebius does also, although far more influenced by his religion than either Tacitus or Thucydides had been by Greek and Roman polytheism); Ovid and his *Metamorphoses* explore the same Greek myths again in new ways. It can be argued, and has been, that the Roman authors, far from being mindless copycats, improved on the genres already established by their Greek predecessors. For example Ovid's *Metamorphoses* creates a form which is a clear predecessor of the stream of consciousness genre. What is undeniable is that the Romans, in comparison with the Greeks, innovate relatively few literary styles of their own.

Satire is one of the few Roman additions to literature—Horace was the first to use satire extensively as a tool for argument, and Juvenal made it into a weapon. Augustine of Hippo and his *The City of God* do for religious literature essentially what Plato had done for philosophy, but Augustine's approach was far less conversational and more didactive. His *Confessions* is perhaps the first true autobiography, and it gave rise to the genre of confessional literature which is now more popular than ever.

Indian Literature

Indian epics such as *Ramayana* and *Mahabharata,* have influenced countless other works, including Balinese Kecak and other performances such as shadow puppetry (wayang), and many European works. Pali literature has an important position in the rise of Buddhism. Classical Sanskrit literature flowers in the Maurya and Gupta periods, roughly spanning the 2nd century BC to the 8th century AD.

European Literature

After the fall of Rome (in roughly 476), many of the

literary approaches and styles invented by the Greeks and Romans fell out of favor in Europe. In the millennium or so that intervened between Rome's fall and the Florentine Renaissance, medieval literature focused more and more on faith and faith-related matters, in part because the works written by the Greeks had not been preserved in Europe, and therefore there were few models of classical literature to learn from and move beyond. What little there was became changed and distorted, with new forms beginning to develop from the distortions. Some of these distorted beginnings of new styles can be seen in the literature generally described as Matter of Rome, Matter of France and Matter of Britain.

Following Rome's fall, Islam's spread across Asia and Africa brought with it a desire to preserve and build upon the work of the Greeks, especially in literature. Although much had been lost to the ravages of time (and to catastrophe, as in the burning of the Library of Alexandria), many Greek works remained extant: they were preserved and copied carefully by Muslim scribes.

In Europe Hagiographies, or "lives of the saints", are frequent among early medieval texts. The writings of Bede—*Historia ecclesiastica gentis Anglorum*—and others continue the faith-based historical tradition begun by Eusebius in the early 300s. Playwriting essentially ceased, except for the mystery plays and the passion plays that focused heavily on conveying Christian belief to the common people. Around 400 AD the *Prudenti Psychomachia* began the tradition of allegorical tales. Poetry flourished, however, in the hands of the troubadours, whose courtly romances and *chanson de geste* amused and entertained the upper classes who were their patrons. Geoffrey of Monmouth wrote works which he claimed were histories of Britain. These were highly fanciful and included stories of Merlin the magician and King Arthur. Epic poetry continued to develop with the addition of the mythologies of Northern Europe: *Beowulf* and the Norse sagas have much in common with Homer and Virgil's approaches to war and honor, while poems such as Dante's *Divine Comedy* and Geoffrey Chaucer's *The Canterbury Tales* take much different stylistic directions.

In November 1095 - Pope Urban II preached the First Crusade at the Council of Clermont. The crusades would affect everything in Europe and the Middle East for many years to come and literature would, along with everything else, be transformed by the wars between these two cultures. For instance the image of the knight would take on a different significance. Also the Islamic emphasis on scientific investigation and the presevation of the Greek philosophical writings would eventually affect European literature.

Between Augustine and *The Bible*, religious authors had numerous aspects of Christianity that needed further explication and interpretation. Thomas Aquinas, more than any other single person, was able to turn theology into a kind of science, in part because he was heavily influenced by Aristotle, whose works were returning to Europe in the 1200s.

Japanese Literature

Classical Japanese literature generally refers to literature produced during the Heian Period, what some would consider a golden era of art and literature. *The Tale of Genji* (early eleventh century) by Murasaki

Shikibu is considered the pre-eminent masterpiece of Heian fiction and an early example of a work of fiction in the form of a novel. It is sometimes called the world's first novel, the first modern novel, the first romance novel, the first psychological novel, or the first novel to still be considered a classic.

Other important works of this period include the *Kokin Wakashû* (905), a waka-poetry anthology, and *The Pillow Book* (990s), the latter written by Murasaki Shikibu's contemporary and rival, Sei Shônagon, as an essay about the life, loves, and pastimes of nobles in the Emperor's court. The *iroha* poem, now one of two standard orderings for the Japanese syllabary, was also written during the early part of this period.

The 10th century Japanese narrative, *The Tale of the Bamboo Cutter*, can be considered an early example of proto-science fiction. The protagonist of the story, Kaguya-hime, is a princess from the Moon who is sent to Earth for safety during a celestial war, and is found and raised by a bamboo cutter in Japan. She is later taken back to the Moon by her real extraterrestrial family. A manuscript illustration depicts a disc-shaped flying object similar to a flying saucer.

In this time the imperial court patronised the poets, most of whom were courtiers or ladies-in-waiting. Editing anthologies of poetry was a national pastime. Reflecting the aristocratic atmosphere, the poetry was elegant and sophisticated and expressed emotions in a rhetorical style.

Renaissance Literature

Had nothing occurred to change literature in the 1400s but the Renaissance, the break with medieval approaches would have been clear enough. The 1400s, however, also brought Johann Gutenberg and his invention of the printing press, an innovation (for Europe, at least) that would change literature forever. Texts were no longer precious and expensive to produce—they could be cheaply and rapidly put into the marketplace. Literacy went from the prised possession of the select few to a much broader section of the population (though by no means universal). As a result, much about literature in Europe was radically altered in the two centuries following Gutenberg's unveiling of the printing press in 1455.

William Caxton was the first English printer and published English language texts including *Le Morte d'Arthur* (a collection of oral tales of the Arthurian Knights which is a forerunner of the novel) and Geoffrey Chaucer's *Canterbury Tales*. These are an indication of future directions in literature. With the arrival of the printing press a process begins in which folk yarns and legends are collected within a frame story and then mass published.

In the Renaissance, the focus on learning for learning's sake causes an outpouring of literature. Petrarch popularised the sonnet as a poetic form; Giovanni Boccaccio's *Decameron* made romance acceptable in prose as well as poetry; François Rabelais rejuvenates satire with *Gargantua and Pantagruel*; Michel de Montaigne single-handedly invented the essay and used it to catalog his life and ideas. Perhaps the most controversial and important work of the time period was a treatise printed in Nuremberg, entitled *De Revolutionibus Orbium Coelestium*: in it, the astronomer Nicolaus Copernicus removed the Earth from its privileged position in the universe, which had far-reaching effects, not only in science, but in literature and its approach to humanity, hierarchy, and truth.

Islamic Literature

The most well known fiction from the Islamic world was *The Book of One Thousand and One Nights* (*Arabian Nights*), which was a compilation of many earlier folk tales told by the Persian Queen Scheherazade. The epic took form in the 10th century and reached its final form by the 14th century; the number and type of tales have varied from one manuscript to another. All Arabian fantasy tales were often called "Arabian Nights" when translated into English, regardless of whether they appeared in *The Book of One Thousand and One Nights*, in any version, and a number of tales are known in Europe as "Arabian Nights" despite existing in no Arabic manuscript.

This epic has been influential in the West since it was translated in the 18th century, first by Antoine Galland. Many imitations were written, especially in France. Various characters from this epic have themselves become cultural icons in Western culture, such as Aladdin, Sinbad and Ali Baba. However, no medieval Arabic source has been traced for Aladdin, which was incorporated into *The Book of One Thousand and One Nights* by its French translator, Antoine Galland, who heard it from an Arab Syrian Christian storyteller from Aleppo. Part of its popularity may have sprung from the increasing historical and geographical knowledge, so that places of which little was known and so marvels were plausible had to be set further "long ago" or farther "far away"; this is a process that continues, and finally culminate in the fantasy world having little connection, if any, to actual times and places. A number of elements from Arabian mythology and Persian mythology are now common in modern fantasy, such as genies, bahamuts, magic carpets, magic lamps, etc. When L. Frank Baum proposed writing a modern fairy tale that banished stereotypical elements, he included the genie as well as the dwarf and the fairy as stereotypes to go.

A number of stories within the *One Thousand and One Nights* (*Arabian Nights*) also feature science fiction elements. One example is "The Adventures of Bulukiya", where the protagonist Bulukiya's quest for the herb of immortality leads him to explore the seas, journey to the Garden of Eden and to Jahannam, and travel across the cosmos to different worlds much larger than his own world, anticipating elements of galactic science fiction; along the way, he encounters societies of jinns, mermaids, talking serpents, talking trees, and other forms of life. In another *Arabian Nights* tale, the protagonist Abdullah the Fisherman gains the ability to breathe underwater and discovers an underwater submarine society that is portrayed as an inverted reflection of society on land, in that the underwater society follows a form of primitive communism where concepts like money and clothing do not exist.

Other *Arabian Nights* tales deal with lost ancient technologies, advanced ancient civilisations that went astray, and catastrophes which overwhelmed them. "The City of Brass" features a group of travellers on an archaeological expedition across the Sahara to find an ancient lost city and attempt to recover a brass vessel that Solomon once used to trap a jinn, and, along the way, encounter a mummified queen, petrified inhabitants, life-like humanoid robots and automata, seductive marionettes dancing without strings, and a brass horseman robot who directs the party towards the ancient city. "The Ebony Horse" features a robot in the form of a flying mechanical horse controlled using keys that could fly into outer space and towards the Sun, while the "Third Qalandar's Tale" also features a robot in the form of an uncanny boatman. "The City of Brass" and "The Ebony Horse" can be considered early examples of proto-science fiction.

A famous example of Arabic poetry and Persian poetry on romance (love) is *Layla and Majnun,* dating back to the Umayyad era in the 7th century. It is a tragic story of undying love much like the later *Romeo and Juliet,* which was itself said to have been inspired by a Latin version of *Layli and Majnun* to an extent.

Dante Alighieri's *Divine Comedy,* considered the greatest epic of Italian literature, derived many features of and episodes about the hereafter directly or indirectly from Arabic works on Islamic eschatology: the *Hadith* and the *Kitab al-Miraj* (translated into Latin in 1264 or shortly before as *Liber Scale Machometi,* "The Book of Muhammad's Ladder") concerning Muhammad's ascension to Heaven, and the spiritual writings of Ibn Arabi.

The Moors also had a noticeable influence on the works of George Peele and William Shakespeare. Some of their works featured Moorish characters, such as Peele's *The Battle of Alcazar* and Shakespeare's *The Merchant of Venice, Titus Andronicus* and *Othello,* which featured a Moorish Othello as its title character. These works are said to have been inspired by several Moorish delegations from Morocco to Elizabethan England at the beginning of the 17th century.

Ibn Tufail (Abubacer) and Ibn al-Nafis were pioneers of the philosophical novel. Ibn Tufail wrote the first fictional Arabic novel *Hayy ibn Yaqdhan* (*Philosophus Autodidactus*) as a response to al-Ghazali's *The Incoherence of the Philosophers,* and then Ibn al-Nafis also wrote a novel *Theologus Autodidactus* as a response to Ibn Tufail's *Philosophus Autodidactus.* Both of these narratives had protagonists (Hayy in *Philosophus Autodidactus* and Kamil in *Theologus Autodidactus*) who were autodidactic feral children living in seclusion on a desert island, both being the earliest examples of a desert island story. However, while Hayy lives alone with animals on the desert island for the rest of the story in *Philosophus Autodidactus,* the story of Kamil extends beyond the desert island setting in *Theologus Autodidactus,* developing into the earliest known coming of age plot and eventually becoming the first example of a science fiction novel.

Theologus Autodidactus, written by the Arabian polymath Ibn al-Nafis (1213-1288), is the first example of a science fiction novel. It deals with various science fiction elements such as spontaneous generation, futurology, the end of the world and doomsday, resurrection, and the afterlife. Rather than giving supernatural or mythological explnations for these events, Ibn al-Nafis attempted to explain these plot elements using the scientific knowledge of biology, astronomy, cosmology and geology known in his time. His main purpose behind this science fiction work was to explain Islamic religious teachings in terms of science and philosophy through the use of fiction.

A Latin translation of Ibn Tufail's work, *Philosophus Autodidactus,* first appeared in 1671, prepared by Edward Pococke the Younger, followed by an English translation by Simon Ockley in 1708, as well as German and Dutch translations. These translations later inspired Daniel Defoe to write *Robinson Crusoe,* regarded as the first novel in English. *Philosophus Autodidactus* also inspired Robert Boyle to write his own philosophical novel set on an island, *The Aspiring Naturalist.* The story also anticipated Rousseau's *Emile: or, On Education* in some ways, and is also similar to Mowgli's story in Rudyard Kipling's *The Jungle Book* as well as Tarzan's story, in that a baby is abandoned but taken care of and fed by a mother wolf. Among other innovations in Arabic literature was Ibn Khaldun's perspective on chronicling past events—by fully rejecting supernatural explanations, Khaldun essentially invented the scientific or sociological approach to history.

Persian Literature

From Persian culture the book which would, eventually, become the most famous in the west is the *Rubaiyat of Omar Khayyam.* The Rubáiyát is a collection of poems by the Persian mathematician and astronomer Omar Khayyám (1048-1122). "Rubaiyat" means "quatrains": verses of four lines.

Ferdowsi's *Shahnameh,* the national epic of Iran, is a mythical and heroic retelling of Persian history. *Amir Arsalan* was also a popular mythical Persian story, which has influenced some modern works of fantasy fiction, such as *The Heroic Legend of Arslan.*

Examples of early Persian proto-science fiction include Al-Farabi's *Opinions of the residents of a splendid city* about a utopian society, Al-Qazwini's futuristic tale of *Awaj bin Anfaq* about a man who travelled to Earth from a distant planet, and elements such as the flying carpet.

Ottoman Literature

The two primary streams of Ottoman written literature are poetry and prose. Of the two, poetry—specifically, Divan poetry—was by far the dominant stream. Moreover, it should be noted that, until the 19th century, Ottoman prose did not contain any examples of fiction; that is, there were no counterparts to, for instance, the European romance, short story, or novel (though analogous genres did, to some extent, exist in both the Turkish folk tradition and in Divan poetry).

Until the 19th century, Ottoman prose never managed to develop to the extent that contemporary Divan poetry did. A large part of the reason for this was that much prose was expected to adhere to the rules of *sec'*, or rhymed prose, a type of writing descended from the Arabic *saj'* and which prescribed that between each adjective and noun in a sentence, there must be a rhyme.

Early Modern Literature

A new spirit of science and investigation in Europe was part of a general upheaval in human understanding which began with the European invasion of the New World in 1492 and continues through the subsequent centuries, even up to the present day.

The form of writing now commonplace across the world—the novel—originated from the early modern period and grew in popularity in the next century. Before the modern novel became established as a form there first had to be a transitional stage when "novelty" began to appear in the style of the epic poem.

Plays for entertainment (as opposed to religious enlightenment) returned to Europe's stages in the early modern period. William Shakespeare is the most notable of the early modern playwrights, but numerous others made important contributions, including Christopher Marlowe, Molière, and Ben Jonson. From the 16th to the 18th century Commedia dell'arte performers improvised in the streets of Italy and France. Some Commedia dell'arte plays were written down. Both the written plays and the improvisation were influential upon literature of the time, particularly upon the work of Molière. Shakespeare, and his associate Robert Armin, drew upon the arts of jesters and strolling players in creating new style comedies. All the parts, even the female ones, were played by men (*en travesti*) but that would change, first in France and then in England too, by the end of the 17th century.

The epic Elizabethan poem *The Faerie Queene* by Edmund Spenser was published, in its first part, in 1590 and then in completed form in 1597. *The Fairie Queen* marks the transitional period in which "novelty" begins to enter in to the narrative in the sense of overturning and playing with the flow of events. Theatrical forms known in Spenser's time such as The Masque and the Mummers' Play are incorporated into the poem in ways which *twist tradition* and turn it to political propaganda in the service of Queen Elizabeth I.

The earliest work considered an opera in the sense the work is usually understood dates from around 1597. It is *Dafne,* (now lost) written by Jacopo Peri for an elite circle of literate Florentine humanists who gathered as the "Camerata".

Miguel de Cervantes's *Don Quixote de la Mancha* has been called "the first novel" by many literary scholars (or the first of the modern European novels). It was published in two parts. The first part was published in 1605 and the second in 1615. It might be viewed as a parody of *Le Morte d'Arthur* (and other examples of the chivalric romance), in which case the novel form would be the direct result of poking fun at a collection of heroic folk legends. This is fully in keeping with the spirit of the age of enlightenment which began from about this time and delighted in giving a satirical twist to the stories and ideas of the past. It's worth noting that this trend toward satirising previous writings was only made possible by the printing press. Without the invention of mass produced copies of a book it would not be possible to assume the reader will have seen the earlier work and will thus understand the references within the text.

The new style in English poetry during the 17th century was that of the metaphysical movement. The metaphysical poets were John Donne, George Herbert, Andrew Marvell, Thomas Traherne, Henry Vaughan and others. Metaphysical poetry is characterised by a spirit of intellectual investigation of the spiritual, rather than the mystical reverence of many earlier English poems. The metaphysical poets were clearly trying to *understand* the world around them and the spirit behind it, instead of accepting dogma on the basis of faith.

In the middle of the century the king of England was overthrown and a republic declared. In the new regime (which lasted from 1649 to 1653) the arts suffered. In England and the rest of the British Isles Oliver Cromwell's rule temporarily banned all theatre, festivals, jesters, mummers plays and frivolities. The ban was lifted when the monarchy was restored with Charles II. Thomas Killigrew and the Drury Lane theatre were favorites of King Charles.

In contrast to the metaphysical poets was John Milton's *Paradise Lost,* an epic religious poem in blank verse. Milton had been Oliver Cromwell's chief propagandist and suffered when the Restoration came. *Paradise Lost* is one of the highest developments of the epic form in poetry immediately preceding the era of the modern prose novel.

2

History of Writing

The history of writing follows the art of expressing words by letters or other marks. In the history of how systems of representation of language through graphic means have evolved in different human civilisations, more complete writing systems were preceded by proto-writing, systems of ideographic and/or early mnemonic symbol. Language expresses thought, preserves thought, and also suggests or creates thought. It has been considered obvious that, so long as language is unwritten, it can accomplish these ends only in a very imperfect measure. Hence it may well be supposed that, at a very early stage of man's history, attempts were made to present in some way to the eye the thought which spoken language conveyed to the ear, and thus give it visible form and permanence. However, this understanding does not necessarily go unquestioned. True writing, or phonetic writing, records were developed independently in four different civilisations in the world, namely Sumeria, Egypt, China, and Mesoamerica.

Writing Systems

Writing systems are distinguished from other possible symbolic communication systems in that one must usually understand something of the associated spoken language to comprehend the text. By contrast, other possible symbolic systems such as information signs, painting, maps, and mathematics often do not require prior knowledge of a spoken language. Every human community possesses language, a feature regarded by many as an innate and defining condition of mankind. However the development of writing systems, and the process by which they have supplanted traditional oral systems of communication has been sporadic, uneven and slow. Once established, writing systems on the whole change more slowly than their spoken counterparts, and often preserve features and expressions which are no longer current in the spoken language. The great benefit of writing systems is their ability to maintain a persistent record of information expressed in a language, which can be retrieved.

The various kinds of writing which have been in use in different ages and in different parts of the world may be classified in two great divisions, according as the object of their inventors was to present the ideas to which they wished to give visible expression directly and immediately to the mind, or indirectly, through the medium of spoken language. Scholars make reasonable definition between prehistory and history with writing. Scholars have disagreed concerning when prehistory becomes history and when proto-writing became "true writing"; the definition is largely subjective. Writing, in its most general terms, is just a drawn device to indicate a message and is composed of glyphs.

The various methods — the ideographic and the phonographic or phonetic — has its attendant advantages and disadvantages; but the advantages of the latter method greatly preponderate. The principal recommendation of the former method, in which the depicted idea is caught up immediately by the mind, is that it addresses itself to a much wider circle than the latter, being intelligible by all classes and in all countries; whereas the latter, in which the sound is depicted, not the idea, is of course intelligible only to those who are acquainted with the language to which the depicted word belongs. On the other hand, the very serious drawbacks attendant upon the direct method are:

1. That it is capable of giving distinct expression only to a very limited range of ideas, viz. the ideas of sensible objects and qualities, and if it attempts to go beyond that range at once becomes arbitrary and obscure; and

2. That in its representation even of the limited class of ideas to which it is capable of giving distinct expression, it is cumbrous and altogether unfitted for general use.

The emergence of writing in a given area is usually followed by several centuries of fragmentary inscriptions. With the presence of coherent texts (such that is from the various writing systems and the system's associated literature), historians mark the "historicity" of that culture. The sacred writing of the Egyptians may be regarded as forming a stage of transition between the ideographic and the phonetic sorts of writing described. Till the 20th century, the received opinion was that the ancient Egyptian was an exclusively ideographic writing, and to this conclusion the testimonies of those ancient writers who have given any account of it seemed to point. But the labors of various scholars, during the end of the 19th-century, threw light on those ancient characters; and, though very possibly a picture writing originally, the hieroglyphic, in the form in which it appears on the most ancient monuments, and which it retains unchanged down to the early centuries after Christ, bears a composite character, being in part ideographic, in part phonetic. Accordingly, the characters are used in three different ways:

1. Pictorial use, in which the character is designed to convey to the mind the idea of the object it represents, and nothing more. This pictorial representation sometimes stands instead of a phonetic name for the object, but the most common use of it is to make the phonetic group of characters more intelligible by being subjoined to them. Thus, to the names of individuals the figure of a man is subjoined.
2. Hieroglyphical writing is the symbolical, in which the object delineated is not meant to convey to the mind the idea of itself, but of something associated with it and suggested by it.
3. Phonetic writing, is really by far the most extensive. The greater part of the characters are as truly letters as if the language were English or Greek; syllable characters are the exception, not the rule.

In the ancient Egyptian inscription of any length it is found these three modes of writing in use together, but with a great predominance of phonetic.

Developmental Stages

A conventional "proto-writing to true writing" system follows a general series of developmental stages:

1) *Picture writing system*: glyphs represent directly objects and ideas or objective and ideational

situations. In connection with this the following substages may be distinguished:

a) The mnemonic: glyphs primarily a reminder;

b) The pictographic (pictography): glyphs represent directly an object or an objective situation such as (a)chronological, (b) notices, (c) communications, (d) totems, titles, and names, (e) religious, (f) customs, (g) historical, and (h) biographical;

c) The ideographic (ideography): glyphs represent directly an idea or an ideational situation.

2) *Transitional system*: glyphs refer not only to the object or idea which it represents but to its name as well.

3) *Phonetic system*: glyphs refer to sounds or spoken symbols irrespective of their meanings. This resolves itself into the following substages:

a) The verbal: glyphs represents a whole word;

b) The syllabic: glyphs represent a syllable;

c) The alphabetic: glyphs represent an elementary sound.

The best known picture 'writing system of ideographic and/or early mnemonic symbols are:

1) Jiahu Script, symbols on tortoise shells in Jiahu, ca. 6600 BC

2) Vinca script (Tartaria tablets), ca. 4500 BC

3) Early Indus script, ca. 3500 BC

True writing, or phonetic writing, records were developed independently in four different civilisations in the world. Writing systems developed from neolithic writing in the Early Bronze Age (4th millennium BC). The invention of the phonetic system is roughly contemporary with the beginning of the Bronze Age in the late Neolithic of the late 4th millennium BC. The Sumerian archaic cuneiform script and the Egyptian hieroglyphs are generally considered the earliest writing systems, both emerging out of their ancestral proto-literate symbol systems from 3400–3200 BC with earliest coherent texts from about 2600 BC. The Chinese and Mesopotamian Phonetic systems have especially been influential in the development of the systems of writing in use in the world today.

Literature and Writing

Literature and writing, though obviously connected, are not synonymous. The very first writings from ancient Sumer by any reasonable definition do not constitute literature — the same is true of some of the early Egyptian hieroglyphics or the thousands of logs from ancient Chinese regimes. The *history of literature* begins with the history of writing and the notion of "literature" has different meanings depending on who is using it. Scholars have disagreed concerning when written record-keeping became more like "literature" than anything else and is largely subjective. It could be applied broadly to mean any symbolic record, encompassing everything from images and sculptures to letters. The oldest literary texts that have come down to us date to a full millennium after the invention of writing, to the late 3rd millennium BC. The earliest literary authors known by name are Ptahhotep and Enheduanna, dating to ca. the 24th and 23rd centuries BC, respectively. In the early literate societies, as much as 600 years passed from the first inscriptions to the first coherent textual sources.

Locations and Timeframes

Proto-writing

The history of human communication dates back to the earliest era of humanity. Symbols were developed about 30,000 years ago, and writing about 7,000. The early writing systems of the late 4th millennium BC are not considered a sudden invention. Rather, they were based on ancient traditions of symbol systems that cannot be classified as writing proper, but have many characteristics strikingly reminiscent of writing. These systems may be described as *proto-writing*. They used ideographic and/or early mnemonic symbols to convey information yet were probably devoid of direct linguistic content. These systems emerged in the early Neolithic period, as early as the 7th millennium BC.

Europe and Near East

The Vinca signs show an evolution of simple symbols beginning in the 7th millennium, gradually increasing in complexity throughout the 6th millennium and culminating in the Tartaria tablets of the 5th millennium with their rows of symbols carefully aligned, evoking the impression of a "text". The "Slavic runes" mentioned by a few medieval authors may also have been a system of proto-writing. The Quipu of the Incas (sometimes called "talking knots") may have been of a similar nature. A historical example is the system of pictographs invented by Uyaquk before the developed of the Yugtun syllabary.

The Dispilio Tablet of the late 6th millennium is similar. The hieroglyphic scripts of the Ancient Near East (Egyptian, Sumerian proto-Cuneiform and Cretan) seamlessly emerge from such symbol systems, so that it is difficult to say at what point precisely writing emerges from proto-writing. Adding to this difficulty is the fact that very little is known about the symbols' meanings.

India and Asia

The 4th to 3rd millennium BC Indus script may similarly constitute proto-writing, possibly already influenced by the emergence of writing in Mesopotamia. In 2003, tortoise shells were discovered in China, which had Jiahu Script carved into them. These shells were determined as dating back to the 6th millennium BC, via radiocarbon dating. The shells were found buried with human remains, in 24 Neolithic graves unearthed at Jiahu, Henan province, northern China. According to some archaeologists, the writing on the shells had similarities to the 2nd millennium BC Oracle bone script. Others, however, have dismissed this claim as insufficiently substantiated, claiming that simple geometric designs such as those found on the Jiahu Shells, cannot be linked to early writing.

Bronze Age Writing

Writing emerged in a variety of different cultures in the Bronze age. In the hieroglyphic, it is found that the point of meeting between the two great classes of written characters, the ideographic and phonetic, and, as it seems, there has been some light thrown on their mutual relation, and the manner in which the one arose, or, at least, may have arisen, out of the other. It has been affirmed, indeed, that the two kinds of writing are so entirely distinct that it is impossible to entertain the idea of a historical relationship between them. But the fact is, that in the hieroglyphic that such a relationship is already established. No nation which had made any considerable advance towards civilisation remained satisfied with a pictorial or symbolic writing, more particularly if it be disposed to cultivate to any extent intercourse with other nations. To represent by means of such a method of writing foreign words and names is a matter of the utmost difficulty; and it is not improbable that the origin of the phonetic writing may be traced to the intercourse of nations speaking different languages. Thus compelled to employ ideographic characters phonetically in writing foreign words.

From this there is but a step to the discovery of an alphabet, viz. the employment of the same sign to represent not the combination of sounds forming the word, but the initial sound. It is true such correspondence cannot be traced through the whole of the phonetic alphabet. But when considering how very imperfect is the knowledge which even the most distinguished scholars possess of the ancient language, it is fully warranted in putting aside this negative evidence, and receiving the hypothesis just mentioned (such as that of Champollion with the ancient Egyptian language), as furnishing a very probable explanation of the origin of what may be called the alphabet.

The Ge'ez writing system of Ethiopia is considered Semitic it is likely of semi-independent origin, having roots in the Meroitic Sudanese ideogram system. The Chinese script likely developed independently of the Middle Eastern scripts, around 1600 BC. The pre-Columbian Mesoamerican writing systems (including among others Olmec and Maya scripts) are also generally believed to have had independent origins. It is thought that the first true alphabetic writing appeared around 2000 BC, as a representation of language developed for Semitic slaves in Egypt by Egyptians. Most other alphabets in the world today either descended from this one innovation, many via the Phoenician alphabet, or were directly inspired by its design. In the case of Italy, about 500 years passed from the early Old Italic alphabet to Plautus (750 to 250 BC), and in the case of the Germanic peoples, the corresponding time span is again similar, from the first Elder Futhark inscriptions to early texts like the *Abrogans* (ca. 200 to 750 CE).

Cuneiform Script

The original Sumerian writing system derives from a system of clay tokens used to represent commodities. By the end of the 4th millennium BC, this had evolved into a method of keeping accounts, using a round-shaped stylus impressed into soft clay at different angles for recording numbers.

This was gradually augmented with pictographic writing using a sharp stylus to indicate what was being counted. Round-stylus and sharp-stylus writing was gradually replaced about 2700-2500 BC by writing using a wedge-shaped stylus (hence the term cuneiform), at first only for logograms, but developed to include phonetic elements by the 29th century BC.

About 2600 BC cuneiform began to represent syllables of the Sumerian language. Finally, cuneiform writing became a general purpose writing system for logograms, syllables, and numbers. From the 26th century BC, this script was adapted to the Akkadian language, and from there to others such as Hurrian, and Hittite. Scripts similar in appearance to this writing system include those for Ugaritic and Old Persian.

Egyptian Hieroglyphs

Writing was very important in maintaining the Egyptian empire, and literacy was concentrated among an educated elite of scribes. Only people from certain backgrounds were allowed to train to become scribes, in the service of temple, pharisaic, and military authorities. The hieroglyph system was always difficult to learn, but in later centuries may have purposely made even more so, as this preserved the scribes' position.

> Various scholars believe that Egyptian hieroglyphs "came into existence a little after Sumerian script, and... probably [were]... invented under the influence of the latter...", although it is pointed out and held that "the evidence for such direct influence remains flimsy" and that "a very credible argument can also be made for the independent development of writing in Egypt..."

Chinese Writing

In China, historians have found out a lot about the early Chinese dynasties from the written documents left behind. From the Shang Dynasty most of this writing has survived on bones or bronze implements (*bronze script*). Markings on turtle shells, or *jiaguwen,* have been carbon-dated to around 1500 BC. Historians have found that the type of media used had an effect on what the writing was documenting and how it was used.

There have recently been discoveries of tortoise-shell carvings dating back to c. 6000 BC, like Jiahu Script, Banpo Script, but whether or not the carvings are of sufficient complexity to qualify as writing is under debate. At Damaidi in theNingxia Hui Autonomous Region, 3,172 cliff carvings dating to

6,000-5,000 BCE have been discovered featuring 8,453 individual characters such as the sun, moon, stars, gods and scenes of hunting or grazing. These pictographs are reputed to be similar to the earliest characters confirmed to be written Chinese. If it is deemed to be a written language, writing in China will predate Mesopotamian cuneiform, long acknowledged as the first appearance of writing, by some 2000 years, however it is more likely that the inscriptions are rather a form of proto-writing, similar to the contemporary European Vinca script. Undisputed evidence of writing in China dates from ca. 1600 BC.

Elamite Scripts

The undeciphered Proto-Elamite script emerges from as early as 3200 BC and evolves into Linear Elamite by the later 3rd millennium, which is then replaced by Elamite Cuneiform adopted from Akkadian.

Anatolian Hieroglyphs

Anatolian hieroglyphs are an indigenous hieroglyphic script native to western Anatolia first appears on Luwian royal seals, from ca. the 20th century BC, used to record the Hieroglyphic Luwian language.

Cretan Scripts

Cretan hieroglyphs are found on artifacts of Crete (early to mid 2nd millennium BC, MM I to MM III, overlapping with Linear A from MM IIA at the earliest). Linear B has been deciphered while Linear A has yet to be deciphered.

Early Semitic Alphabets

The first pure alphabets (properly, "abjads", mapping

single symbols to single phonemes, but not necessarily each phoneme to a symbol) emerged around 1800 BC in Ancient Egypt, as a representation of language developed by Semitic workers in Egypt, but by then alphabetic principles had a slight possibility of being inculcated into Egyptian hieroglyphs for upwards of a millennium. These early abjads remained of marginal importance for several centuries, and it is only towards the end of the Bronze Age that the Proto-Sinaitic script splits into the Proto-Canaanite alphabet (ca. 1400 BC) Byblos syllabary and the South Arabian alphabet (ca. 1200 BC). The Proto-Canaanite was probably somehow influenced by the undeciphered Byblos syllabary and in turn inspired the Ugaritic alphabet (ca. 1300 BC).

Indus Scripts

The Middle Bronze Age Indus script which dates back to the early Harrapan phase of around 3000 BC in Pakistan, has not yet been deciphered. It is unclear whether it should be considered an example of proto-writing (a system of symbols or similar), or if it is actual writing of the logographic-syllabic type of the other Bronze Age writing systems. Mortimer Wheeler recognises the style of writing as boustrophedon, where "this stability suggests a precarious maturity"

Mesoamerica

A stone slab with 3,000-year-old writing was discovered in the Mexican state of Veracruz, and is an example of the oldest script in the Western Hemisphere preceding the oldest Zapotec writing dated to about 500 BC.Of several pre-Columbian scripts in Mesoamerica, the one that appears to have been best developed, and fully deciphered, is the Maya script. The earliest inscriptions which are identifiably

Maya date to the 3rd century BC, and writing was in continuous use until shortly after the arrival of the Spanish conquistadores in the 16th century AD. Maya writing used logograms complemented by a set of syllabic glyphs, somewhat similar in function to modern Japanese writing.

Iron Age Writing

The Phoenician alphabet is simply the Proto-Canaanite alphabet as it was continued into the Iron Age (conventionally taken from a cut-off date of 1050 BC). This alphabet gave rise to the Aramaic and Greek, as well as, likely via Greek transmission, to various Anatolian and Old Italic (including the Latin) alphabets in the 8th century BC. The Greek alphabet for the first time introduces vowel signs. The Brahmic family of India originated independently. The Greek and Latin alphabets in the early centuries of the Common Era gave rise to several European scripts such as the Runes and the Gothic and Cyrillic alphabets while the Aramaic alphabet evolved into the Hebrew, Syriac and Arabic abjads and the South Arabian alphabet gave rise to the Ge'ez abugida.

Writing in Antiquity

In history of the Greek alphabet, the Greeks borrowed the Phoenician alphabet and adapted it to their own language. The letters of the Greek alphabet are the same as those of the Phoenician alphabet, and both alphabets are arranged in the same order. Several varieties of the Greek alphabet developed. One, known as Western Greek or Chalcidian, was west of Athens and in southern Italy. The other variation, known as Eastern Greek, was used in present-day Turkey, and the Athenians, and eventually the rest of the world that spoke Greek adopted this variation. After first writing right to left, the Greeks eventually chose to write from left to right, unlike the Phoenicians who wrote from right to left. Greek is in turn the source for all the modern scripts of Europe.

A tribe known as the Latins, who became known as the Romans, also lived in the Italian peninsula like the Western Greeks. From the Etruscans, a tribe living in the first millennium BCE in central Italy, and the Western Greeks, the Latins adopted writing in about the fifth century. The Anglo-Saxons began using Roman letters to write Old English as they converted to Christianity, following Augustine of Canterbury's mission to Britain in the sixth century.

Middle Ages Writing

With the end of the Western Roman Empire and urban centers in decline, literacy decreased in the West. Education became the preserve of monasteries and cathedrals. A "Renaissance" of classical education would appear in Carolingian Empire in the 8th century. In the Eastern Roman Empire (Byzantium), learning (in the sense of formal education involving literature) was maintained at a higher level than in the West. Further to the east, Islam conquered many of the Eastern Patriarchates, and it outstripped Christian lands in science, philosophy, and other intellectual endeavors in a "golden age"

Modern Writing

The nature of writing has been constantly evolving, particularly due to the development of new technologies over the centuries. The pen, the printing press, the computer and the mobile phone are all technological developments which have altered what is written, and the medium through which the written word is produced. Particularly with the advent of digital technologies, namely the computer and the mobile phone, characters can be formed by the press of a button, rather than making the physical motion with the hand.

The nature of the written word had evolved over time to make way for an informal, colloquial written style, where an everyday conversation can occur through writing rather than speaking. Written communication can also be delivered with minimal time delay (e-mail, SMS), and in some cases, with an imperceptible time delay (instant messaging). Writing creates the possibility to break spatial boundaries and travel through time, since a word normally spoken could only exist in the time and space it is spoken in. It creates a certain immortality, that could not be experienced without writing. Socially, writing is seen as an authoritative means of communication, from legal documentation, law and the media all produced through the medium. The growth of multimedia literacy can be seen as the first steps toward a postliterate society.

Materials of Writing

There is no very definite statement as to the material which was in most common use for the purposes of writing at start of the early writing systems. In all ages it has been customary to engrave on stone or metal, or other durable material, with the view of securing the permanency of the record; and accordingly, in the very commencement of the national history of Israel, it is read of the two tables of the law written in stone, and of a subsequent writing of the law on stone. In the latter case there is this peculiarity, that plaster (sic, lime or gypsum) was used along with stone, a combination of materials which is illustrated by comparison of the practice of the Egyptian engravers, who, having first carefully smoothed the stone, filled up the faulty places with gypsum or cement, in order to obtain a perfectly uniform surface on which to execute their engravings. Metals, such as stamped coins, are mentioned as a material of writing; they include lead, brass, and gold. To the engraving of gems there is reference also, such as with seals or signets.

The common materials of writing were the tablet and the roll, the former probably having a Chaldean origin, the latter an Egyptian. The tablets of the Chaldeans are among the most remarkable of their remains There are small pieces of clay, somewhat rudely shaped into a form resembling a pillow, and thickly inscribed with cuneiform characters. Similar use has been seen in hollow cylinders, or prisms of six or eight sides, formed of fine terra cotta, sometimes glazed, on which the characters were traced with a small stylus, in some specimens so minutely as to be capable of decipherment only with the aid of a magnifying-glass.

In Egypt the principal writing material was quite of a different sort. Wooden tablets are indeed found pictured on the monuments; but the material which was in common use, even from very ancient times, was the papyrus. This reed, found chiefly in Lower Egypt, had various economic means for writing, the pith was taken out, and divided by a pointed instrument into the thin pieces of which it is composed; it was then fattened by pressure, and the strips glued together, other strips being placed at right angles to them, so that a roll of any length might be manufactured. Writing seems to have become more widespread with the invention of papyrus in Egypt. That this material was in use in Egypt from a very early period is evidenced by still existing papyrus of the earliest Theban dynasties. As the papyrus, being in great demand, and exported to all parts of the world, became very costly, other materials were often used instead of it, among which is mentioned leather, a few leather mills of an early period having been found in the tombs. Parchment, using sheepskins left after the wool was removed for cloth, was sometimes cheaper than papyrus, which had to be imported outside Egypt. With the invention of wood-pulp paper, the cost of writing material began a steady decline.

Writing System

A writing system is a type of symbolic system used to represent elements or statements expressible in language. Writing systems are distinguished from other possible symbolic communication systems in that one must usually understand something of the associated spoken language to comprehend the text. By contrast, other possible symbolic systems such as information signs, painting, maps and mathematics often do not require prior knowledge of a spoken language.

Every human community possesses language, a feature regarded by many as an innate and defining condition of mankind. However the development of writing systems, and the process by which they have supplanted traditional oral systems of communication has been sporadic, uneven and slow. Once established, writing systems on the whole change more slowly than their spoken counterparts, and often preserve features and expressions which are no longer current in the spoken language. The great benefit of writing systems is their ability to maintain a persistent record of information expressed in a language, which can be retrieved independently of the initial act of formulation.

All writing systems require:

1) at least one set of defined base elements or symbols, individually termed *characters* and collectively called a script;
2) at least one set of rules and conventions (orthography) understood and shared by a community, which arbitrarily assign meaning to the base elements (graphemes), their ordering and relations to one another;
3) at least one language (generally spoken) whose constructions are represented and able to be recalled by the interpretation of these elements and rules;
4) some physical means of distinctly representing the symbols by application to a permanent or semi-permanent medium, so they may be interpreted (usually visually, but tactile systems have also been devised).

The study of writing systems has developed along partially independent lines in the examination of individual scripts and as such the terminology employed differs somewhat from field to field.

The generic term *text* may be used to refer to an individual product of a writing system. The act of composing a text may be referred to as *writing*, and the act of interpreting the text as *reading*. In the study of writing systems, *orthography* refers to the method and rules of observed writing structure (literal meaning, "correct writing"), and in particular for alphabetic systems, includes the concept of *spelling*.

A grapheme is the technical term coined to refer to the specific base or atomic units of a given writing system. Graphemes are the *minimally significant* elements which taken together comprise the set of "building blocks" out of which texts of a given writing system may be constructed, along with rules of correspondence and use. The concept is similar to that of the phoneme used in the study of spoken languages. For example, in the Latin-based writing system of standard contemporary English, examples of graphemes include the majuscule and minuscule forms of the twenty-six letters of the alphabet (corresponding to various phonemes), marks of punctuation (mostly non-phonemic), and a few other symbols such as those for numerals (logograms for numbers).

Note that an individual grapheme may be represented in a wide variety of ways, where each variation is visually distinct in some regard, but all are interpreted as representing the "same" grapheme. These individual variations are known as allographs of a grapheme (compare with the term allophone used in linguistic study). For example, the minuscule a letter has different allographs when written as a cursive, block, or typed letter. The selection between different allographs may be influenced by the medium used, the writing instrument, the stylistic choice of the writer and the largely unconscious features of an individual's handwriting.

The terms *glyph, sign* and *character* are sometimes used to refer to a grapheme. Common usage varies from discipline to discipline; compare cuneiform sign, Maya glyph, Chinese character. The glyphs of most writing systems are made up of lines (or strokes) and are therefore called linear, but there are glyphs in non-linear writing systems made up of other types of marks, such as Cuneiform and Braille.

Writing systems are conceptual systems, as are the languages to which they refer. Writing systems may be regarded as *complete* according to the extent to which they are able to represent all that may be expressed in the spoken language.

History of Writing Systems

Writing systems were preceded by proto-writing, systems of ideographic and/or early mnemonic symbols. The best known examples are:

1) Jiahu Script, symbols on tortoise shells in Jiahu, ca. 6600 BC
2) Vinca script (Tartaria tablets), ca. 4500 BC
3) Early Indus script, ca. 3500 BC

The invention of the first writing systems is roughly contemporary with the beginning of the Bronze Age in the late Neolithic of the late 4th millennium BC. The Sumerian archaic cuneiform script and the Egyptian hieroglyphs are generally considered the earliest writing systems, both emerging out of their ancestral proto-literate symbol systems from 3400–3200 BC with earliest coherent texts from about 2600 BC.

The Chinese script likely developed independently of the Middle Eastern scripts, around 1600 BC.

The pre-Columbian Mesoamerican writing systems (including among others Olmec and Maya scripts) are also generally believed to have had independent origins.

It is thought that the first true alphabetic writing appeared around 2000 BC, as a representation of language developed for Semitic slaves in Egypt by Egyptians. Most other alphabets in the world today either descended from this one innovation, many via the Phoenician alphabet, or were directly inspired by its design.

Functional Classification

This textbook for Puyi shows the English alphabet. Although the English letters run from left to right, the Chinese explanations run from top to bottom, as traditionally written.

The oldest-known forms of writing were primarily logographic in nature, based on pictographic and ideographic elements. Most writing systems can be broadly divided into three categories: logographic, syllabic, and alphabetic (or segmental); however, all three may be found in any given writing system in varying proportions, often making it difficult to categorise a system uniquely. The term complex system is sometimes used to describe those where the admixture makes classification problematic.

Logographic Writing Systems

As each character represents a single word (or, more precisely, a morpheme), many logograms are required to write all the words of language. The vast array of logograms and the memorization of what they mean are the major disadvantage of the logographic systems over alphabetic systems. However, since the meaning is inherent to the symbol, the same logographic system can theoretically be used to represent different languages. In practice, this is only true for closely related languages, like the Chinese languages, as syntactical constraints reduce the portability of a given logographic system. Japanese uses Chinese logograms extensively in its writing systems, with most of the symbols carrying the same or similar meanings. However, the semantics, and especially the grammar, are different enough that a long Chinese text is not readily understandable to a Japanese reader without any knowledge of basic Chinese grammar, though short and concise phrases such as those on signs and newspaper headlines are much easier to comprehend.

While most languages do not use wholly logographic writing systems many languages use some logograms. A good example of modern western logograms are the Hindu-Arabic numerals – everyone who uses those symbols understands what 1 means whether he or she calls it *one, eins, uno, yi, ichi, ehad* or *jedan*.

Logograms are sometimes called ideograms, a word that refers to symbols which graphically represent abstract ideas, but linguists avoid this use, as Chinese characters are often semantic–phonetic compounds, symbols which include an element that represents the meaning and an element that represents the pronunciation. Some nonlinguists distinguish between lexigraphy and ideography, where symbols in lexigraphies represent words and symbols in ideographies represent words or morphemes.

The most important (and, to a degree, the only surviving) modern logographic writing system is the

Chinese one, whose characters are or were used, with varying degrees of modification, in Chinese, Japanese, Korean, Vietnamese, and other east Asian languages. Ancient Egyptian hieroglyphs and the Mayan writing system are also systems with certain logographic features, although they have marked phonetic features as well and are no longer in current use.

Syllabic Writing Systems

As logographic writing systems use a single symbol for an entire word, a syllabary is a set of written symbols that represent (or approximate) syllables, which make up words. A symbol in a syllabary typically represents a consonant sound followed by a vowel sound, or just a vowel alone.

In a "true syllabary", there is no systematic graphic similarity between phonetically related characters (though some do have graphic similarity for the vowels). That is, the characters for /ke/, /ka/ and /ko/ have no similarity to indicate their common "k" sound (voiceless velar plosive). More recent creations such as the Cree syllabary embody a system of varying signs, which can best be seen when arranging the syllabogram set in an onset–coda or onset–rime table.

Syllabaries are best suited to languages with relatively simple syllable structure, such as Japanese. The English language, on the other hand, allows complex syllable structures, with a relatively large inventory of vowels and complex consonant clusters, making it cumbersome to write English words with a syllabary. To write English using a syllabary, every possible syllable in English would have to have a separate symbol, and whereas the number of possible syllables in Japanese is no more than about fifty to sixty, in English there are many thousands. Other languages that use true syllabaries include Mycenaean Greek (Linear B) and Native American languages such as Cherokee. Several languages of the Ancient Near East used forms of cuneiform, which is a syllabary with some non-syllabic elements.

Segmental Writing Systems

An alphabet is a small set of *letters* — basic written symbols — each of which roughly represents or represented historically a phoneme of a spoken language. The word *alphabet* is derived from alpha and beta, the first two symbols of the Greek alphabet.

In a perfectly phonemic alphabet, the phonemes and letters would correspond perfectly in two directions: a writer could predict the spelling of a word given its pronunciation, and a speaker could predict the pronunciation of a word given its spelling. Each language has general rules that govern the association between letters and phonemes, but, depending on the language, these rules may or may not be consistently followed.

Perfectly phonemic alphabets are very easy to use and learn and languages that have them (for example Serbocroatian or Finnish) have much lower barriers to literacy than languages such as English, which has a very complex and irregular spelling system. As languages often evolve independently of their writing systems, and writing systems have been borrowed for languages for which they were not designed, the degree to which letters of an alphabet correspond to phonemes of a language varies greatly from one language to another and even within a single language. In modern times, when linguists invent a writing system for a language that didn't previously have one, the goal is usually to develop a phonemic alphabet. It should be noted that a truly phonetic alphabet for a natural spoken language would be very cumbersome, as it would have to have a huge variety of phonetic variation. An example of such a writing system is the International Phonetic Alphabet (IPA).

Consonantal Writing Systems

The first type of alphabet that was developed was the abjad. An abjad is an alphabetic writing system where there is one symbol per consonant. Abjads differ from other alphabets in that they have characters only for consonantal sounds. Vowels are not usually marked in abjad.

All known abjads (except maybe Tifinagh) belong to the Semitic family of scripts, and derive from the original Northern Linear Abjad. The reason for this is that Semitic languages and the related Berber languages have a morphemic structure which makes the denotation of vowels redundant in most cases.

Some abjads (such as Arabic and Hebrew) have markings for vowels as well, but use them only in special contexts, such as for teaching. Many scripts derived from abjads have been extended with vowel symbols to become full alphabets, the most famous case being the derivation of the Greek alphabet from the Phoenician abjad. This has mostly happened when the script was adapted to a non-Semitic language.

Inherent-vowel Writing Systems

An abugida is an alphabetic writing system whose basic signs denote consonants with an inherent vowel and where consistent modifications of the basic sign indicate other following vowels than the inherent one. Thus, in an abugida there may or may not be a sign for "k" with no vowel, but also one for "ka" (if "a" is the inherent vowel), and "ke" is written by modifying the "ka" sign in a way that is consistent with how one would modify "la" to get "le". In many abugidas the modification is the addition of a vowel sign, but other possibilities are imaginable (and used), such as rotation of the basic sign, addition of diacritical marks and so on.

The contrast with "true syllabaries" is that the latter have one distinct symbol per possible syllable, and the signs for each syllable have no systematic graphic similarity. The graphic similarity of most abugidas comes from the fact that they are derived from abjads, and the consonants make up the symbols with the inherent vowel and the new vowel symbols are markings added on to the base symbol.

In the Ge'ez script, for which the linguistic term *abugida* was named, the vowel modifications do not always appear systematic, although they originally were more so. Canadian Aboriginal syllabics can be considered abugidas, although they are rarely thought of in those terms. The largest single group of abugidas is the Brahmic family of scripts, however, which includes nearly all the scripts used in India and Southeast Asia.

Featural Writing Systems

A featural script represents finer detail than an alphabet. Here symbols do not represent whole phonemes, but rather the elements (features) that make up the phonemes, such as voicing or its place of articulation. Theoretically, each feature could be written with a separate letter; and abjads or abugidas, or indeed syllabaries, could be featural, but the only prominent system of this sort is Korean hangul. In hangul, the featural symbols are combined into alphabetic letters, and these letters are in turn joined into syllabic blocks, so that the system combines three levels of phonological representation.

Many scholars, e.g. DeFrancis, reject this class or at least labeling hangul as such. The Korean script is a conscious script creation by literate experts, which Daniels calls a "sophisticated grammatogeny". These include stenographies and constructed scripts of hobbyists and fiction writers, many of which feature advanced graphic designs corresponding to phonologic properties. The basic unit of writing in these systems can map to anything from phones to words. It has been shown that even the roman script has sub-character "features".

Ambiguous Writing Systems

Most writing systems are not purely one type. The English writing system, for example, includes numerals and other logograms such as #, $, and &, and the phonemic letter clusters are a complex match to sound. As mentioned above, all logographic systems have phonetic components as well, whether that's along the lines of a syllabary, such as Chinese ("logo-syllabic"), or an abjad, as in Egyptian ("logo-consonantal").

Some scripts, however, are truly ambiguous. The semi-syllabaries of ancient Spain were syllabic for plosives such as *p*, *t*, *k*, but alphabetic for other consonants. In some versions, vowels were written redundantly after syllabic letters, conforming to an alphabetic orthography. Old Persian cuneiform was similar. Of 23 consonants (including null), seven were fully syllabic, thirteen were purely alphabetic, and for the other three, there was one letter for /Cu/ and another for both /Ca/ and /Ci/. However, all vowels were written overtly regardless; as in the Brahmic abugidas, the /Ca/ letter was used for a bare consonant.

The zhuyin phonetic glossing script for Chinese divides syllables in two or three, but into onset, medial, and rime rather than consonant and vowel. Pahawh Hmong is similar, but can be considered to divide syllables into either onset-rime or consonant-vowel (all consonant clusters and diphthongs are written with single letters); as the latter, it is equivalent to an abugida but with the roles of consonant and vowel reversed. Other scripts are intermediate between the categories of alphabet, abjad and abugida, so there may be disagreement on how they should be classified.

Graphic Classification of Writing Systems

Perhaps the primary graphic distinction made in classifications is that of *linearity*. Linear writing systems are those in which the characters are composed of lines, such as the Latin alphabet and Chinese characters. Chinese characters are considered linear whether they're written with a ball-point pen or a calligraphic brush, or cast in bronze. Similarly, Egyptian hieroglyphs and Maya glyphs were often painted in linear outline form, but in formal situations they were carved in bas-relief. Non-linear systems, on the other hand, such as braille, are not composed of lines, no matter which instrument is used to write them. The earliest examples of writing are linear: the Sumerian script of c. 3300 BCE was linear, though its cuneiform descendants were not. Cuneiform was probably the earliest non-linear writing. Its glyphs were formed by pressing the end of a reed stylus into moist clay, not by tracing lines in the clay with the stylus as had been done previously. The result was a radical transformation of the appearance of the script.

Braille is a non-linear adaptation of the Latin alphabet that completely abandoned the Latin forms. The letters are composed of raised bumps on the writing substrate, which can be leather (Louis Braille's original material), stiff paper, plastic or metal.

There are also transient non-linear adaptations of the Latin alphabet, including Morse code, the manual alphabets of various sign languages, and semaphore, in which flags or bars are positioned at prescribed angles. However, if "writing" is defined as a potentially permanent means of recording information, then these systems do not qualify as writing at all, since the symbols disappear as soon as they are used.

Directionality

Scripts are also graphically characterized by the direction in which they are written. Egyptian hieroglyphs were written in either horizontal direction, with the animal and human glyphs turned to face the beginning of the line. The early alphabet could be written in multiple directionshorizontally (left-to-right or right-to-left) or vertically (up or down). It was commonly written boustrophedonically: starting in one (horizontal) direction, then turning at the end of the line and reversing direction.

The Greek alphabet and its successors settled on a left-to-right pattern, from the top to the bottom of the page. In Timed Text (TT) Authoring Format, this pattern is abbreviated LRTB. Other scripts, such as Arabic and Hebrew, came to be written right-to-left. Scripts that incorporate Chinese characters have traditionally been written vertically (top-to-bottom), from the right to the left of the page, but nowadays are frequently written left-to-right, top-to-bottom, due to Western influence, a growing need to accommodate terms in the Roman alphabet, and technical limitations in popular electronic document formats. The Uighur alphabet and its descendants are unique in being the only scripts written top-to-bottom, left-to-right; this direction originated from an ancestral Semitic direction by rotating the page 90° counter-clockwise to conform to the appearance of vertical Chinese writing. Several scripts used in the Philippines and Indonesia, such as Hanuno'o, are traditionally written with lines moving away from the writer, from bottom to top, but are read horizontally left to right.

Calligraphy

Calligraphy is a type of visual art. It is often called the art of writing. A contemporary definition of calligraphic practice is "the art of giving form to signs in an expressive, harmonious and skillful manner" The story of writing is one of aesthetic evolution framed within the technical skills, transmission speed(s) and materials limitations of a person, time and place. A style of writing is described as a script, hand or alphabet.

Modern calligraphy ranges from functional hand lettered inscriptions and designs to fine art pieces where the abstract expression of the handwritten mark may or may not supersede the legibility of the letters. Classical calligraphy differs from typography and non-classical hand-lettering, though a calligrapher may create all of these; characters are historically disciplined yet fluid and spontaneous, improvised at the moment of writing.

Calligraphy continues to flourish in the forms of wedding and event invitations, font design/ typography, original hand-lettered logo design, religious art, announcements/graphic design/ commissioned calligraphic art, cut stone inscriptions and memorial documents. It is also used for props and moving images for film and television, testimonials, birth and death certificates, maps, and other works involving writing.

Western calligraphy is recognizable by the use of the Roman alphabet, which evolved from the Phoenician, Greek, and Etruscan alphabets. The first Roman alphabet appeared about 600 BC, in Rome, and by the first century developed into Roman imperial capitals carved on stones, Rustic capitals painted on walls, and Roman cursive for daily use. In the second and third centuries the Uncial lettering style developed. As writing withdrew to monasteries, uncial was found more suitable for copying the Bible and other religious texts. It was the monasteries which preserved the calligraphic traditions during the fourth and fifth centuries, when the Roman Empire fell and Europe entered the Dark Ages.

At the height of the Roman Empire its power reached as far as Great Britain; when the empire fell, its literary influence remained. The Semi-uncial generated the Irish Semi-uncial, the small Anglo-Saxon. Each region seems to have developed its own standards following the main monastery of the region (i.e. Merovingian script, Laon script, Luxeuil script,

Visigothic script, Beneventan script), which are mostly cursive and hardly readable.

The rising Carolingian Empire encouraged setting a new standardized script, which was developed by several famous monasteries (including Corbie Abbey and Beauvais) around the eighth century. The script from Saint Martin of Tours was ultimately set as the Imperial standard, named the Carolingian script (or "the Caroline"). From the powerful Carolingian Empire, this standard also became used in neighboring kingdoms.

In the eleventh century, the Caroline evolved into the Gothic script, which was more compact and made it possible to fit more text on a page. The Gothic calligraphy styles became dominant in northern Europe; and in 1454 AD, when Johannes Gutenberg developed the first printing press in Mainz, Germany, he adopted the Gothic style, making it the first typeface.

Century, the rediscovery of old Carolingian texts encouraged the creation of the Antiqua script (about 1470). The seventeenth century saw the Batarde script from France, and the eighteenth century saw the English script spread across Europe and world by their books. The contemporary typefaces found on every computer, from simple word processing programs like Microsoft Word or Apple Pages to professional designer's software packages like Adobe InDesign, owe a considerable debt to the past and to a small number of professional typeface designers today.

Western Calligraphy

Sacred Western calligraphy has some special features, such as the illumination of the first letter of each book or chapter in medieval times. A decorative "carpet page" may precede the literature, filled with ornate, geometrical depictions of bold-hued animals. The Lindisfarne Gospels (715-720 AD) are an early example. As with Chinese or Arabian calligraphies, Western calligraphic script had strict rules and shapes. Quality writing had a rhythm and regularity to the letters, with a "geometrical" order of the lines on the page. Each character had, and often still has, a precise stroke order.

Unlike a typeface, irregularity in the characters' size, style and colors adds meaning to the Greek translation "beautiful letters". The content may be completely illegible, but no less meaningful to a viewer with some empathy for the work on view. Many of the themes and variations of today's contemporary Western calligraphy are found in the pages of the Saint John's Bible. A particularly modern example is The Holy Bible,Timothy Botts Illustrated edition, with 360 calligraphic images as well as a calligraphy typeface.

Slavonic Lettering

The history of the slavonic and consequently Russian writing systems differs fundamentally from the one of the Latin language.

Glagolitic Script

Alphabets that became a basis for slavonic writing were called "Glagolitic" and "Cyrillic" alphabets. The history of their emergence is totally unknown. The extant monuments of glagolitsa are dated no later than the end of the 10th century. Symbols as a rule are composed of two elements that are combined one above the other.

Such construction can be seen in the decoration of kirillitsa. It usually does not include simple forms. They are connected with straights. Some letters correspond to their modern form. Regarding the form of letters there are two types of glagolitsa. The first one – Bulgarian glagolitsa – has roundish letters, and Croatian glagolitsa – called as well illyrian or dalmatian – has an angular forms of letters. Neither of the two types has strict border zones of spreading. Later glagolitsa borrowed many sounds from kirillitsa. West slavic glagolitsa existed for only a short time and was replaced with the Latin writing. But glagolitsa did not perish in modern times. It was used up to the beginning of World War II, and was even used for newspapers. It is currently being used in Croatian settlements of Italy.

Cyrillic Alphabet

Its origin remains unexplained. The title appeared later than the alphabet. Kirill, while travelling across slavic countries during the 9th century definitely composed a new slavonic alphabet. It is not known whether it was a glagolitic script or not. It was necessary to translate religious texts into the slavonic language. To do that it would be necessary to simplify intricate and difficult-to-write symbols of glagolitsa, but at the same time introduce the lacking letters for sound denotations in the spoken slavonic language.

Many sources of the time describe this, but mention only one slavonic alphabet though there were already two. The Cyrillic alphabet has 43 letters, 24 of them were borrowed from the Byzantium paternal writing and the other 19 were invented anew, but in the graphic decorations similar to the first ones. But not all the borrowed letters kept the denotations of the same sound in the Greek language – some received new denotations peculiar to their slavonic phonetic features.

Bulgarians have preserved the Cyrillic alphabet to a greater extent than other slavonians. Nowadays their writing (i.e. the Serbian language) is similar to Russian writing except several symbols designating specific phonetic features. The ancient form of kirillitsa is called "uncial". Uncial and glagolitic alphabet are wholly handwritten scripts. Uncial, as well as glagolitic alphabet, has a peculiar trait – clearness and straightness of tracings (writings).

Most letters are angular and have graceless features. Exceptions are narrow roundish letters with round curves, and among other letters these seem out of place. Lower elongations of certain letters are idiosyncratic to this type of writing. They appear to be light decorative elements in the context of calligraphy. As for the diacritical symbols, their origin is still unclear. Uncial letters are all of a big size and are set separately from each other. The old uncial has no intervals between words.

Semi-uncial

Semi-uncial was the second type of writing, that had been developed from the 14th century and later replaced the uncial. This script is brighter and more roundish. Its letters are more shallow: they have many superscript marks and the whole system of punctuation marks. Letters are more flexible and wide in comparison with the uncial writing and have lower and upper elongations. The broad-pen technique used while writing the uncial is seldom applied in the semi-uncial. Semi-uncial was used with cursive and ligature in the 14th–18th centuries along with the other writing styles.

To use semi-uncial in writing was more comfortable. Feudal atomism caused the development of unique uncial styles and even an uncial language in some remote districts. Military novels and chronicles occupy the bulk of these manuscripts, but some manuscripts recount historical events in Russia during that period. During Ivan III's reign when the land integration and consolidation around Moscow was finished, Moscow became not only a national, but also a cultural center; and the national Russian state was created under a new autocratic regime. So a local Moscow culture became an icon of Russian character. Along with the growing demands of everyday life, the necessity of a new and more simple script was born in the society of Moscow, and thus Russia at large.

Nursive

The term "cursive writing" corresponds to the Latin cursive. At the first stage of scripts development the ancient Greeks had a widely spread writing culture. Some of the south-west Slavonians also had their own scripts. Cursive writing as a separate type of writing emerged in the 15th century in Russia. The partly-bound letters and bright patterns differed from other scripts' letters. But since the letters had different marks and signs, pigtails, and additional symbols, it was difficult to read texts. Although cursive writing reflected semi-uncial, there were fine lines that bound letters, a feature that contrasts with the semi-uncial. This script is also more flexible and fluent. Letters of cursive writing were written with elongations.

In the beginning the symbols were composed of elongations as is specific to uncial and semi-uncial. In the second half of the 16th century, and especially in the beginning of the 17th century the semi-roundish lines became the major lines. In a broader historical perspective, it is possible to see some elements of the Greek cursive script.

By the second half of the 17th century, when many different variants of writing appeared, the cursive script showed more roundish elements and ligature. The roundish contour of letters became more decorative and smooth near the end of the century. Cursive writing of that time misses elements of the Greek cursive writing and discards some semi-uncial forms. Later straights and cursives attained balance and letters became more symmetrical and roundish. At that period the uncial was transformed into a civil writing cursive.

Eastern Asian Calligraphy

Traditional East Asian writing uses ink brushes to write Chinese characters. The way of writing (in Chinese, *Shufa,* in Korean, *Seoye,* in Japanese *Shodo*) is an important aspect of East Asian culture. Calligraphy has influenced ink and wash painting, which is accomplished using similar tools and techniques. Calligraphy has influenced most major art styles in East Asia, including Ink and wash painting, a style of Chinese, Korean, Japanese painting, and Vietnamese painting based entirely on calligraphy.

In ancient China, the oldest Chinese characters existing are Jiaguwen characters carved on ox scapula and tortoise plastrons, because brush-written ones have decayed over time. During the divination ceremony, after the cracks were made, the characters were written with a brush on the shell or bone to be later carved. With the development of *Jinwen* (Bronzeware script) and *Dazhuan* "cursive" signs continued. Moreover, each archaic kingdom of current China had its own set of characters.

Imperial China

In Imperial China, the graphs on old steles – some dating from 200 BC, and in Xiaozhuan style – are still accessible. About 220 BC, the emperor Qin Shi Huang, the first to conquer the entire Chinese basin, imposed several reforms, among them Li Si's character unification, which created a set of 3300 standardized Xiao*zhuan* characters. Despite the fact that the main writing implement of the time was already the brush, few papers survive from this period, and the main examples of this style are on steles.

The Lishu style (clerical script) which is more regularized, and in some ways similar to modern text, have been also authorised under Qin Shi Huangdi.

Kaishu style (traditional regular script) – still in use today – and attribute to Wang Xizhi and his followers, is even more regularized. Its spreading was encourage by Emperor Mingzong of Later Tang (926-933), who ordered the printing of the classic using new wooden block and such Kaishu. Printing technologies here allowed a shape stabilization. The Kaishu shape of characters 1000 years ago was mostly similar to that at the end of Imperial China. But small changes have be made, for example in the shape of which is not absolutely the same in the Kangxi dictionary of 1716 as in modern books. The Kangxi and current shapes have tiny differences, while stroke order is still the same, according to old style.

Styles which did not survive include Bâfçnshû, a mix made of Xiaozhuan style at 80%, and Lishu at 20%. Some Variant Chinese characters were unorthodox or locally used for centuries. They were generally understood but always rejected in official texts. Some of these unorthodox variants, in addition to some newly created characters, compose the Simplified Chinese character set.

Cursive styles and hand-written styles

Cursive styles such as *Xingshu* (semi-cursive or running script) and Caoshu (cursive or grass script) are less constrained and faster, where more movements made by the writing implement are visible. These styles' stroke orders vary more, sometimes creating radically different forms. They are descended from Clerical script, in the same time as Regular script (Han dynasty), but Xingshu and Caoshu were use for personal notes only, and were never used as standard. Caoshu style was highly appreciated in Emperor Wu of Han reign (140-87).

Printed and computer styles

Examples of modern printed styles are Song from the Song Dynasty's printing press, and sans-serif. These are not considered traditional styles, and are normally not written.

Indian Calligraphy

Asoka's edicts were committed to stone. These inscriptions are stiff and angular in form. Following the Aœoka style of Indic writing, two new calligraphic types appear: Kharostiand Brahmi. Kharosti was used in the northwestern regions of India from the 3rd century BC to the 4th century of the Christian Era, and it was used in Central Asia until the 8th century. Copper was a favoured material for Indic inscriptions. In the north of India, birch bark was used as a writing surface as early as the 2nd century AD. Many Indic manuscripts were written on palm leaves, even after the Indian languages were put on paper in the 13th century. Both sides of the leaves were used for writing. Long rectangular strips were gathered on top of one another, holes were drilled through all the leaves, and the book was held together by string. Books of this manufacture were common to Southeast Asia. The palm leaf was an excellent surface for penwriting, making possible the delicate lettering used in many of the scripts of southern Asia.

Arabic Calligraphy

Islamic or Arabic calligraphy (*calligraphy* in Arabic is *Khatt ul-Yad*) is an aspect of Arabic art that has evolved alongside the religion of Islam and the Arabic language.

Arabic calligraphy is associated with geometric Islamic art (arabesque) on the walls and ceilings of mosques as well as on the page. Contemporary artists in the Islamic world draw on the heritage of calligraphy to use calligraphic inscriptions or abstractions.

Instead of recalling something related to the spoken word, calligraphy for Muslims is a visible expression of the highest art of all, the art of the spiritual world. Calligraphy has arguably become the most venerated form of Islamic art because it provides a link between the languages of the Muslims with the religion of Islam. The holy book of Islam, al-Qur'an, has played an important role in the development and evolution of the Arabic language, and by extension, calligraphy in the Arabic alphabet. Proverbs and passages from the Qur'an are still sources for Islamic calligraphy. There was a strong parallel tradition to that of the Islamic, among Aramaic and Hebrew scholars, seen in such works as the Hebrew illuminated bibles of the 9th and 10th centuries.

3

Literature: Oral Tradition

Oral tradition, oral culture and oral lore are messages or testimony transmitted orally from one generation to another. The messages or testimony are verbally transmitted in speech or song and may take the form, for example, of folktales, sayings, ballads, songs, or chants. In this way, it is possible for a society to transmit oral history, oral literature, oral law and other knowledges across generations without a writing system.

For the purposes of some disciplines, a narrower definition of oral tradition may be appropriate. Sociologists might also emphasise a requirement that the material is held in common by a group of people, over several generations, and might distinguish oral tradition from testimony or oral history. In a general sense, "oral tradition" refers to the transmission of cultural material through vocal utterance, and was long held to be a key descriptor of folklore (a criterion no longer rigidly held by all folklorists). As an academic discipline, it refers both to a set of objects of study and a method by which they are studied— the method may be called variously "oral traditional theory," "the theory of Oral-Formulaic Composition" and the "Parry-Lord theory" (after two of its founders)

The study of oral tradition is distinct from the academic discipline of oral history, which is the recording of personal memories and histories of those who experienced historical eras or events. It is also distinct from the study of orality, which can be defined as thought and its verbal expression in societies where the technologies of literacy (especially writing and print) are unfamiliar to most of the population.

History of Oral Tradition

Oral tradition as a field of study had its origins in the work of the Serb scholar Vuk Stefanovic Karadsic (1787-1864), a contemporary and friend of the Brothers Grimm. Vuk pursued similar projects of "salvage folklore" (similar to rescue archaeology) in the cognate traditions of the Southern Slavic regions which would later be gathered into Yugoslavia, and with the same admixture of romantic and nationalistic interests (he considered all those speaking Serbo-Croat as Serbs). Somewhat later, but as part of the same scholarly enterprise of nationalist studies in folklore, the turcologist Vasily Radlov (1837-1918) would study the songs of the Kara-Kirghiz in what would later become the Soviet Union; Karadzic and Radloff would provide models for the work of Parry.

Milman Parry and Albert Lord

Shortly thereafter, Milman Parry (1902-1935), pursuing a degree in Classics at the University of California, Berkeley, would begin to grapple with what was then called the "Homeric Question," usually framed as "who was Homer?" and "what are the Homeric poems?" The Homeric question actually consists of a series of related inquiries, and Parry's contribution, which drew upon and synthesised the insights of previous scholars including Marcel Jousse, Matija Murko and Arnold van Gennep, was to reconsider the foundational assumptions which framed the inquiries, a re-ordering that would have consequences for a great many literatures and disciplines.

> Parry's work under Antoine Meillet at the Sorbonne led to his crucial insight into the "formula," which he originally defined as "a group of words which is regularly employed under the same metrical conditions to express a given essential idea." In Homeric verse, for example, phrases like *eos rhododaktylos* ("rosy fingered dawn") or *oinops pontos* ("winedark sea") occupy a certain metrical pattern that fits, in modular fashion, into the six-colon Greek hexameter, and aids the *aioidos* or bard in extempore composition.

In Parry's view, formulas were not individual and idiosyncratic devices of particular artists, but the shared inheritance of a tradition of singers. They were easily remembered, making it possible for the singer to execute an improvisational composition-in-performance. A later scholar commented on the potential for Parry's concept to be seen as disparaging of Homeric genius: "The meaning of the Greek term 'rhapsodise', *rhapsoidein*, 'to stitch song together' could then be taken in a negative sense: Homer stitched together pre-fabricated parts."

The idea indeed met with immediate resistance, because it seemed to make the fount of Western literary eloquence the slave of a system of cliches, but it accounted for such otherwise inexplicable features of the Homeric poems as gross anachronisms (revealed by advances in historical and archaeological knowledge), the presence of incompatible dialects, and the deployment of locally unsuitable epithets ("blameless Aegisthos" for the murderer of Agamemnon, or the almost comic use of "swift-footed Achilles" for the hero in conspicuously sedentary moments).

Parry was appointed to a junior professorship at Harvard, and during this time became aware of living oral traditions in the Balkan region. In two field expeditions with his young assistant Albert Lord (1912-1991) he would record thousands of songs on aluminum disks. The collection would provide the basis for an empirical documentation of the dynamics of composition of metrical narrative in traditional oral performance. This analysis included the patterns and types of variation at lexical and other levels which would yield a structural account of a work's multiformity. This phenomenon could only be accounted for in standard literary methodology by concepts of "corruption" and "distortion" of a pristine, original "ur-text" or hypothetical "lost Q" ("Quelle", German for "source"), hypothesised via stemmatology. Thus the work of Parry and Lord reduced the prominence of the historic-geographic method in folkloristics.

Parry died in 1935. His work was posthumously published by his son Adam Parry as *The Making of Homeric Verse*. Lord, however, had meanwhile published *The Singer of Tales* (1960), a work which summarised both Parry's response to the Homeric Question, and the joint work he had done with Parry in the Balkans. The Parry-Lord work exercised great influence on other scholars, notably Francis P. Magoun, whose application of their model to Anglo-Saxon traditions demonstrated the explicative and problem-solving power of the theory – a process that would be repeated by other scholars in numerous independent traditions.

Walter Ong

In a separate development, the media theorist Marshall McLuhan (1911-1980) would begin to focus attention on the ways that communicative media shape the nature of the content conveyed. He would serve as mentor to the Jesuit, Walter Ong (1912-2003), whose interests in cultural history, psychology and rhetoric would result in *Orality and Literacy* (Methuen, 1980) and the important but less-known *Fighting for Life: Contest, Sexuality and Consciousness*. These two works articulated the contrasts between cultures defined by primary orality, writing, print, and the secondary orality of the electronic age.

Ong's works also made possible an integrated theory of oral tradition which accounted for both production of content (the chief concern of Parry-Lord theory) and its reception. This approach, like McLuhan's, kept the field open not just to the study of aesthetic culture but to the way physical and behavioral artifacts of oral societies are used to store, manage and transmit knowledge, so that oral tradition provides methods for investigation of cultural differences, other than the purely verbal, between oral and literate societies.

Orality and Literacy concerns the "psychodynamics of orality" which defines the fundamental characteristics of 'primary' orality and summarises a series of descriptors to use index of the relative orality or literacy of a given text or society.

John Miles Foley

In advance of Ong's synthesis, John Miles Foley, who studied with Robert Creed (who had in turn studied with Magoun), began a series of papers based on his own fieldwork on South Slavic oral genres, emphasising the dynamics of performers and audiences. Foley effectively consolidated oral tradition as an academic field when he compiled *Oral-Formulaic Theory and Research* in 1985. The bibliography gives a summary of the progress scholars made in evaluating the oral tradition up to that point, and includes a list of all relevant scholarly articles relating to the theory of Oral-Formulaic Composition. Foley established both the journal *Oral Tradition* and founded the *Center for Studies in Oral Tradition* at the University of Missouri. Foley developed Oral Theory beyond the somewhat mechanistic notions presented in earlier versions of Oral-Formulaic Theory, by extending Ong's interest in cultural features of oral societies beyond the verbal, by drawing attention to the agency of the bard and by describing how oral traditions bear meaning.

The bibliography would establish a clear underlying methodology which accounted for the findings of scholars working in the separate Linguistics fields (primarily Ancient Greek, Anglo-Saxon and Serbo-Croatian). Perhaps more importantly, it would stimulate conversation among these specialties, so that a network of independent but allied investigations and investigators could be established.

Theory of Oral Tradition

The theory of oral tradition would undergo elaboration and development as it grew in acceptance. While the number of formulas documented for various traditions proliferated, the concept of the formula remained lexically-bound. However, numerous innovations appeared, such as the "formulaic system" with structural "substitution slots" for syntactic, morphological and narrative necessity (as well as for artistic invention). Sophisticated models such as Foley's "word-type placement rules" followed. Higher levels of formulaic composition were defined over the years, such as "ring composition," "responsion" and the "type-scene" (also called a "theme" or "typical scene"). Examples include the "Beasts of Battle" and the "Cliffs of Death" Some of these characteristic patterns of narrative details, (like "the arming sequence;" "the hero on the beach;" "the traveler recognises his goal" would show evidence of global distribution.

At the same time, the fairly rigid division between oral and literate was replaced by recognition of transitional and compartmentalised texts and societies, including models of diglossia (Brian Stock Frans Bäuml, and Eric Havelock). Perhaps most importantly, the terms and concepts of "orality" and "literacy" came to be replaced with the more useful and apt "traditionality" and "textuality." Very large units would be defined (The Indo-European Return Song) and areas outside of military epic would come under investigation: women's song, riddles." and other genres.

The methodology of oral tradition now conditions a large variety of studies, not only in folklore, literature and literacy, but in philosophy, communication theory, Semiotics, and including a very broad and continually expanding variety of languages and ethnic groups, and perhaps most conspicuously in biblical studies, in which Werner Kelber has been especially prominent; the annual bibliography is indexed by 100 areas, most of which are ethnolinguistic divisions.

Present developments explore the implications of the theory for rhetoric and composition, interpersonal communication, cross-cultural communication, postcolonial studies, rural community development, popular culture and film studies, and many other areas. The most significant areas of theoretical development at present may be the construction of systematic hermeneutics and aesthetics specific to oral traditions.

The theory of oral tradition encountered early resistance from scholars who perceived it as potentially supporting either one side or another in the controversy between what were known as "unitarians" and "analysts" – that is, scholars who believed Homer to have been a single, historical figure, and those who saw him as a conceptual "author function," a convenient name to assign to what was essentially a repertoire of traditional narrative. A much more general dismissal of the theory and its implications simply described it as "unprovable". Some scholars, mainly outside the field of oral tradition, represent (either dismissively or with approval) this body of theoretical work as reducing the great epics to children's party games like "telephone" or "Chinese whispers".

While games provide amusement by showing how messages distort content via uncontextualised transmission, Parry's supporters argue that the theory of oral tradition reveals how oral methods optimised the signal-to-noise ratio and thus improved the quality, stability and integrity of content transmission.

There were disputes concerning particular findings of the theory. For example, those trying to support or refute Crowne's hypothesis found the "Hero on the Beach" formula in numerous Old English poems. It was also discovered in other works of Germanic origin, Middle English poetry, and even an Icelandic prose saga. J.A. Dane, in an article characterised as "polemics without rigor" claimed that the appearance of the theme in Ancient Greek poetry, a tradition without known connection to the Germanic, invalidated the notion of "an autonomous theme in the baggage of an oral poet."

Within Homeric studies specifically, Lord's *The Singer of Tales*, which focused on problems and questions that arise in conjunction with applying oral-formulaic theory to problematic texts such as the *Iliad, Odyssey,* and even *Beowulf,* influenced nearly all of the articles written on Homer and oral-formulaic composition thereafter. However, in response to Lord, Geoffrey Kirk published "The Songs of Homer," questioning Lord's extension of the oral-formulaic nature of Serbian and Croatian literature (the area from which the theory was first developed) to Homeric epic. Kirk argues that Homeric poems differ from those traditions in their "metrical strictness," "formular system[s]", and creativity.

In other words, Kirk argued that Homeric poems were recited under a system that gave the reciter much more freedom to choose words and passages to get to the same end than the Serbo-Croatian poet, who was merely "reproductive". Shortly thereafter, Eric Havelock's *Preface to Plato* revolutionised how scholars looked at Homeric epic by arguing not only that it was the product of an oral tradition, but also that the oral-formulas contained therein served as a way for ancient Greeks to preserve cultural knowledge across many different generations. Adam Parry, in his 1966 work "Have we Homer's *Iliad*?", theorised the existence of the most fully developed oral poet to his time, a person who could (at his discretion) creatively and intellectually create nuanced characters in the context of the accepted, traditional story. In fact, he discounted the Serbo-Croatian tradition to an "unfortunate" extent, choosing to elevate the Greek model of oral-tradition above all others. Lord reacted to Kirk's and Parry's essays with "Homer as Oral Poet," published in 1968, which reaffirmed Lord's belief in the relevance of Yugoslav poetry and its similarities to Homer and downplayed the intellectual and literary role of the reciters of Homeric epic.

Many of the criticisms of the theory have been absorbed into the evolving field as useful refinements and modifications. For example, in what Foley called a "pivotal" contribution, Larry Benson introduced the concept of "written-formulaic" to describe the status of some Anglo-Saxon poetry which, while demonstrably written, contains evidence of oral influences, including heavy reliance on formulas and themes. A number of individual scholars in many areas continue to have misgivings about the applicability of the theory or the aptness of the South Slavic comparison, and particularly what they regard as its implications for the creativity which may legitimately be attributed to the individual artist. However, at present, there seems to be little systematic or theoretically coordinated challenge to the fundamental tenets of the theory; as Foley put it, ""there have been numerous suggestions for revisions or modifications of the theory, but the majority of controversies have generated further understanding.

4

Ancient Greek Literature

The Ancient Greeks wrote a great deal, and a surprising amount of what they wrote is still available to us today, 2500 years later. The earliest extant European literary works are the *Iliad* and the *Odyssey,* both written in ancient Greek probably before 700 B.C., and attributed to Homer. Among other early epic poems, most of which have perished, those of Hesiod, the first didactic poet, remain. The poems dealing with mythological subjects and known as the *Homeric Hymns* are dated 800-300 B.C. Only fragments survive of the works of many early Greek poets, including the elegiasts Tyrtaeus, Theognis, Solon, Semonides of Amorgos, Archilochus, and Hipponax. The most personal Greek poems are the lyrics of Alcaeus, Sappho and Anacreon. The Dorian lyric for choral performance, developed with Alcman, Ibycus, and Stesichorus, achieved perfection in Pindar, Simonides of Ceos, and Bacchylides.

Classical and Pre-Classical Antiquity

This period of Greek literature stretches from Homer until the 4th century BC and the rise of Alexander the Great. Alfred North Whitehead once claimed that all of philosophy is but a footnote to Plato. To suggest that all of Western literature is no more than a footnote to the writings of ancient Greece is an exaggeration, but it is nevertheless true that the Greek world of thought was so far-ranging that there is scarcely an idea discussed today not already debated by the ancient writers.

The earliest known Greek writings are Mycenaean, written in the Linear B syllabary on clay tablets. These documents contain prosaic records largely concerned with trade (lists, inventories, receipts, etc.); no real literature has been discovered. Several theories have been advanced to explain this curious absence. One is that Mycenaean literature, like the works of Homer and other epic poems, was passed on orally, since the Linear B syllabary is not well-suited to recording the sounds of Greek (phonemic principle). Another is that literary works, being the preserve of an elite, were written on finer materials such as parchment, which have not survived.

Epic Poetry

At the beginning of Greek literature stand the two monumental works of Homer, the *Iliad* and the *Odyssey*. The figure of Homer is shrouded in mystery. Although the works as they now stand are credited to him, it is certain that their roots reach far back before his time. The *Iliad* is the famous story about the Trojan War. It centers on the person of Achilles, who embodied the Greek heroic ideal.

While the *Iliad* is pure tragedy, the *Odyssey* is a mixture of tragedy and comedy. It is the story of Odysseus, one of the warriors at Troy. After ten years fighting the war, he spends another ten years sailing back home to his wife and family. During his ten-year voyage, he loses all of his comrades and ships and makes his way home to Ithaca disguised as a beggar. Both of these works were based on ancient legends. The stories are told in language that is simple, direct, and eloquent. Both are as fascinatingly readable today as they were in ancient Greece.

The other great poet of the preclassical period was Hesiod. Unlike Homer, Hesiod speaks of himself in his poetry; it remains true that nothing is known about him from any external source. He was a native of Boeotia in central Greece, and is thought to have lived and worked around 700 BC. His two works were *Works and Days* and *Theogony*.

The first is a faithful depiction of the poverty-stricken country life he knew so well, and it sets forth principles and rules for farmers. *Theogony* is a systematic account of creation and of the gods. It vividly describes the ages of mankind, beginning with a long-past Golden Age. Together the works of Homer and Hesiod made a kind of bible for the Greeks. Homer told the story of a heroic past, and Hesiod dealt with the practical realities of daily life.

Lyric Poetry

The type of poetry called lyric got its name from the fact that it was originally sung by individuals or a chorus accompanied by the instrument called the lyre. The first of the lyric poets was probably Archilochus of Paros, circa 700 BC. Only fragments remain of his work, as is the case with most of the poets. The few remnants suggest that he was an embittered adventurer who led a very turbulent life.

Tragedy

The Greeks invented the epic and lyric forms and used them skillfully. They also invented drama and produced masterpieces that are still reckoned as drama's crowning achievement. In the age that followed the Greco-Persian Wars, the awakened national spirit of Athens was expressed in hundreds of superb tragedies based on heroic and legendary themes of the past. The tragic plays grew out of simple choral songs and dialogues performed at festivals of the god Dionysus. Wealthy citizens were chosen to bear the expense of costuming and training the chorus as a public and religious duty. Attendance at the festival performances was regarded as an act of worship. Performances were held in the great open-air theater of Dionysus in Athens. All of the greatest poets competed for the prizes offered for the best plays.

Comedy

Like tragedy, comedy arose from a ritual in honor of Dionysus, but in this case the plays were full of frank obscenity, abuse, and insult. At Athens the comedies became an official part of the festival celebration in 486 BC, and prizes were offered for the best productions. As with the tragedians, few works still remain of the great comedic writers. Of the works of earlier writers, only some plays by Aristophanes exist. These are a treasure trove of comic presentation. He poked fun at everyone and every institution. For boldness of fantasy, for merciless insult, for unqualified indecency, and for outrageous and free political criticism, there is nothing to compare to the comedies of Aristophanes. In *The Birds* he held up Athenian democracy to ridicule. In *The Clouds* he attacked the philosopher

Socrates. In *Lysistrata* he denounced war. Only 11 of his plays have survived.

Historiography

Two of the most famous historians who have ever written flourished during Greece's classical age: Herodotus and Thucydides. Herodotus is commonly called the father of history, and his "History" contains the first truly literary use of prose in Western literature. Of the two, Thucydides was the more careful historian. His critical use of sources, inclusion of documents, and laborious research made his History of the Peloponnesian War a significant influence on later generations of historians.

A third historian of ancient Greece, Xenophon, began his 'Hellenica' where Thucydides ended his work about 411 BC and carried his history to 362 BC. His writings were superficial in comparison to those of Thucydides, but he wrote with authority on military matters. He therefore is at his best in the Anabasis, an account of his participation in a Greek mercenary army that tried to help the Persian Cyrus expel his brother from the throne. Xenophon also wrote three works in praise of the philosopher Socrates: *Apology, Symposium,* and *Memorabilia.* Although both Xenophon and Plato knew Socrates, their accounts are very different, and it is interesting to compare the view of the military historian to that of the poet-philosopher.

Philosophy

The greatest achievement of the 4th century was in philosophy. There were many Greek philosophers, but three names tower above the rest: Socrates, Plato, and Aristotle. It is impossible to calculate the enormous influence these thinkers have had on Western society. Socrates himself wrote nothing, but his thought (or a reasonable presentation of it) is believed to be given by Plato's early socratic dialogues. Aristotle is virtually without rivals among scientists and philosophers. The first sentence of his *Metaphysics* reads: "All men by nature desire to know." He has, therefore, been called the "Father of those who know." His medieval disciple Thomas Aquinas referred to him simply as "the Philosopher." Aristotle was a student at Plato's Academy, and it is known that like his teacher he wrote dialogues, or conversations. None of these exists today. The body of writings that has come down to the present probably represents lectures that he delivered at his own school in Athens, the Lyceum. Even from these books the enormous range of his interests is evident. He explored matters other than those that are today considered philosophical. The treatises that exist cover logic, the physical and biological sciences, ethics, politics, and constitutional government. There are also treatises on *The Soul* and *Rhetoric*. His *Poetics* has had an enormous influence on literary theory and served as an interpretation of tragedy for more than 2,000 years. With his death in 322 BC, the classical era of Greek literature drew to a close.

Hellenistic Age

By 338 BC all of the Greek city-states except Sparta had been conquered by Philip II of Macedon. Philip's son Alexander the Great extended his father's conquests greatly. In so doing he inaugurated what is called the Hellenistic Ages. Alexander's conquests were in the East, and Greek culture shifted first in that direction. Athens lost its preeminent status as the leader of Greek culture, and it was replaced temporarily by Alexandria, Egypt.

The city of Alexandria in northern Egypt became, from the 3rd century BC, the outstanding center of Greek culture. It also soon attracted a large Jewish population, making it the largest center for Jewish scholarship in the ancient world. In addition, it later became a major focal point for the development of Christian thought. The Museum, or Shrine to the Muses, which included the library and school, was founded by Ptolemy I. The institution was from the beginning intended as a great international school and library. The library, eventually containing more than a half million volumes, was mostly in Greek. It served as a repository for every Greek work of the classical period that could be found.

Hellenistic Poetry

Later Greek poetry flourished primarily in the 3rd century BC. The chief poets were Theocritus, Callimachus, and Apollonius of Rhodes. Theocritus, who lived from about 310 to 250 BC, was the creator of pastoral poetry, a type that the Roman Virgil mastered in his Eclogues. Of his rural-farm poetry, Harvest Home is considered the best work. He also wrote mimes, poetic plays set in the country as well as minor epics and lyric poetry.

Callimachus, who lived at the same time as Theocritus, worked his entire adult life at Alexandria, compiling a catalogue of the library. Only fragments of his poetry survive. The most famous work was Aetia (Causes). It is a kind of poem called an elegy and in four books explains the legendary origin of obscure customs, festivals, and names. Its structure became a model for the work of the Roman poet Ovid. Of his elegies for special occasions, the best known is the

'Lock of Berenice', a piece of court poetry that was later adapted by the Roman Catullus. Callimachus also wrote short poems for special occasions and at least one short epic, the 'Ibis', which was directed against his former pupil Apollonius.

Apollonius of Rhodes was born about 295 BC. He is best remembered for his epic the 'Argonautica', about Jason and his shipmates in search of the golden fleece. Apollonius studied under Callimachus, with whom he later quarreled. He also served as librarian at Alexandria for about 13 years. Apart from the 'Argonautica', he wrote poems on the foundation of cities as well as a number of epigrams. The Roman poet Virgil was strongly influenced by the 'Argonautica' in writing his Aeneid. Lesser 3rd-century poets include Aratus of Soli and Herodas. Aratus wrote the 'Phaenomena', a poetic version of a treatise on the stars by Eudoxus of Cnidus, who had lived in the 4th century. Herodas wrote mimes reminiscent of those of Theocritus. His works give a hint of the popular entertainment of the times. Mime and pantomime were a major form of entertainment during the early Roman Empire

Hellenistic and Roman Periods

While the transition from city-state to empire affected philosophy a great deal, shifting the emphasis from political theory to personal ethics, Greek letters continued to flourish both under the Successors (especially the Ptolemies) and under Roman rule. Romans of literary or rhetorical inclination looked to Greek models, and Greek literature of all types continued to be read and produced both by native speakers of Greek and later by Roman authors as well.

A notable characteristic of this period was the expansion of literary criticism as a genre, particularly as exemplified by Demetrius, Pseudo-Longinus and Dionysius of Halicarnassus. The Greek novel, typified by Chariton's *Callirhoe* and the *Hero and Leander* of Pseudo-Musaeus, also emerged. The New Testament, written by various authors in varying qualities of Koine Greek also hails from this period, the most important works being the Gospels and the Epistles of Saint Paul.

Historiography

The significant historians in the period after Alexander were Timaeus, Polybius, Diodorus Siculus, Dionysius of Halicarnassus, Appian of Alexandria, Arrian, and Plutarch. The period of time they cover extended from late in the 4th century BC to the 2nd century AD.

Timaeus was born in Sicily but spent most of his life in Athens. His 'History', though lost, is significant because of its influence on Polybius. In 38 books it covered the history of Sicily and Italy to the year 264 BC, which is where Polybius began his work. Timaeus wrote the 'Olympionikai', a valuable chronological study of the Olympic Games. Polybius was born about 200 BC and brought to Rome as a hostage in 168. At Rome a friend of the general Scipio Aemilianus became his friend.

Theocritus probably accompanied the general to Spain and North Africa in the wars against Carthage and was with Scipio at the destruction of Carthage in 146. The history on which his reputation rests consisted of 40 books, five of which have been preserved along with various excerpts. They are a vivid recreation of Rome's rise to world power. A lost book, 'Tactics', was on military matters.

Diodorus Siculus lived in the 1st century BC, the time of Julius Caesar and Augustus. Diodorus wrote 'Bibliotheca historica', in 40 books. Of these, the first five and the 11th through the 20th remain. The first two parts covered history through the early Hellenistic era. The third part takes the story to the beginning of Caesar's wars in Gaul, now France. Dionysius of Halicarnassus lived late in the 1st century BC. His history of Rome from its origins to the First Punic War (264 to 241 BC) is written from a Roman point of view, but it is carefully researched. Diodorus also wrote a number of other treatises, including 'On Imitation', 'Commentaries on the Ancient Orators', and 'On the Arrangement of Words'.

Appian and Arrian both lived in the 2nd century AD. Appian wrote on Rome and its conquests, while Arrian is remembered for his work on the campaigns of Alexander the Great. Arrian served in the Roman army. His book therefore concentrates heavily on the military aspects of Alexander's life. Arrian also wrote a philosophical treatise, the 'Diatribai', based on the teachings of his mentor Epictetus. Best known of the late Greek historians to modern readers is Plutarch, who died about AD 119. His 'Parallel Lives' of great Greek and Roman leaders has been read by every generation since the work was first published. His other surviving work is the 'Moralia', a collection of essays on ethical, religious, political, physical, and literary topics.

Scientific and Mathematical Writings

Eratosthenes of Alexandria, who died about 194 BC, wrote on astronomy and geography, but his work is known mainly from later summaries. Eratosthenes is credited with being the first person to measure the Earth's circumference. Much that was written by the mathematicians Euclid and Archimedes has been preserved. Euclid is known for his *Elements,* much of which was drawn from his predecessor Eudoxus of Cnidus. The *Elements* is a treatise on geometry, and it has exerted a continuing influence on mathematics. From Archimedes several treatises have come down to the present. Among them are *Measurement of the Circle,* in which he worked out the value of pi; *The Method of Mechanical Theorems,* on his work in mechanics; *The Sand Reckoner*; and *On Floating Bodies*. A manuscript of his works is currently being studied.

The physician Galen, in the history of ancient science, is the most significant person in medicine after Hippocrates, who laid the foundation of medicine in the 5th century BC. Galen lived during the 2nd century AD, a careful student of anatomy, and his works exerted a powerful influence on medicine for the next 1,400 years. Strabo, who died about AD 23, was a geographer and historian. His 'Historical Sketches' in 47 volumes has nearly all been lost. His *Geographical Sketches* remain as the only existing ancient book, covering the whole range of people and countries known to the Greeks and Romans through the time of Augustus. Pausanias, who lived in the 2nd century AD, was also a geographer.

His *Description of Greece* is an invaluable guide to what are now ancient ruins. His book takes the form of a tour of Greece, starting in Athens. The accuracy of his descriptions has been proved by archaeological excavations. The scientist of the Roman period who had the greatest influence on later generations was undoubtedly the astronomer Ptolemy, lived during the

2nd century AD, though little is known of his life. His masterpiece, originally entitled *The Mathematical Collection,* has come to the present under the title *Almagest,* as it was translated by Arab astronomers with that title. It was Ptolemy who devised a detailed description of an Earth-centered universe, a notion that dominated astronomical thinking for more than 1,300 years. The Ptolemaic view of the universe endured until Copernicus, Galileo, Kepler, and other early modern astronomers replaced it with heliocentrism.

Late Philosophical Works

Later philosophical works were no match for Plato and Aristotle. Epictetus, who died about AD 135, was associated with the moral philosophy of the Stoics. His teachings were collected by his pupil Arrian in the 'Discourses' and the 'Encheiridion' (Manual of Study). Diogenes Laertius, who lived in the 3rd century, wrote 'Lives, Teachings, and Sayings of Famous Philosophers', a useful sourcebook. Another major philosopher of his period was Plotinus transformed Plato's philosophy into a school called Neoplatonism. His 'Enneads' had a wide-ranging influence on European thought until at least the 17th century.

5

Ancient Latin Literature

Latin literature, the body of written works in the Latin language, remains an enduring legacy of the culture of ancient Rome. The Romans produced many works of poetry, comedy, tragedy, satire, history, and rhetoric, drawing heavily on the traditions of other cultures and particularly on the more matured literary tradition of Greece. Long after the Western Roman Empire had fallen, the Latin language continued to play a central role in western European civilisation.

Latin literature is conventionally divided into distinct periods. Few works remain of Early and Old Latin; among these few surviving works, however, are the plays of Plautus and Terence, which have remained very popular in all eras down to the present, while many other Latin works, including many by the most prominent authors of the Classical period, have disappeared, sometimes being re-discovered after centuries, sometimes not. Such lost works sometimes survive as fragments in other works which have survived, but others are known from references in such works as Pliny the Elder's Naturalis Historia or the De Architectura of Vitruvius.

Classical Latin

The period of Classical Latin, when Latin literature is widely considered to have reached its peak, is divided into the Golden Age, which covers approximately the period from the start of the 1st century BC up to the mid-1st century AD, and the Silver Age, which extends into the 2nd century AD. Literature written after the mid-2nd century has often been disparaged and ignored; in the Renaissance, for example, when many Classical authors were re-discovered and their style consciously imitated. Above all, Cicero was imitated, and his style praised as the pinnacle of Latin style. Medieval Latin was often dismissed as inferior; but in fact, many great works of Latin literature were produced throughout Late Antiquity and the Middle Ages, although they are no longer as widely known as those written in the Classical period. Three works survived to inspire architects and engineers in the Renaissance, the Naturalis Historia of Pliny the Elder, the books by Frontinus on the aqueducts of Rome and the De Architectura of Vitruvius.

Philological Constructs

The Classical

Good Latin in philology is "classical" Latin literature. The term refers to the canonicity of works of literature written in Latin in the late Roman republic and the early to middle Roman empire: "that is to say, that of belonging to an exclusive group of authors (or works) that were considered to be emblematic of a certain genre." The term *classicus* (masculine plural *classici*) was devised by the Romans themselves to translate Greek (enkrithentes), "select", referring to authors who wrote in Greek that was considered model. Prior to then *classis,* in addition to being a naval fleet, was a social class in one of the diachronic divisions of Roman society according to property ownership by the Roman constitution. The word is a transliteration into the Latin alphabet of Greek (klsis), a "calling" of draftees for the army by property: first class, second class, etc., down to fifth class.

Classicus is anything *primae classis,* "first class", such as the authors of the polished works of *Latinitas,* or *sermo urbanus.* It had nuances of the certified and the authentic: *testis classicus,* "reliable witness." It was in this sense that Marcus Cornelius Fronto (an African-Roman lawyer and language teacher) in the 2nd century AD used *scriptores classici,* "first-class" or "reliable authors" whose works could be relied upon as model of good Latin. This is the first known reference, possibly innovated at this time, to classical applied to authors by virtue of the authentic language of their works.

The Canonical

In imitation of the Greek grammarians, the Roman ones, such as Quintilian, drew up lists termed *indices* or *ordines* on the model of the Greek lists, termed *pinakes,* considered classical: the *recepti scriptores,* "select writers." Aulus Gellius includes many authors, such as Plautus, who are currently considered writers of Old Latin and not strictly in the period of classical Latin. The classical Romans distinguished Old Latin as *prisca Latinitas* and not *sermo vulgaris.* Each author (and work) in the Roman lists was considered equivalent to one in the Greek; for example Ennius was the Latin Homer, the Aeneid was a new Iliad, and so on. The lists of classical authors were as far as the Roman grammarians went in developing a philology. The topic remained at that point while interest in the *classici scriptores* declined in the medieval period as the best Latin yielded to medieval Latin, somewhat less than the best by classical standards.

The Renaissance brought a revival of interest in restoring as much of Roman culture as could be restored and with it the return of the concept of classic, "the best." Thomas Sebillet in 1548 (*Art Poétique*) referred to "les bons et classiques poètes françois", meaning Jean de Meun and Alain Chartier, which was the first modern application of the word. According to Merriam Webster's Collegiate Dictionary, the term classical, from *classicus*, entered modern English in 1599, some 50 years after its re-introduction on the continent. Governor William Bradford in 1648 referred to synods of a separatist church as "classical meetings" in his *Dialogue*, a report of a meeting between New-England-born "young men" and "ancient men" from Holland and England. In 1715 Laurence Echard's *Classical Geographical Dictionary* was published. In 1736 Robert Ainsworth's *Thesaurus Linguae Latinae Compendarius* turned English words and expressions into "proper and classical Latin." In 1768 David Ruhnken (*Critical History of the Greek Orators*) recast the mold of the view of the classical by applying the word canon to the *pinakes* of orators, after the Biblical canon or list of authentic books of the Bible. Ruhnken had a kind of secular catechism in mind.

The Ages of Latin

In 1870 Wilhelm Sigismund Teuffel in *Geschichte der Römischen Literatur* (*A History of Roman Literature*) innovated the definitive philological classification of classical Latin based on the metaphoric uses of the ancient myth of the Ages of Man, a practice then universally current: a Golden Age and a Silver Age of classical Latin were to be presumed. The practice and Teuffel's classification, with modifications, are still in use. His work was translated into English as soon as published in German by Wilhelm Wagner, who corresponded with Teuffel. Wagner published the English translation in 1873. Teuffel divides the chronology of classical Latin authors into several periods according to political events, rather than by style. Regarding the style of the literary Latin of those periods he had but few comments.

Teuffel was to go on with other editions of his history, but meanwhile it had come out in English almost as soon as it did in German and found immediate favorable reception. In 1877 Charles Thomas Cruttwell produced the first English work along the same lines. In his Preface he refers to "Teuffel's admirable history, without which many chapters in the present work could not have attained completeness" and also gives credit to Wagner.

Cruttwell adopts the same periods with minor differences; however, where Teuffel's work is mainly historical, Cruttwell's work contains detailed analyses of style. Nevertheless like Teuffel he encounters the same problem of trying to summarize the voluminous detail in a way that captures in brief the gist of a few phases of writing styles. Like Teuffel, he has trouble finding a name for the first of the three periods (the current Old Latin phase), calling it mainly "from Livius to Sulla." The language, he says, is ..."marked by immaturity of art and language, by a vigorous but ill-disciplined imitation of Greek poetical models, and in prose by a dry sententiousness of style, gradually giving way to a clear and fluent strength...." These abstracts have little meaning to those not well-versed in Latin literature. In fact, Cruttwell admits "The ancients, indeed, saw a difference between Ennius, Pacuvius, and Accius, but it may be questioned whether the advance would be perceptible by us."

Some of Cruttwell's ideas have become stock in Latin philology for better or for worse. While praising the application of rules to classical Latin, most intensely in the Golden Age, he says "In gaining accuracy, however, classical Latin suffered a grievous loss. It became cultivated as distinct from a natural language .... Spontaneity, therefore, became impossible and soon invention also ceased.... In a certain sense, therefore, Latin was studied as a dead language, while it was still a living." These views are certainly debatable; one might ask how the upper classes of late 16th century Britain, who shared the Renaissance zealousness for the classics, managed to speak spontaneous Latin to each other officially and unofficially after being taught classical Latin by tutors hired for the purpose. *Latinitas* in the Golden Age was in fact *sermo familiaris,* the spoken Latin of the Roman upper classes, who sent their children to school to learn it. The debate continues.

A second problem is the appropriateness of Teuffel's scheme to the concept of classical Latin, which Teuffel does not discuss. Cruttwell addresses the problem, however, altering the concept of the classical. As the best Latin is defined as golden Latin, the second of the three periods, the other two periods considered classical are left hanging. While on the one hand assigning to Old Latin the term pre-classical and by implication the term post-classical (or post-

Augustan) to silver Latin Cruttwell realizes that this construct is not according to ancient usage and asserts "... the epithet classical is by many restricted to the authors who wrote in it [golden Latin]. It is best, however, not to narrow unnecessarily the sphere of classicity; to exclude Terence on the one hand or Tacitus and Pliny on the other, would savour of artificial restriction rather than that of a natural classification." (This from a scholar who had just been complaining that golden Latin was not a natural language.) The contradiction remains; Terence is and is not a classical author depending on context.

Stylistic Shifts

The style of language refers to repeatable features of speech that are somewhat less general than the fundamental characteristics of the language. The latter give it a unity allowing it to be referenced under a single name. Thus Old Latin, Classical Latin, Vulgar Latin, etc., are not considered different languages, but are all referenced under the name of Latin. This is an ancient practice continued by moderns rather than a philological innovation of recent times. That Latin had case endings is a fundamental feature of the language. Whether a given form of speech prefers to use prepositions such as *ad, ex, de* for "to", "from" and "of" rather than simple case endings is a matter of style. Latin has a large number of styles. Each and every author has a style, which typically allows his prose or poetry to be identified by experienced Latinists. The problem of comparative literature has been to group styles finding similarites by period, in which case one may speak of Old Latin, Silver Latin, Late Latin as styles or a phase of styles.

The ancient authors themselves first defined style by recognizing different kinds of *sermo,* or "speech." In making the value judgement that classical Latin was "first class" and that it was better to write with *Latinitas* they were themselves selecting the literary and upper-class language of the city as a standard style and all *sermo* that differed from it was a different style; thus in rhetoric Cicero was able to define sublime, intermediate and low styles (within classical Latin) and St. Augustine to recommend the low style for sermons (from *sermo*). Style therefore is to be defined by differences in speech from a standard. Teuffel defined that standard as Golden Latin.

Literature of Medieval World

Medieval Latin was the form of Latin used in the Middle Ages, primarily as a medium of scholarly exchange and as the liturgical language of the medieval Roman Catholic Church, but also as a language of science, literature, law, and administration. Despite the clerical origin of many of its authors, Medieval Latin should not be confused with Ecclesiastical Latin. There is no real consensus on the exact boundary where Late Latin ends and Medieval Latin begins. Some scholarly surveys begin with the rise of early Christian Latin in the middle of the 4th century, others around the year 500, and still others with the replacement of written Late Latin by written Romance languages starting around the year 900.

Medieval Latin was characterized by an enlarged vocabulary, which freely borrowed from other sources. It was heavily influenced by the language of the Vulgate, which contained many peculiarities alien to Classical Latin that were the consequence of more or less direct translation from Greek and Hebrew; these peculiarities were mirrored not only in its vocabulary, but also in its grammar and syntax. Greek provided much of the technical vocabulary of Christianity. The various Germanic languages spoken by the Germanic tribes, who invaded western Europe, were also major sources of new words. Germanic leaders became the rulers of western Europe, and words from their languages were freely imported into the vocabulary of law. Other more ordinary words were replaced by coinages from Vulgar Latin or Germanic sources because the classical words had fallen into disuse.

Latin was also spread to areas such as Ireland and Germany, where Romance languages were not spoken and which had never known Roman rule. Works written in these lands where Latin was a learned language with no relation to the local vernacular also influenced the vocabulary and syntax of medieval Latin.

Since abstract subjects like science and philosophy were communicated in Latin, the Latin vocabulary developed for them is the source of a great many technical words in modern languages. English words like *abstract, subject, communicate, matter, probable* and their cognates in other European languages generally have the meanings given to them in medieval Latin.

The influence of Vulgar Latin was also apparent in the syntax of some Medieval Latin writers, although Classical Latin continued to be held in high esteem and studied as models for literary compositions. The high point of development of medieval Latin as a literary language came with the Carolingian renaissance, a rebirth of learning kindled under the patronage of Charlemagne, king of the Franks. Alcuin was Charlemagne's Latin secretary and an important writer in his own right; his influence led to a rebirth of Latin literature and learning after the depressed period following the final disintegration of Roman authority in Western Europe.

Although it was simultaneously developing into the Romance languages, Latin itself remained very conservative, as it was no longer a native language and there were many ancient and medieval grammar books to give one standard form. On the other hand, strictly speaking there was no single form of "Medieval Latin". Every Latin author in the medieval period spoke Latin as a second language, to varying degrees of fluency, and syntax, grammar, and vocabulary were often influenced by an author's native language. This was especially true beginning around the 12th century, after which the language became increasingly adulterated: late-medieval Latin documents written by French speakers tend to show similarities to medieval French grammar and vocabulary; those written by Germans tend to show similarities to German, etc. For instance, rather than following the classical Latin practice of generally placing the verb at the end, medieval writers would often follow the conventions of their own native language instead. Whereas Latin had no definite or indefinite articles, medieval writers sometimes used forms of *unus* as an indefinite article, and forms of *ille* (reflecting usage in the Romance languages) or even *quidam* (meaning "a certain one/thing" in Classical Latin) as something like a definite article. Unlike in classical Latin, where *esse* ("to be") was used as the only auxiliary verb, Medieval Latin writers might use *habere* ("to have"), as Germanic and Romance languages do. The accusative infinitive construction in classical Latin was often ignored, in favour of introducing a subordinate clause with the word *quod* or *quia*. This is almost identical, for example, to the use of *que* in similar constructions in French.

In every age from the late eighth century onwards, there were learned writers (especially within the Church) who were familiar enough with classical syntax to be aware that these forms and usages were 'wrong' and able to resist their use. Thus the Latin of a theologian like St. Thomas Aquinas or an erudite clerical historian such as William of Tyre tends to avoid most of the characteristics described above, showing its period in vocabulary and spelling alone; the features listed are much more prominent in the language of lawyers (e.g. the 11th-century English Domesday Book), physicians, technical writers and secular chroniclers. However, the last-mentioned point — the indirect-statement construction with *quod* — was especially pervasive and is found at all levels.

For most of the Medieval era, Latin was the dominant written language in use in western Europe. After the Roman Empire split into its Western and Eastern halves, Greek, which had been widely used all over the Empire, faded from use in the West, all the more so as the political and religious distance steadily grew between the Catholic West and the Orthodox, Greek East. The vernacular languages in the West, the languages of modern-day western Europe, developed for centuries as spoken languages only: most people did not write, and it seems that it very seldom occurred to those who wrote to write in any language other than Latin, even when they spoke French or Italian or English or another vernacular in their daily life. Very gradually, in the late Middle Ages and the early Renaissance, it became more and more common to write in the Western vernaculars.

It was probably only after the invention of printing, which made books and pamphlets cheap enough that a mass public could afford them, and which made possible modern phenomena such as the newspaper, that a large number of people in the West could read and write who were not fluent in Latin. Still, many people continued to write in Latin, although they were mostly from the upper classes and/ or professional academics. As late as the 17th century, there was still a large audience for Latin poetry and drama; it was not unusual, for example, that Milton wrote many poems in Latin, or that Francis Bacon or Baruch Spinoza wrote mostly in Latin. The use of Latin as a lingua franca continued in smaller European lands until the 20th century.

Although the number of works of non-fiction and drama, history and philosophy written in Latin has continued to dwindle, the Latin language is still not dead. Well into the twentieth century, some knowledge of Latin was required for admission into many universities, and theses and dissertations written for graduate degrees were often required to be written in Latin. Treatises in chemistry and biology and other natural sciences were often written in Latin as late as the early 20th century. Up to the present day, the editors of Latin and Greek texts in such series as the Oxford Classical Texts, the Bibliotheca scriptorum Graecorum et Romanorum Teubneriana and some others still write the introductions to their editions in polished and vital Latin. Among these Latin scholars of the 20th and 21st centuries are R.A.B. Mynors, R.J. Tarrant, L.D. Reynolds and John Brisco.

The first half of the 5th century saw the literary activities of the great Christian authors Jerome (c. 347–420) and Augustine of Hippo (354–430), whose texts had an enormous influence on theological thought of the Middle Ages, and of the latter's disciple Prosper of Aquitaine (c. 390-455). Of the later 400s and early 500s, Sidonius Apollinaris (c. 430 – after 489) and Ennodius (474–521), both from Gaul, are well-known for their poems, as is Venantius Fortunatus (c. 530–600). This was also a period of transmission: the Roman patrician Boethius (c. 480–524) translated part of Aristotle's logical corpus, thus preserving it for the Latin West, and wrote the influential literary and philosophical treatise *De consolatione Philosophiae;* Cassiodorus (c. 485–585) founded an important library at the monastery of Vivarium near Squillace where many texts from Antiquity were to be preserved. Isidore of Seville (c. 560-636) collected all scientifical knowledge still available in his time into what might be called the first encyclopedia, the *Etymologiae.*

Etymologiae

Etymologiae was compiled by Isidore of Seville (died 636) towards the end of his life, which forms a bridge between a condensed epitome of classical learning at the close of Late Antiquity and the inheritance received, in large part through Isidore's work, by the early Middle Ages. according to the prefatory letters, the work was composed at the urging of his friend Braulio, Bishop of Saragossa, to whom Isidore, at the end of his life, sent his *codex inemendatus* ("unedited book"), which seems to have begun circulating before Braulio was able to revise it, and issue it, with a dedication to the late Visigothic King Sisebut. Partly as a consequence, three families of texts have been distinguished, including a "compressed" text with many omissions, and an expanded text with interpolations.

Etymologiae presents in abbreviated form much of that part of the learning of antiquity that Christians thought worth preserving. Etymologies, often very learned and far-fetched, a favorite *trope* of Antiquity, form the subject of just one of the encyclopedia's twenty books, but perceived linguistic similarities permeate the work. Isidore's vast encyclopedia systematizing ancient learning includes subjects from theology to furniture and provided a rich source of classical lore and learning for medieval writers.

In all, Isidore quotes from 154 authors, both Christian and pagan. Many of the Christian authors he read in the originals; of the pagans, many he consulted in current compilations. Bishop Braulio, to whom Isidore dedicated it and sent it for correction, divided it into its twenty books

W. M. Lindsay noted in 1911, having recently edited Isidore for the Clarendon Press, with the further observation, however, that a portion of the texts quoted have otherwise been lost: the *Prata* of Suetonius can only be reconstructed from Isidore's excerpts. In the second book, dealing with dialectic and rhetoric, Isidore is heavily indebted to translations from the Greek by Boethius, and in treating logic, Cassiodorus, who provided the gist of Isidore's treatment of arithmetic in Book III. Caelius Aurelianus contributes generously to that part of the fourth book which deals with medicine. Isidore's view of Roman law in the fifth book is viewed through the lens of the Visigothic compendiary called the *Breviary of Alaric*, which was based on the Code of Theodosius, which Isidore never saw. Through Isidore's condensed paraphrase a third-hand memory of Roman law passed to the Early Middle Ages. Lactantius is the author most extensively quoted in the eleventh book, concerning man. The twelfth, thirteenth, and fourteenth books are largely based on the writings of Pliny and Solinus; whilst the lost *Prata* of Suetonius, which can be partly pieced together from its quoted passages in *Etymolgiae,* seems to have inspired the general plan of the "Etymologiae", as well as many of its details.

Isidore's Latin, replete with nonstandard Vulgar Latin, some of which is identified as such, also stands at the cusp of Latin and the local Romance language of Hispania.

Through the Middle Ages *Etymologiae* was the textbook most in use, regarded so highly as a depository of classical learning that, in a great measure, it superseded the use of the individual works of the classics themselves, full texts of which were no longer copied and thus were lost. The book was not only one of the most popular compendia in medieval libraries but was printed in at least ten editions between 1470 and 1530, showing Isidore's continued popularity in the Renaissance, rivalling Vincent of Beauvais.

A stylized T and O map featuring the world as a wheel appeared in the *editio princeps,* the first printed edition, published at Augsburg, 1472. The continent Asia is peopled by descendants of Sem or Shem, Africa by descendants of Ham and Europe by descendants of Japheth, the sons of Noah.

Isidore taught in the *Etymologiae* that the Earth was round. His meaning was ambiguous and some writers think he referred to a disc-shaped Earth; his other writings make it clear, however, that he considered the Earth to be globular. He also admitted the possibility of people dwelling at the antipodes, considering them as legendary and noting that there was no evidence for their existence. Isidore's disc-shaped analogy continued to be used through the Middle Ages by authors clearly favouring a spherical Earth, e.g. the 9th century bishop Rabanus Maurus who compared the habitable part of the northern hemisphere (Aristotle's northern temperate clime) with a wheel, imagined as a slice of the whole sphere.

The 13th century Codex Gigas, the largest extant medieval manuscript, contains a copy of the *Etymologiae*. The modern critical edition, superceeding W.M. Lindsay's of 1911, supervised by an Intenational Committee of Isidorian Studies, (B. Bischoff, M.C. Díaz, J. Fontaine, J.N. Hilgarth, eds.) was announced in 1974, intended to appear in twenty volumes, one for each book, with an additional volume discussing the manuscript history and presenting a general introduction.

Gregory of Tours (c. 538–594) wrote a lengthy history of the Frankish kings. Gregory came from a Gallo-Roman aristocratic family, and his Latin, which shows many aberrations from the classical forms, testifies to the declining significance of classical education in Gaul. At the same time, good knowledge of Latin and even of Greek was being preserved in monastic culture in Ireland and was brought to England and the European mainland by missionaries in the course of the 6th and 7th centuries, such as Columbanus (543–615), who founded the monastery of Bobbio in Northern Italy. Ireland was also the birthplace of a strange poetic style known as Hisperic

Latin. Other important Insular authors include the historian Gildas (c. 500–570) and the poet Aldhelm (c. 640–709). Benedict Biscop (c. 628–690) founded the monastery of Wearmouth-Jarrow and furnished it with books which he had taken home from a journey to Rome and which were later used by Bede (c. 672–735) to write his *Ecclesiastical History of the English People.*

Ecclesiastical History of the English People

It is considered to be one of the most important original references on Anglo-Saxon history. It is believed to have been completed in 731, when Bede was approximately 60 years old.

Bede's best-known work is the *Historia ecclesiastica gentis Anglorum*, or *An Ecclesiastical History of the English People.* Completed in about 731, the first of the five books begins with some geographical background, and then sketches the history of England, beginning with Caesar's invasion in 55 B.C. A brief account of Christianity in Roman Britain, including the martyrdom of St Alban, is followed by the story of Augustine's mission to England in 597, which brought Christianity to the Anglo-Saxons.

The second book begins with the death of Gregory the Great in 604, and follows the further progress of Christianity in Kent and the first attempts to evangelize Northumbria. These ended in disaster when Penda, the pagan king of Mercia, killed the newly Christian Edwin of Northumbria at the Battle of Hatfield Chase in about 632. The setback was temporary, and the third book recounts the growth of Christianity in Northumbria under kings Oswald of Northumbria and Oswy. The climax of the third book is the account of the Council of Whitby, traditionally seen as a major turning point in English history. The fourth book begins with the consecration of Theodore as Archbishop of Canterbury, and recounts Wilfrid's efforts to bring Christianity to the kingdom of Sussex. The fifth book brings the story up to Bede's day, and includes an account of missionary work in Frisia, and of the conflict with the British church over the correct dating of Easter. Bede wrote a preface for the work, in which he dedicates it to Ceolwulf, king of Northumbria.

The preface mentions that Ceolwulf received an earlier draft of the book; presumably Ceolwulf knew enough Latin to understand it, and he may even have been able to read it. The preface makes it clear that Ceolwulf had requested the earlier copy, and Bede had asked for Ceolwulf's approval; this correspondence with the king indicates that Bede's monastery had excellent connections among the Northumbrian nobility.

Divided into five books (about 400 pages), the *Historia* covers the history of England, ecclesiastical and political, from the time of Julius Caesar to the date of its completion. The first twenty-one chapters, covering the period before the mission of Augustine, are compiled from earlier writers such as Orosius, Gildas, Prosper of Aquitaine, the letters of Pope Gregory I, and others, with the insertion of legends and traditions.

After AD 596, documentary sources, which Bede took pains to obtain throughout England and from Rome, are used, as well as oral testimony, which he employed along with critical consideration of its authenticity.

The *Historia,* like other historical writing from this period has a lower degree of objectivity than modern historical writings. It is a mixture of fact, legend and literature. For example, Bede quotes some speeches at length, by people who were not his contemporaries, and yet whose speeches do not appear in any other source.

The monastery at Jarrow had an excellent library. Both Benedict Biscop and Ceolfrith had acquired books from the Continent, and in Bede's day the monastery was a renowned centre of learning.

For the period prior to Augustine's arrival in 597, Bede drew on earlier writers, including Orosius, Eutropius, Pliny, and Solinus. He used Constantius's *Life of Germanus* as a source for Germanus's visits to Britain. Bede's account of the invasion of the Anglo-Saxons is drawn largely from Gildas's *De Excidio et Conquestu Britanniae.* Bede would also have been familiar with more recent accounts such as Eddius Stephanus's *Life of Wilfrid,* and anonymous *Lives* of Gregory the Great and Cuthbert. He also drew on Josephus's *Antiquities,* and the works of Cassiodorus, and there was a copy of the *Liber Pontificalis* in Bede's monastery.

Bede also had correspondents who supplied him with material. Albinus, the abbot of the monastery in Canterbury, provided much information about the church in Kent, and with the assistance of Nothhelm, at that time a priest in London, obtained copies of Gregory the Great's correspondence from Rome relating to Augustine's mission. Almost all of Bede's information regarding Augustine is taken from these letters. Bede acknowledged his correspondents in the preface to the *Historia Ecclesiastica;* he was in contact with Daniel, the Bishop of Winchester, for information about the history of the church in Wessex, and also wrote to the monastery at Lastingham for information about Cedd and Chad. Bede also mentions an Abbot Esi as a source for the affairs of the East Anglian church, and Bishop Cynibert for information about Lindsey.

The History of the English Church and People has a clear polemical and didactic purpose. Bede sets out, not just to tell the story of the English, but to advance his views on politics and religion. In political terms he is a partisan of his native Northumbria, amplifying its role in English history over and above that of Mercia, its great southern rival. He takes greater pains in describing events of the seventh century, when Northumbria was the dominant Anglo-Saxon power, than the eighth, when it was not. The only criticism he ventures of his native Northumbria comes in writing about the death of King Ecgfrith in fighting the Picts at Nechtansmere in 685.

Bede attributes this defeat to God's vengeance for the Northumbrian attack on the Irish in the previous year. For while Bede is loyal to Northumbria he shows an even greater attachment to the Irish and the Irish Celtic missionaries, whom he considers to be far more effective and dedicated than their rather complacent English counterparts.

His final preoccupation is over the precise date of Easter, which he writes about at length. It is here, and only here, that he ventures some criticism of St Cuthbert and the Irish missionaries, who celebrated the event, according to Bede, at the wrong time. In the end he is pleased to note that the Irish Church was saved from error by accepting the correct date for Easter.

6

Ancient Indian Literature

The ancient literature is the crowning glory of the Indian civilization. No other part of the world has produced such voluminous literature of knowledge and wisdom. The Vedas are the most celebrated possessions of the mankind. The Rig Veda is the oldest literary work in the history of the world. The Vedas are the exquisite expressions of the Divinity. They are the first significant utterances on the lips of man. The ancient Indian literature is the glorious gift of the Indian civilization to the world. It comprises of the illustrious scriptures. The Indian scriptures can be broadly classified into two categories:

(1) The *Shruti* literature

(2) The *Smriti* literature.

Shruti is concerned with 'the heard' or 'the revealed'. *Smriti* is concerned with 'the remembered.'

The Vedas and the Upanishads are considered as the *Shruti* literature. The Sanskrit root *'shrut'* means 'to hear'. In ancient times, while doing their *tapasya* and *sadhana,* the great sages 'heard' the divine truths. Whatever was 'heard' was presented in the Vedas and the Upanishads. Thus they came to be known as the *Shruti* literature.

Smriti literature is concerned with 'that what is remembered'. The literature which was based on the knowledge acquired through the experience or the tradition was the *Smriti* literature.

Generally, the *Smriti* literature is based on the *Shruti*. The famous Manu-Smriti and other *smritis* and *shastras* constitute the *Smriti* literature. The guidelines for ethics, moral obligations, social codes, customs etc. are found in the *Smriti* literature. The great epics Mahabharata and Ramayana also belong to the *Smriti* literature.

While the *Shruti* literature is veritable and inviolable, the *Smriti* literature may get modified under the influence of time and place.

Vedic Literature

The Vedas represent the most sacred heritage of the mankind.

The Vedas reflect the growth and development of human thought over a span of scores of centuries. They vividly present a picture of the transformation of a *prakrit* man into a *sanskrit* man.

The Vedas are regarded as divine in origin. They are referred to as *apaurusheya*. They are not produced by a couple of individuals. They are not composed by some poets or authors. The Vedas constitute the sublime knowledge revealed to our great ancestors while they were doing their penance. It is not an acquired knowledge. It is the sublime knowledge revealed to them in their meditation by the Supreme Divinity. The ancient sages, while doing their *tapasya* and *sadhana*, 'heard' the divine truths. Whatever was 'heard' or 'revealed' to the great sages was presented in the Vedas and the Upanishads.

The Vedas are eternal. They are timeless. They are without a beginning. They were not composed at a certain time. No doubt, they might have acquired the verbal form during certain period in history. They are timeless in the sense that they are beyond the confines of time. They are the eternal truths beyond the influence of time. Time or place can not affect the significance of the knowledge 'contained' in the Vedas.

The Vedas are divine and eternal. The Vedas are truly considered to be the boundless repository of "knowledge par excellence".

The Vedas are known as the *Shruti* literature.

The *Shruti* is treated as the supreme and ultimate authority. The authentic *Smriti* literature has had its basis in the *Shruti*. Whenever a difference arises between the *Shruti* and the *Smriti*, the *Shruti* statement is accepted as the final word. Needless to say, the *Smriti* is to be interpreted in consonance with the *Shruti*. From time to time the *Smriti* might undergo modifications, but the *Shruti* can not be altered at all.

The ancient Rishis led a very pious life which was further sanctified by the austerity of penance. They could 'hear' the silence of the Divinity and could 'see' the Infinite. The Vedic Rishi is referred to as a *drashta* or a seer. The Vedic Rishis could 'see' even the transcendental truth as they were great 'seers'. The 'divine truths' were revealed to them while they were in meditation on higher spiritual planes. The Vedas contain the 'divine knowledge' revealed to the great Rishis in their "Supra-normal Consciousness", as Shri Aurobindo says.

The Vedas present the sublime form of knowledge. This knowledge is impersonal. It is divine. It is absolute, veritable and inviolable. It is eternal; it is timeless. It remains unaffected at all times, at all places, under all circumstances. Hence the Vedas are adjudged the *Swatah Pramana* or self-evident. That means their truths do not need any proof, support or elaboration.

The Vedas encompass the human life. They do not belong to a particular religion or a race or a country. They are the holy scriptures of Hinduism, but they equally belong to the human race. Dr. Radhakrishnan refers to the Vedas as "the earliest documents of the human mind."

The Vedas contain the *mantras*. These *mantras* have different specific purposes.

Most of them are symbolic. Some of them are hymns addressed to the deities. Some of them are for ceremonial purposes or for the rites and rituals. Some deal with the social life. There are references to the sciences and mathematics also. Discussions on the topics of chemistry, astronomy, botany, zoology, physiology, medical therapeutics and bio-sciences are also found in the Vedas.

The Vedas reflect all the aspects of existence. They throw light on the *Srishti* (the creation), the Brahman, the *atman*, the life and all the related issues of spiritualism. The Vedas present a record of the philosophical progress of man.

However it should be remembered that neither the Vedas nor the Upanishads propagate a specific ideology or a doctrine. As such they are not philosophical treatises. Yet one finds ample evidence of subtle philosophical thoughts from the verses.

In the Vedas, several portions are repeated in toto. A large number of *mantras* are found to be repetitious.

It may be noted that the chapters or the *mantras* are not sequential. The ideas and thoughts in a single chapter may seem to be illogical or incoherent. There are instances of unexplainable digressions from a theme within a chapter. Hence one may not find a systematic, logical development of a doctrine. However, it does not undermine the significance of the Vedas.

A great deal of scholastic ability is required to interpret the Vedas. A single word may have different meanings in different contexts. Many *mantras* are cryptic statements to a lay man. Some of them are too enigmatic to be followed. They are ambiguous or symbolic.

This is why the Vedas have often been misinterpreted even by learned scholars of reputation. Unfortunately, some of the Western philosophers have not done justice to the Vedas. Many of them failed to understand them correctly and presented distorted views on several counts. Some of the Indian scholars have been influenced by their Western counterparts.

On the other hand, Dayananda Saraswati, Shri Aurobindo and others have challenged the Westerners and made great efforts to re-evaluate the Vedas. One may now remember that the Vedas could only be interpreted with the help of an elaborate explanation by an expert. Once understood thoroughly, they open up new vistas of knowledge and radically transform life.

Meaning of the Word "Veda"

The word 'Veda' is interpreted in more than one ways by different scholars. Swami Dayananda Saraswati has brought out four diverse meanings of the word. Thus, the word 'Veda' can be defined in more than one ways.

The word 'Veda' originates from the Sanskrit root *Vid*. The Sanskrit verb 'Vid' means 'to know'. The word 'Veda' literally means knowledge. The Veda is concerned with "knowledge par excellence". When the man was in a primitive stage enveloped in darkness, the philosophy of the Veda was the unprecedented glow of knowledge. The knowledge which transformed a *prakrit* man to a *Sanskrit* man is the Veda.

The word 'Veda' means 'to be'. It is concerned with *astitva* - the existence. That which creates awareness in a man about his own existence is the Veda.

One of the interpretations of the word 'Veda' is 'to think'. The word 'Veda' is suggestive of 'thought'. Thinking awakens discretion in a man's mind. It makes a man wise and judicious. The knowledge which helps to distinguish between *Sat* and *Asat* is the Veda.

The word 'Veda' also refers to accomplishment. The knowledge which helps a man in realizing his supreme goal is the Veda.

Four Vedas

Shri Veda Vyasa (also known as Badarayana or Krishna Dvaipayana Vyasa) was one of the greatest of all the sages of India.

His contribution in compilation of the Vedas is an example of unparalleled erudition. With great perseverance, he searched for all the work of the Rishis. He collected all the *mantras* and categorized them.

The *mantra* which is in the metered form and recited for the praise of the deity is called *rik* or *richa*. The *mantra* that can be chanted melodiously is called *sama*. The *mantra* in the prose form is called *yajus*. The *mantra* meant for daily rites and rituals in prose or poetic form is known as *atharva*.

Thus Veda Vyasa categorized all the *mantras* and compiled them in four parts. The four parts thus compiled came to be known as the four Vedas.

The four Vedas are the Rig Veda, the Yajur Veda, the Sama Veda and the Atharva Veda.

The Rig Veda is the oldest of all the Vedas. The Rig Veda is composed of 10552 *mantras*. It is believed to be the work of 403 sages. The person who knows all the *mantras* is known as *Ritwik*.

The Yajur Veda is the smallest of all the four Vedas. The knower of this Veda is known as *Adhvaryu*.

The Sama Veda has 1875 *mantras*. The knower of this Veda is known as *Udgata*.

The Atharva Veda has a special place in the field of philosophy and spiritualism. The knower of this Veda is known as *Brahma*.

The Parts of the Vedas

In simple terms, the Vedas are the compilation of the *mantras* or the hymns. The word *'mantra'* originates from the *Sanskrit* word *'manan'* which suggests 'thinking', 'pondering' or 'contemplating'. Most of the *mantras* are in the form of the metered verse.

Originally, the Vedas were not in a written form. In the early years, they were chanted orally. For centuries together, they were transmitted orally to the successive generations. They have been preserved by accurate verbal transmission in the *Guru-Shishya* tradition and are passed from a generation to the next one. The Vedas acquired the written form hundreds of centuries later.

In order to study the Vedas in details, six *shastras* are helpful. These *shastras* are known as the *Vedangas*. The six *Vedangas* are: *Shiksha, Kalp, Vyakaran, Nirukta, Jyotish* and *Chhanda*.

The Vedas are voluminous literary work. In the formative phases, they have never had been in written form. The scholars differ on the issue of "parts" or the "sections" of the Vedas.

In the opinion of some scholars, the Vedas are constituted of two parts: The *Samhitas* and the *Brahmanas*. Other scholars opine that each of the Vedas is divided into four parts (or the sections): the *Samhitas*, the *Brahmanas*, the *Aranyakas* and the Upanishads.

The *Samhitas* and the *Brahmanas* form the *Karma-Kanda* segment of the Vedas. They are apparently concerned with the ceremonial rites and rituals. The *Aranyakas* and the Upanishads form the *Gyan-Kanda* segment of the Vedas. They explicitly focus on the philosophy and spiritualism.

The Samhitas

The *Samhitas* form the first part of each of the Vedas. A Samhita is a collection of *mantras*, so the *Samhitas* are sometimes also referred to as the '*mantras*'. Most of the *mantras* or hymns were concerned with the nature and the deities. The ancient man worshipped the elements of nature as deities though it is believed that these deities are symbolic.

Generally, the *mantras* are addressed to the Gods and Goddesses. Some Western scholars believe that the Vedic man used the *mantras* in sacrificial ceremonies and for performing mystic rituals. This may be true for a number of *mantras*. Apparently, many *mantras* or hymns were meant for devotional or ceremonial purposes. In fact, they seem to be symbolic and need exceptional scholastic efforts to decipher them.

Swami Dayananda Saraswati made extraordinary efforts to bring out the significance of the *mantras* of the Vedas. Shri Aurobindo also challenged the Western philosophers and opined that the *mantras* are found to express esoteric truths which the Westerners can not grasp. He strove hard to elucidate the cryptic meanings of the Vedic words and the hymns.

The *Samhitas* are named after the Vedas they belong to. For example, the *Samhita* of the Rig Veda is called the *Rig-Veda-Samhita* or the *Rig-Samhita*.

The *Rig-Samhita* contains the *mantras* or the hymns known as *'richas'*. These hymns are metered verses. The *Sam-Samhita* contains *mantras* in the form of songs meant for liturgy or public worship. The *Yajur-Samhita* contains verities of *mantras* composed in the poetical and the prose forms. The *Atharva-Samhita* contains *mantras* meant for routine rites and rituals.

The Brahmanas

The *Brahmanas* constitute the second part of the Vedas.

With the passage of time, the newer generations found the *mantras* of the *Samhitas* difficult to understand. An elaborate explanation of the *mantras* became necessary. The result was the *Brahmanas*. The *Brahmanas* are explanatory in nature.

The *Brahmanas,* the second part of the Vedas, are mostly in prose. The word *'Brahmana'* has its root in the word *'brahman'* which means 'prayer' or 'devotion'. The word *'brahman'* is distinct from the word *'Brahman'* which means 'the immanent Power'. The *Brahmanas* hint at 'the magic' or 'the secret power' of the sacrificial rituals.

The *Brahmanas* are concerned with the religious rites and rituals. But their covert meanings often baffle the researchers. The Indian scholars differ from their Western counterparts.

The Rig Veda has two *Brahmanas* – *Aitereya Brahmana* and *Shankhayana Brahmana.*

The *Shat-Patha Brahmana* of Yajur Veda is the largest of all the *Brahmanas* of all the Vedas.

The Aranyakas

The *Aranyakas* form the third part of the Vedas. However, it should be noted that the *Aranyakas* are sometimes considered as parts of the *Brahmanas.*

The Sanskrit word *'aranya'* means a forest.

The *Aranyakas* were developed by the hermits, living in the forests. Due to the limited resources in the forests, they could not perform the conventional sacrifices, nor could they adhere to the rituals. It was then that the *Aranyakas* were developed.

With the advent of the *Aranyakas,* the emphasis on the sacrificial rites seems to be diluting. The shift towards philosophic and spiritual interpretation of the rituals and ceremonials is evident.

The *Aranyakas* reflect an explicit transition in the philosophy of life of man. The speculative and intuitive thinking seems to be developing. Meditative thinking is conspicuous. The Vedic man seems to be turning from the gross to the subtle. His quest for knowledge seems to be intensified.

The Upanishads

The Upanishads are the concluding portions of the Vedas. The Upanishads are at the end of the Vedas.

The Upanishads are referred to as the *Vedanta*. The word *Vedanta* is a compound word made up of two Sanskrit words: *'Veda'* and *'Anta'*. The word *'anta'* means an end. *The Vedanta* essentially refers to the philosophy pronounced in the Upanishads, the final parts of the Vedas. The *Vedanta* broadly covers the philosophy enunciated by the holy Scriptural Trinity – the Upanishads, the *Brahma-Sutra* and the *Bhagavad Gita*.

Some scholars consider the Upanishads as the extended portions of the *Aranyakas* or the *Brahmanas*. For e.g., *Brihdaranyaka* Upanishad is considered to be the final chapter of the *Shat-Patha Brahmana*. Some scholars treat the Vedas and the Upanishads altogether separately.

The word 'Upanishad' is derived from the Sanskrit root *Sad*. The Sanskrit verb *sad* refers to the knowledge or the *satya*. The words *'upa'* + *'ni'* suggests 'sitting (before someone) with a determination'. The word 'Upanishad' can be understood as: To sit near (close to) a *guru* with an objective to acquire knowledge.

Most of the Upanishads are in forms of dialogues between a master and a disciple. In Upanishads, a seeker raises a topic and the enlightened guru satisfies the query aptly and convincingly. Thus, the Upanishads contain the sublime knowledge that deals with the topic at great depth. The Upanishads enrich the human mind immensely as they discuss the Brahman, the *atman*, the existence, life and death, *moksha(mukti)*, the *jagat*, the knowledge (the *para-vidya* and the *apara-vidya*), the *Brahma-gyana* (or the *atma-gyana*) and many other related issues elaborately.

It is not known how many Upanishads existed originally. We do not know who composed them. Some of the Upanishads are in the prose form and some others in the verse form. Some of them are partly composed in prose and partly in verse. Some of the Upanishads have been composed in recent times. It is difficult to ascertain the precise number of the original, ancient Upanishads. One hundred and eight Upanishads are believed to belong to the ancient times. Of the 108 Upanishads, ten Upanishads are considered exquisite by distinguished scholars.

The ten outstanding Upanishads are: *Isha, Kena, Katha, Prashna, Mundaka, Mandukya, Chhandogya, Brahadaranyaka, Aitereya and Taitteriya.*

Some scholars also attach due importance to *Shvetashvatara* and *Maitri*. Some others opine that even *Kautishaki* is equally valuable.

It is believed that the Rig Veda has 10 Upanishads. The number of Upanishads for *Shukla* Yajur Veda is 19, for *Krishna* Yajur Veda 32 and for Sama Veda it is 16. Atharva Veda has 31 Upanishads.

Aiteriya Upanishad is associated with Rig Veda. *Kena* Upanishad is associated with Sama Veda.

Isha Upanishad is a part of *Shukla* Yajur Veda. *Katha* Upanishad is associated with *Krishna* Yajur Veda.

Prashna Upanishad is associated with Atharva Veda.

The most exalted Rishis and the enlightened celebrities have contributed to the Upanishads. Some of them are Maharshi Yagnavalkya, Rajarshi Janak, Mandukya Muni, Pippalad Muni etc. Maharshi Yagnavalkya contributed significantly to the *Brahadaranyaka* Upanishad.

Philosophy of the Vedas

In the beginning, it seems that the Vedas propagate the philosophy of polytheism. This illusion gradually disappears as one approaches the Upanishadic period. The Upanishads inconspicuously pronounce the philosophical thoughts that may lead one to the realization of the Ultimate Truth.

After all, the Vedic Rishis are in search of the Ultimate Truth. What they are seeking is knowledge par excellence. They have set out in the quest of Divine Truth. Their search intensifies as they enter the era of the Upanishads. As Shri Aurobindo says: "The Upanishadic hymns are the epic hymns of self-knowledge, world-knowledge and God-knowledge."

The Rishis are inquisitive and they pose diverse questions: What is the Ultimate Truth? What is the *Srishti*? Who is the creator? How and why is the *Samsara* (*Jagat*) created? What is the Brahman? What is the *jiva* or the *jivatma*? Is there any relationship between the Brahman and the *jivatma*? What is life? What is death? What is *moksha*?

The Vedic philosophical thoughts reach the peak in the Upanishads. The Upanishads unveil the Ultimate Truth. The philosophy expressed in the Upanishads is referred to as the Vedanta.

Truly speaking, the Upanishads reflect the sublime knowledge and wisdom of man in its most exalted form. But the significance of the other parts of the Vedas - with their seemingly cryptic statements expressing esoteric truth and profound philosophy – should not be undermined.

The Prasthatrayi

The *Prasthantrayi* refers to three holy books. They are: The Upanishads, the *Brahma-Sutra* and the *Bhagavad Gita*. These three books are collectively known as the *Prasthantrayi* or the *Prasthantrayam*. They form the Scriptural Trinity of the *Sanatan Dharma* or the Hinduism.

The Upanishads present the cream of the Vedas. The Upanishads pronounce the Ultimate Truth. The Upanishadic philosophy puts an end to all forms of ignorance in life and leads to the realization of the self. The different systems of philosophy in India find their roots in the Upanishads.

Badarayana (Ved Vyasa) was a great scholar with exceptional erudition. He initiated the challenging task of systematizing the Vedas. He meticulously studied the vast philosophical doctrines of the Upanishads. He pioneered the efforts to simplify the Upanishadic philosophy what we know as the Vedanta.

The result of his efforts was one of the most illustrious works on the Vedanta. Badarayana's work is known as *Brahma-Sutra*.

The *Brahma-Sutra* is also referred to as *Vedanta-Sutra* or *Uttar-Mimamsa-Sutra*.

The *Bhagavad Gita* is a part of the great epic, the Mahabharat.

The Mahabharat, authored by the great sage Veda Vyasa, is an epic that vividly depicts the different facets of human life. There are unsurmountable aspirations, ceaseless activities and inspiring achievements in Mahabharat. Amongst all these shine out the philosophy of the *Bhagavad Gita.*

The *Bhagavad Gita* sheds a flood of light on all questions associated with life. It proclaims the relationship between the Supreme Self and the self, the Brahman and the *atman,* between God and man. One finds solutions to all the problems of life in the *Bhagavad Gita.*

If ever a controversy arises on any philosophical issue in Hinduism, the interpretation of the *Prasthantrayi* is final and binding. If there is a difference in the statements of the *Prasthantryi* and any other book of Hinduism, the former is considered supreme.

The Vedanta

The Vedanta essentially refers to the philosophy pronounced in the Upanishads, the final parts of the Vedas. In a broad sense, the Vedanta covers the fundamental philosophy enunciated by the *Prasthantrayi* – the Upanishads, the *Brahma-Sutra* and the *Bhagavad Gita.*

The *Brahma-Sutra* (*Vedanta-Sutra*) and the *Bhagavad Gita* are based on the philosophy of the Upanishads. The Vedanta offers the sublime knowledge in its most exalted form. The knowledge may be relative or absolute. Relative knowledge pertains to the senses and the intellect. It is concerned with the physical world and worldly objects. But the Vedanta transcends beyond the realms of relative knowledge. It leads a seeker to transcendental knowledge and finally to absolute knowledge.

The *Brahma-Sutra* is also referred to as *Vedanta-Sutra* or *Uttar-Mimamsa-Sutra*. The *Brahma-Sutra* has 555 *sutras*. Most of them are aphoristic. Being cryptic, they are almost unintelligible at first sight and need elaborate explanation by an expert. Hence, a number of commentaries were written to interpret them.

Shamkaracharya, Ramanujacharya and Madhavacharya wrote commentaries on the *Brahma-Sutra*. This lead to the rise of three schools of the *Vedanta* as mentioned earlier. They were: Shamkaracharya's *Advaita Vedanta*, Ramanujacharya's *Vishishtadvaita Vedanta* and Madhavacharya's *Dvaita Vedanta*.

Though the three schools differ on several counts, the underlying basic concepts of the Vedanta are similar. We shall study only the basic Vedanta concepts here. All the three schools of the Vedanta present three categories of 'realities'. The first category is the *Jagat* or the Universe. The second category is the *Jiva* (individual) or the *atma* (*Atman* or the soul) that lives in the *jagat* or the world. The third category is the Brahman, the substratum behind the *Jagat* and all the *Jivas*. The Brahman is the Supreme Being and governs the destiny of the *Jagat* and the *Jivas*.

The Vedanta philosophy is focused on the *Jagat*(the universe), the *Jiva*(individual soul) and the *Brahman* (the Supreme Being). *Brahman* is the repository of all knowledge and power. *Jivas*, out of ignorance, gets trapped in the *Jagat*. Attached to the physical world and driven by passions and desires, they are tempted to act with selfish, mundane motives. They remain chained to ceaseless actions (*karma*). As a result, they subject themselves to countless births in various forms. Their transmigration from this birth (life) to the next depends on the *karma* (the quality of action). *Moksha* or *mukti* (liberation) is the goal of life. This philosophy, in general, is accepted by all the three schools. These are the basic concepts common to all three schools of the Vedanta. Now let us see how they differ.

Dvaita means dualism. This system believes that the Brahman and the *Jiva* are two different entities. This system believes that the God, the soul and the Universe are three separate realities. God governs the world. The soul in its ignorance remains attached to the physical world. By developing faith and devotion in God, he can seek God's mercy and then the soul may migrate to the Heaven above. Such a *jiva* may attain *Mukti*.

Vishishtadvaita literally means "qualified non-dualism". Ramanujacharya stresses that God alone exists. He says that *Brahman* is God. He is not formless. The Cosmos and the *Jivas* form his body. When the *Jiva* (soul) realizes that he is a part of *Paramatman* (God), the soul is liberated. With self-realization and liberation the soul enjoys infinite consciousness and eternal bliss of God. *Advaita* literally means non-dualism. This system contends that the Brahman and the *atman* (individual soul) are not different entities. Brahman is the Ultimate, Supreme Reality. Brahman is beyond names and forms. Brahman can not be described in words. Brahman is *Sat-Chit-Ananda*. Brahman and *atman* are not different realities. They are identical. They are the eternal, all-pervading realities underlying all existence.

Classical Sanskrit Literature

Sanskrit literature came into being with the making of Vedas and left a rich legacy of literary knowledge for the times to come. However, the language of the Vedas differs from the language used in poetry and drama. Classical Sanskrit literature is found to be in vogue when it comes to writing poetry and dance dramas. This form of classic literature in Sanskrit is a huge contribution in the field of literary knowledge. Sanskrit poetry is different from Vedic poetry. Read on further about literature in classical Sanskrit and check our related sections on Sanskrit plays and Sanskrit poetry.

Sanskrit drama evolved as early as 2nd century B.C. Shudraka, the great Sanskrit writer wrote the earliest play in Sanskrit Mricchakatika around this time. The central theme of these dramas and plays used to be based on heroic tales of the protagonist. The Natya Shastra, which was written by Bharata, literally means the Science of Theater. It contained all the essential elements that go into making a successful dance drama. Other famous dramatists are Kalidasa, Bhasa, Asvaghosa, etc. Check our related sections for further information on their works.

Classical Sanskrit poetry is a varied genre and has many forms of poetry in it. The most famous examples of epic poetry are Ramayana and Mahabharata, the two epics that are held in high reverence by Indians. Romantic poetry was given a boost during the time of Kalidasa, the great poet of India. The epics poems can be recited as well as sung. Thus, one can say that classical music also started from classical Sanskrit literature. Classic literature in Sanskrit is indeed a valuable treasure of Indian cultural heritage.

The classical period of Sanskrit literature dates to the Gupta period and the successive pre-Islamic Middle kingdoms of India, spanning roughly the 3rd to 8th centuries CE.

Dramas

The combination of different genres of drama and Sanskrit resulted in a unique amalgamation that gave us the literary treasure of Sanskrit dramas and Sanskrit plays. The famous dramatists of Sanskrit literature were Kalidasa, Bhasa, Shudraka and Asvaghosa who gave us many famous Sanskrit plays. With the revival of Sanskrit theater in modern times, these Sanskrit plays are gaining much popularity again among Sanskrit scholars and theater enthusiasts. Given here are some famous Sanskrit plays that are worth a read.

Abhijnanasakuntalam

Abhijnanasakuntalam is a beautiful tale of love and romance and how one moment can make or break a relation. Written by one of the greatest poets of India, Shakuntalam Kalidasa is synonymous to its author, Kalidasa.

Malavikagnimitram

The first play composed by the great poet Kalidasa is Malavikagnimitram. Often it is called Kalidasa Malavikagnimitram, as an honor to Kalidasa. This beautiful play of intrigue grips its readers and keeps them glued till the very end. The plot of the play is cleverly constructed and it revolves around the King's love interest who is a maid in the royal palace.

Ritusamhara

India has always believed in the harmonious relation between man and forces of nature and the importance of each season has been beautifully brought into light by the great poet Kalidasa in Ritu Samhaara, a poem written by him. It can be called the "Medley of

Seasons" or "Garland of Seasons". The Ritusamharam has been divided into six main chapters, each chapter describing vividly, the seasons of India.

Vikramorvasiyam

Written by the most famous poet Kalidasa, Vikramorvasiyam is a play that tells the tale of a mortal king Vikramaditya who is in love with a heavenly damsel, Urvashi. It tells the story of his effort and determination and how he wins the love of the divine nymph, who is supposed to be the most gorgeous heavenly fairy. Out of desperation, the king wanders through dense forests in search of his love. A truly intriguing tale of love and possessiveness, it contains beautiful verses that describe true love.

Mrichakatika

Regarded as one of the earliest Indian plays written in Sanskrit, Mrichakatika is a beautiful play by Shudraka. The play is a comedy set in the royal backdrop in which love and mistaken identity play a part. Translated in English, the name means little clay cart. It was written around the Gupta Period in Sanskrit.

Natya Shastra

Written by the sage Bharata Muni, this beautiful text was written in Sanskrit around 400 B.C. The text contains information on the minutest details that should be taken care of during dance. Thus, it can be said that Natya Shastra is set of rules and regulations that are implemented in fine arts in India. The Natya Shastra is the first known text on dance and it has had a strong impact on classical dance forms in both olden and modern times.

Bhasa's Plays

Bhasa's plays are generally shorter as compared to other epic poems and plays. This great Sanskrit dramatist lived before Kalidasa and wrote many short plays that are staged even today. Most of his plays were based on the two major epics, Ramayana and Mahabharata. Most of his plays have graphic depictions of violence, something that was frowned upon by the Natya Shastras. Some of his famous plays are Madhyamavyayogam, Urubhangam, Karnabharam, Pancaratram, among others.

Scholarly Treatises

The earliest surviving treatise on astrology is the Yavanajataka "sayings of the Greeks" (3rd century). Classical Hindu astrology is based on early medieval compilations, notably the Brhat Parasara Horasastra and Saravali (7th to 8th century). The earliest surviving treatise on (non-divinatory) Indian astronomy predates the Yavanajataka: the Vedanga Jyotisha of Ladaga documents the state of in the Maurya period. The astronomy of the classical Gupta period, the centuries following Indo-Greek contact, is documented in treatises known as Siddhantas (which means "established conclusions"). Varahamihira in his *Pancha-Siddhantika* contrasts five of these: The Surya Siddhanta besides the Paitamaha Siddhantas (which is more similar to the "classical" Vedanga Jyotisha), the Paulisha and Romaka Siddhantas (directly based on Hellenistic astronomy) and the Vasishta Siddhanta.

The earliest treatise in Indian mathematics is the *Aryabhatiya* (written ca. 500 CE), a work on astronomy and mathematics. The mathematical portion of the *Aryabhatiya* was composed of 33 *Sutras* (in verse form) consisting of mathematical statements or rules, but without any proofs. However, according to (Hayashi 2003, p. 123), "this does not necessarily mean that their authors did not prove them. It was probably a matter of style of exposition." From the time of Bhaskara I (600 CE onwards), prose commentaries increasingly began to include some derivations (*upapatti*).

"Tantra" is a general term for a scientific, magical or mystical treatise and mystical texts both Hindu and Buddhist said to concern themselves with five subjects:

1. the creation,
2. the destruction of the world,
3. the worship of the gods,
4. the attainment of all objects,
5. the four modes of union with the supreme spirit by meditation.

These texts date to the entire lifespan of Classical Sanskrit literature.

Fairy Tales and Fables

Sanskrit fairy tales and fables are chiefly characterised by ethical reflections and proverbial philosophy. A peculiar style, marked by the insertion of a number of different stories within the framework of a single narrative, made its way to Persian and Arabic literatures, exerting a major influence on works such as *One Thousand and One Nights.*

The two most important collections are Panchatantra and Hitopadesha; originally intended as manuals for the instruction of kings in domestic and foreign policy, they belong to the class of literature which the Hindus call *niti-sastra,* or "Science of Political Ethics".

Other notable prose works include a collection of pretty and ingenious fairy tales, with a highly Oriental colouring, the *Vetala-panchavimsati* or "Twenty-five Tales of the Vetala" (a demon supposed to occupy corpses), the *Simhasana-dvatrimçika* or "Thirty-two Stories of the Lion-seat" (i.e. throne), which also goes by the name of *Vikrama-charita,* or "Adventures of Vikrama" and the *Suka-saptati,* or "Seventy Stories of a Parrot". These three collections of fairy tales are all written in prose and are comparatively short.

Somadeva's Katha-sarit-sagara or "Ocean of Rivers of Stories" is a work of special importance: composed in verse and is of very considerable length. It contains more than 22,000 shlokas, equal to nearly one-fourth of the Mahabharata. Fable collections, originally serving as the handbooks of practical moral philosophy, provided an abundant reservoir of ethical maxims that become so popular that works consisting exclusively of poetical aphorisms started to appear. The most important are the two collections by the highly-gifted Bhartrhari, entitled respectively *Niti-sataka,* or "Century of Conduct," and *Vairagya-sataka,* or "Century of Renunciation." The keynote prevailing in this new ethical poetry style is the doctrine of the vanity of human life, which was developed before the rise of Buddhism in the sixth century B.C., and has dominated Indian

Classical Poetry

This refers to the poetry produced from the approximately the 3rd to 8th centuries. Kalidasa is the foremost example of a classical poet. But a striking characteristic of Indian literary tradition is that sometimes poets show off their technical dexterity with highly Oulipian word-games, like stanzas that read the same backwards and forwards, words that can be split in different ways to produce different meanings, sophisticated metaphors, and so on. This style is referred to as Kavya. A classic example is the poet Bharavi and his magnum opus, the Kiratarjuniya (6th-7th century). Magh is noted for his epic poem (mahAkAvya) Shishupala Vadha, the 20 cantos of which are based on the Mahabharata episode where the defiant king Shishupala is beheaded by Krishna's chakra (disc)

Sanskrit poetry is a vast treasure of knowledge that gives us immense information about ancient thoughts and principles. Some of the best works in ancient Sanskrit literature are in the form of Sanskrit poems. Some of the most famous and respected poets have given us the treasure of poetry in Sanskrit. These poets are synonymous with Sanskrit poetry and most poems are followed by the name of the poet. We are covering some great works of these poets in our related sections. Read on further to know more about these Sanskrit poems.

Kumarasambhavam

Anyone interested in the Sanskrit language is sure to know the story of Kumarasambhavam. One of the gems of Sanskrit literature, Kumarasambhava poem is one of the greatest epic poems written by the famous poet Kalidasa. Both the names go hand in hand and the poem is often called Kumarasambhavam Kalidasa.

Meghadutam

A beautiful piece of literary treasure, the Meghadutam Kalidasa is a short poem of a little over 100 verses. The stanzas are uniform in length of four sentences each. This convenient length makes it a favorite among scholars and translators. The Meghaduta poem is a beautiful work of literary art and the descriptions given in it are so vivid that one visualizes what the poet wants to convey.

Ritusamhara

India has always believed in the harmonious relation between man and forces of nature and the importance of each season has been beautifully brought into light by the great poet Kalidasa in Ritu Samhaara, a poem written by him. It can be called the "Medley of Seasons" or "Garland of Seasons". The Ritusamharam has been divided into six main chapters, each chapter describing vividly, the seasons of India.

Raghuvamsa

Raghuvamsa play is a literary magnum opus written by the famous poet Kalidasa. The play is synonymous with the creator and is often called Raghuvamsa Kalidasa. The play basically traces the roots of the great lineage of Lord Rama and his descendants and the great conqueror Raghu. Raghuvamsam basically talks about the valor and strength of the great warrior Raghu.

Later Sanskrit Literature

Some important works from the 11th century include the *Katha-sarit-sagara* and the *Gita Govinda* of Jayadeva. Naganandа, attributed to King Harsha, is an outstanding drama that outlines the story of King Jimutavahana, who sacrifices himself to save the tribe of serpents. It is also unique in that it invokes Lord

Buddha in what is a predominantly Hindu drama.The *Katha-sarita-sagara* (An Ocean of Stories) by Somadeva was an 11th century poetic adaptation in Sanskrit of *Brihat-katha*, written in the 5th century BC in the *Paishachi* dialect. One of the famous series of stories in this work is the *Vikrama and Vetala* series, known to every child in India. On the other side of the spectrum, of the 'Bhana' style of drama, Ubhayabhisarika is a one-person drama of an endearing lecher who knows every courtesan and her family by name.

The *Gita Govinda* (The song of Govinda) by the Oriya composer Jayadeva is the story of Krishna's love for Radha, and is written in spectacularly lyrical and musical Sanskrit.

A central text for several Hindu sects in eastern India, the *Gita Govinda* is recited regularly at major Hindu pilgrimage sites such as Jagannath temple at Puri, Orissa. The *Ashtapadis* of the *Gita Govinda* also form a staple theme in Bharatanatyam and Odissi classical dance recitals.

Beyond the 11th century, the use of Sanskrit for general literature declined, most importantly because of the emergence of literature in vernacular Indian languages. Sanskrit continued to be used, largely for Hindu religious and philosophical literature. Sanskrit literature fueled literature in vernacular languages, and the Sanskrit language itself continued to have a profound influence over the development of Indian literature in general.

7

Ancient Chinese Literature

People in China began writing about 1500 BC, more than a thousand years later than people in West Asia or Egypt, but earlier than anyone in Europe, Africa, or Central America. The earliest writing that we know of from China was on animal bones, which are called "oracle bones" because they were used to tell the future. The writing on these oracle bones is the same writing that people use in modern China, just in an earlier version. The signs they used came from pictures, like earlier Egyptian hieroglyphs or Sumerian cuneiform.

People in early China also wrote on strips of bamboo wood. Later on, people also wrote on silk cloth. The earliest Chinese literature that we know of probably comes from the later part of the Western Chou Dynasty about 800 BC (the same time as Hesiod in Greece) and was written on silk. This is the I Ching, a fortune-telling book, like the earlier oracle bones.

Sometime around 300 BC, in the Warring States period, a general called Sun Tzu wrote a book called the Art of War, about the best ways to organize armies and battles.

Around 100 BC, people in China invented paper to write on. Paper was cheaper to write on than silk, so more people wrote and copied books during the Han Dynasty. During the Tang Dynasty, about 700 AD, people in China invented wood-block printing, which was easier than copying out books by hand and made books much cheaper than they had been before. Many more people learned to read, and many more people wrote books. The poet Bai Juyi wrote a famous poem, the Song of Everlasting Sorrow.

Soon afterward, during the Sung Dynasty, about 1000 AD, people invented movable clay type, and this made books even cheaper and more popular than before. In 1103 AD, Lie Jie published a book setting architectural standards for all of China.

One of the most famous novels of early China is the Romance of the Three Kingdoms, which was written about 1330 AD, during the Yuan Dynasty, by a man named Luo Guanzhong.

China is the only country in the world with a literature written in one language for more than 3,000 consecutive years. This continuity results largely from the nature of the written language itself. It is the use of characters, not letters as in Western languages, that is most important in the Chinese language. The characters stand for things or ideas and so, unlike groups of letters, they cannot and need never be sounded. Thus Chinese could be read by people in all parts of the country in spite of gradual changes in pronunciation, the emergence of regional and local dialects, and modification of the characters.

The dominance of the written language has had significant effects on the development of the literature. In handwriting or in print, a piece of literature has visual appeal. This has given rise to the great respect that calligraphy enjoys in China, where it has been regarded for at least 16 centuries as a fine art comparable to painting. The main disadvantage of written Chinese is the great number of characters it contains: Even basic reading and writing require a knowledge of more than 1,000 characters. This has often made it difficult to spread the skills of reading and writing into certain areas of the country. But even with this disadvantage, Chinese has been a potent factor in shaping and maintaining a cultural continuity for millions of people. Because the written characters tend to keep the language stable, Chinese never developed into distinctly separate languages as did Latin in southern Europe with the formation of the several Romance languages.

China has a very old and rich tradition in literature and the dramatic and visual arts. Early writings generally derived from philosophical or religious essays such as the works of Confucius (551-479 BC) and Lao-tzu (probably 4th century BC). These writings were often about how people should act and how the society and political system should be organized and operated. A strong tradition of historical writing also evolved. After the fall of a dynasty, for example, a grand history of the late dynasty was commissioned and written by scholars in the next dynasty.

In addition to philosophical, religious, and historical writings, China also produced poetry, novels, and dramatic writings from an early date. Poetry became well established as a literary form during the T'ang Dynasty, from AD 618 to 907. One of China's greatest poets, Li Po, wrote during this period. This tradition of poetry, often dealing with the relationship of humans to their natural surroundings, has continued.

Drama is another old and important literary form. Chinese drama usually combines vernacular language with music and song and thus has been popular with the common people. A variety of popular and standard themes are presented in Peking Opera, which is probably the best known of several operatic traditions that developed in China. Chinese opera is a favorite artistic and cultural medium.

Early Chinese novels often stressed character development and usually centered on an adventure or supernatural happening; an example is the classic Ming version of 'Shui-hu chuan' (The Water Margin). Historical themes were also popular, as in the 'Romance of the Three Kingdoms', written in the late Yuan period. There were also love stories such as the extremely popular

"Dream of the Red Chamber', probably China's most famous novel. Many of the early novels were written anonymously. Often these works were written in the vernacular, and many authors felt it was beneath their station to be associated with this type of writing.

China's literary tradition continues to the present, though much 20th-century writing has concentrated on efforts to reform or modernize China. Probably the most famous 20th-century writer is Lu Xun, a poet, essayist, and novelist whose work focused on the need to modernize through revolution. Under Communism, writers have been expected to uphold the values of the socialist state, though the degree of control over their output has varied.

Dynastic Literature

With the unification of China by the short-lived Ch'in Dynasty (221 to 206 BC), the singular feature in literary matters was what is called the "Burning of the Books." The emperor, Shih Huang Ti, was determined to be an absolutist ruler and opposed to writings on good government such as those in the Classics. In 213, it is believed, he ordered the burning of all texts that appeared threatening to him. Whether the books were actually burned or simply kept from the people is uncertain. The result was the same: It was necessary during the next dynasty to reconstruct the texts of the Classics.

The Han Dynasty

The Han Dynasty (206 BC to AD 220) actively promoted the restoration and teaching of the Classics. In 124 BC a national university was opened for the purpose of teaching Confucianism. Probably at about this time civil-service examinations, which determined the appointment and promotion of government officials, began to be based on the Classics. It was also during the Han period that the Classics became established as the basis of Chinese education.

Literature flowered again during the Han Dynasty. Traditional poetry and prose forms, especially the fu prose poems, flourished. But the most notable achievement came with the reactivation of the Yueh Fu, or Music Bureau, in 125 BC. This agency was founded in the previous century to collect traditional songs. One of its achievements was the compiling of folk songs and ballads. The most outstanding folk ballad of the period, about AD 200, was 'Southeast the Peacock Flies'. It tells of the tragedy of a young married couple who committed suicide as the result of the cruelty of the husband's mother.

The major prose authors of the Han Dynasty were Liu An, Ssu-ma Ch'ien, and Pan Ku. Liu An was a prince of Huai-nan in the 2nd century BC. The work attributed to him, but probably done under his patronage, is 'The Master of Huai-nan'. It is a compilation of 21 chapters on cosmology, philosophy, politics, and ethics. Although the book contains little that is not traditional, its cosmology was highly regarded by the Taoists and became part of their accepted teaching. The masterpiece of the period was the 'Shih-chi', meaning "Historical Records," of Ssu-ma Ch'ien. It was completed in about 85 BC and took 18 years to produce. It contains a record of events and personalities for the previous 2,000 years. The text is divided into 130 chapters with more than 520,000 words. It was the first attempt at a national history in China, and it set the pattern for the histories of dynasties in the following centuries.

In the next century Ssu-ma Ch'ien was followed as historian by Pan Ku, who was born about AD 32 and died about AD 92. He was also a poet, soldier, and the author of 'Han shu', meaning "History of the Former Han Dynasty." Completed after 16 years of study, the history contains more than 800,000 words. Because he was court historian, Pan Ku could get all the official records as well as the family histories of the emperors. In addition to information about the rulers, the author added sections on geography, natural phenomena, memorable biographies, and a descriptive account of books in the imperial library.

The Han Dynasty was followed by the period of the Six Dynasties and the Sui Dynasty (AD 221 to 618).

The major poet of this era was T'ao Ch'ien (365-427). In his 20s he became a government official, but after about ten years he resigned and with his family went to live in a farming village to contemplate nature and to write poetry. His verse was in a plain style that was imitated by poets long after. He was a master of the five-word line and has been called the first of China's great nature poets because most of his writings deal with rural activities. Although he was essentially a Taoist, his work also showed elements of Confucianism and Buddhism.

The 3rd and 4th centuries were, for prose writers, a time of individuality and partial rejection of slavish imitation of past models. Lu Chi (261-303) was a renowned poet and literary critic who emphasized originality in creative writing. He wrote a great deal of lyric poetry but is best remembered for his 'Wen fu', an essay on literature.

The revolt against imitative writing was also expressed in a 5th-century style called "pure conversation," an intellectual discussion on lofty matters. Some of these were recorded in a collection of anecdotes entitled `Sayings of the World'. In the 6th century the first book of literary criticism, `Carving of the Literary Dragon', was published by Liu Hsieh (465-522). It was written in the p'ien wen, or parallel prose, style. Two other 6th-century prose masters were Yang Hsien-chih, author of `Record of Buddhist Temples in Lo-yang', and Li Tao-yuan, author of `Commentary on the Water Classic'. Both of these are outstanding records of not only what was happening but also of the folklore of the time.

The period from 618 to 960, the time of the T'ang Dynasty and the Five Dynasties, is considered China's golden age of poetry. The works of more than 2,000 poets, totaling more than 48,900 pieces, have been preserved. The writing adapted traditional verse forms and created new ones. Among the new and popular forms were lu shih, meaning "regulated verse"; chueh chu, "truncated verse"; and a song form called tz'u. Regulated verse consisted of eight lines of five or seven syllables set in accordance with strict tonal patterns. Truncated verse was an outgrowth of regulated verse: It omitted four of the lines but maintained the tonal qualities of regulated verse. The tz'u consisted of lines of irregular length written as lyrics for music. Because the lines varied from 1 to 11 syllables, they were comparable to the natural rhythms of speech and were easily understood when sung. The tz'u served as a major style for poetry during the succeeding Sung Dynasty.

Two of the greatest poets in all Chinese literature lived during the T'ang Dynasty: Li Po (701-762) and Tu Fu (712-770). Li Po was a romantic who celebrated such things as drinking, friendship, and nature as well as solitude and the passage of time. His work showed a great deal of imagination and a fresh approach to old themes. Tu Fu also celebrated the beauties of nature and bemoaned the passage of time, but he was also a satirist and critic. In 'The Army Carts' he condemned the senselessness of war, and in 'The Beautiful Woman' he made fun of the luxuriousness of the imperial court. Tu Fu's great reputation in literature comes in part from his expert use of all types of poetic style. His mastery of the regulated verse form was unmatched.

Chinese prose also underwent a stylistic reform during the T'ang period. The major change was brought about by Han Yu (768-824). He promoted classic Confucian doctrines at a time when they had begun to fall into neglect because of the rising popularity of Buddhism and Taoism. In his writing he advocated a return to the free, simple prose of the ancient philosophers. His own essays are among the most beautiful ever written in Chinese and became models for the style of writing he prized. At his death he was honored with the title "Prince of Letters."

Sung Dynasty

During the Sung Dynasty, especially in the 11th century, the tz'u form of poetry and song was brought to its greatest heights, particularly through the efforts of China's best woman poet, Li Ch'ing-chao (1081-1141). She produced six volumes of poetry and seven volumes of essays, all of which have been lost except for some poetry fragments. Her early poems dealt with the joys of love and were intensely personal. Later in life her writing began to reflect a dark despair, caused by long separations from her husband and, eventually, by his untimely death.

The prose reform continued under followers of Han Yu, and poetry of the conventional type continued to be written by members of rival literary schools. The only real innovation came with the use of everyday speech in local dialects in storytelling. This literature had its origin in unrecorded oral tales recounted by individuals to audiences gathered in marketplaces or temple yards. By the 12th century these tales became fairly lengthy narratives, many dealing with fictionalized history. This style opened new vistas in prose fiction in later periods, though its use was at first despised by professional writers.

Yuan, or Mongol, Dynasty

The best-known ruler of the Yuan, or Mongol, Dynasty was Kublai Khan. In literature Chinese drama came to the fore for the first time, and vernacular fiction was firmly established.

Puppet shows, skits, vaudeville acts, and shadow plays of previous ages had laid the foundation for a full-fledged drama. Plays in four or five acts, including songs and dialect in language quite close to that of the common people, became popular. More than 1,700 musical plays were written, and more than 105 dramatists were recorded. The first, and probably the greatest, playwright of classical theater was Kuan Han-ch'ing, author of about 60 plays. He wrote in a simple and straightforward manner, often about common everyday occurrences. Among his best works were 'Injustice Suffered by Tou-o', 'Meeting Enemies Alone', and 'Saving a Prostitute'.

Wang Shih-fu (1250-1337) wrote one of the best dramas of the period, 'Romance of the Western Chamber', a work that is still popular. It is about the romantic exploits of the poet Yuan Chen, renamed Chang Chun-jui in the play. It is notable for its length, two or three times that of the standard Yuan drama.

In vernacular fiction one of the greatest novelists was Lo Kuan-chung (1330-1400), known for his masterpiece, 'The Romance of the Three Kingdoms'. He is also presumed to be the author of one of China's best-known novels, 'The Story of the Water Margin' (translated by novelist Pearl S. Buck as 'All Men Are Brothers'). The work is a semihistorical collection of stories about a band of enlightened outlaws—social and political dissenters whose exploits were recorded in official dynastic history. This is one of the few traditional novels approved today by Chinese Communist authorities and critics.

Ming Dynasty

Most Ming literature in both prose and poetry was traditional, imitative, and old-fashioned. Two schools of writing challenged this trend, claiming that literature should change with the age instead of slavishly imitating the past. The influence of these schools did not last long, however.

It was in the vernacular literature of the period that writers made significant contributions. The dramatic form ch'uan-chi (tales of marvels) became popular. Some examples were full-length dramas with many changes of scene and many subplots, while others were one-act playlets. This drama form won gradual support from literary figures, and in the 16th century the influential K'un school, which was to dominate the theater until the end of the 18th century, was formed.

In fiction there were some novels that are still considered outstanding. Wu Ch'eng-en (1500?-82?) wrote 'Monkey', the adventures of a cunningly resourceful animal that accompanied the Buddhist monk Hsuan-tsang on a pilgrimage to India. 'Adventure to the Western Ocean' was an expanded tale of the 15th-century explorer Cheng Ho. The author of 'Gold Vase Plum', subtitled "The Adventurous History of Hsi-men and His Six Wives," is unknown. It was the first realistic social novel to appear in China—the first fiction work not derived from popular legends or historical events. In a very naturalistic, somewhat coarse way it describes the life of a well-to-do businessman who has acquired his wealth largely through dishonest means; his goals in life are animal pleasures and heavy drinking. Although the novel was banned in China more than once, and Western translators have occasionally resorted to Latin for offensive passages, it is one of the most popular Chinese novels.

Ch'ing or Manchu Dynasty

Ch'ing was the last imperial ruling house of China. During its reign most Chinese literature tended to be old-fashioned and imitative; genuine creativity was rare. Toward the end of the period, however, China had its first extensive contacts with European powers, and ideas from the West began to filter into the literature through translations of novels and other books.

In native prose fiction two works stand out. P'u Sung-ling (1640-1715) wrote a collection of supernatural tales entitled 'Strange Stories from a Chinese Studio'. The other is one of the great novels in world literature—'Dream of the Red Chamber', by Ts'ao Chan (1715?-63). Partly autobiographical and written in the vernacular, it describes in sometimes lengthy detail the decline of a powerful family and the ill-fated love between two young people. A much later novel, 'The Travels of Lao Ts'an', by Liu E (1857-1909), was significant because it pointed up the problems inherent in the weakening dynasty, which was soon to be overthrown by revolution. The book was published in 1904-07.

Literary Revolutions

The Ch'ing Dynasty was overthrown in the Chinese Revolution of 1911-12, and from that time China was in almost continual turmoil until the success of the Communist revolution in 1949. Even then the turmoil did not altogether cease, for the nation was subject to the whims of the Communist leadership.

The Great Leap Forward, the government program of the 1950s, brought economic disaster to China, and the Cultural Revolution of the late 1960s poisoned the whole cultural and social environment.

Political revolution was followed by literary revolution. In 1915 Youth Magazine (later, New Youth) was founded by Ch'en Tu-hsiu (1879-1942), who soon became a founder of the Chinese Communist party. A leader in developing the intellectual basis of the revolution, Ch'en published an article about the rebellion against traditional and classical literary forms and ideas. Hu Shih (1891-1962) was a proponent of a new national literature in the vernacular.

Another significant writer of this period was Lu Hsun, the pen name of Chou Shu-jen (1881-1936). In 1918 he published a short story, "A Madman's Diary," the first Western-style short story written in Chinese. He followed it in 1921 with "The True Story of Ah Q." Both stories criticized and rejected the old order. He is considered a revolutionary hero.

Political writings and speeches came much into prominence at this time, especially in the works of Sun Yat-sen, known as the father of modern China; Chiang Kai-shek, the leader of Nationalist China; and Mao Zedong, the leader of Communist China. Under Mao's leadership countless literary works were produced, all of which reflected Communist policies and what in the Soviet nion was called "socialist realism."

One of the prominent writers of the early Communist era was Ting Ling, the pen name of

Chiang Wei-chih (1904-86). He wrote 'The Sun Shines over the Sangkan River', a novel about land reform. Chou Li-po (born 1910), author of the novel 'The Hurricane', about rebellious peasants seizing power from armed landlords, was also a major writer. So too was Chou Erh-fu (born 1912), the author of 'Morning in Shanghai', a novel about changes in a textile factory after the revolution.

The one 20th-century giant of Chinese literature whose fame spread far beyond his native land was Lin Yu-tang (1895-1976). The peak of his career in China came with the establishment in 1932 of the satirical magazine Analects Fortnightly. His work reached English-speaking readers with 'My Country and My People', published in 1935. From 1936 he lived mostly in the United States, writing books on Chinese history and philosophy, but he returned to Asia ten years before his death in Hong Kong. He has been acclaimed as one of the most versatile Chinese writers of all time, producing novels, plays, short stories, and essays in addition to historical and philosophical works.

Lu Xun (1881-1936).

Although he died 13 years before the Communist party came to power in China, the writer Lu Xun is considered a revolutionary hero by present-day Chinese Communists. By the 1930s, when his reputation as a writer was established, he hailed Communism as the only means of unifying China and solving its social and economic problems.

Lu Xun was born Chou Shu-jen in Shaoxing in 1881. He attended the School of Railways and Mines of the Kiangnan Military Academy in Nanjing and later studied medicine, literature, and philosophy in Japan.

He returned home a committed foe of the Manchu dynasty, and, after the revolution that overthrew the dynasty in 1911, he joined the new republican government in its ministry of education.

Lu Xun's literary activity began in 1918 when, at the urging of friends, he published a short story, "A Madman's Diary." The first Western-style short story written in Chinese, it was a satiric attack on the traditional Confucian culture of China. Its success laid the foundation for acceptance of the short story as a literary vehicle. "The True Story of Ah Q," published in 1921, was also a repudiation of China's old order. In addition to his stories, Lu Xun wrote essays, of which "Outline History of Chinese Fiction" is by far his best known; made compilations of classical fiction; and translated literature from Russian to Chinese.

His pessimism about the republican government led him to leave Peking in 1926 and settle in Shanghai. There he recruited many fellow writers and countrymen for the Communist party, although he never joined it himself. He died there on Oct. 19, 1936.

Ancient Poetry

In China "poetic education" in the original meaning is learning The Book of Songs. This is the first comprehensive anthology of Chinese poems including including 305 poems of the Zhou Dynasty (1122-256 B.C.). It was originally called Shi (Poems) and Shi Sanbai (Three Hundred Poems). Each poem in The Book of Songs was set to music and could be sung. The compilers classified the 305 poems into folk songs, ceremonial songs, and sacrificial songs, according to their contents and the style of the music. Folk songs, which were popular among the people, made up the best part of The Book of Songs, while ceremonial songs and sacrificial songs were used mainly on sacrificial or ceremonial occasions to eulogize the merits and virtues of the Son of Heaven and of his forefathers.

Confucius, a great philosopher and educator was very fond of The Book of Songs. He used to recite the poems from time to time, and used it as a textbook for his pupils. In the Han Dynasty, The Book of Songs was formally accepted as a classic of the Confucian school, called Shi Jing. The Book of Songs has over a long period of times been highly appreciated, and has exerted a profound and far-reaching influence on the development of Chinese literature, especially that of poetry, over a period of more than 2000 years. It has also served as important historical data for the study of ancient China from the early years of the Western Zhou Dynasty to the Spring and Autumn Period.

All three hundred and five songs were drawn from the region north of the Yellow River. They are typical products of north China, the area administered by the Kings of the House of Zhou in Confucius's time. By the 4th century B.C. China's boundaries had expanded to include the vast area of the Yangtze river valley, where the strong State of Chu became even stronger. This region is very fertile and the life of the inhabitants was more highly developed than that of the northern people. They produced their own type of song, a representative collection of which was compiled under the name of the Chuci. The songs in this collection are more lyrical and romantic. The style is different from that of The Book of Songs. It is called "poetic prose of Chu", or "the Sao style", in the history of Chinese literature. The representative poet is Qu Yuan and his follower Song Yu.

In the following literary history, there were certain periods which were dominated by one distinctive predominant literary genre, such as fu (descriptive prose interspersed with verse) during the Han Dynasty, poetry in Tang, Ci poetry (a special poetic form) of Song and qu (singing verse) of Yuan.

During the Han dynasty (206 B.C.-A.D. 220), the Chu lyrics evolved into the fu, a poem usually in rhymed verse except for introductory and concluding passages that are in prose, often in the form of questions and answers.

The Han was a period of cultural flowering. A poetic form that became the norm for creative writing, began to flourish. Emperor Wu created a music bureau, called "yuefu", in Chinese, specially to collect and record ceremonial chants, but also the songs and ballads of ordinary people. Collected by the Han Music Bureau "Yuefu", many of these songs are anonymous, but also men of letters wrote these tunes, folk ballads, many of them are very narrative. Later, during the Eastern Han, poems with five characters to a line in imitation of the yuefu style appeared. The employment of five characters to the line was found to be a more rewarding measure, permitting a smoother and more melodious effect and the evocation of subtler human feelings.

The yue fu began to develop into shi or classical poetry- the form which was to dominate Chinese poetry until the modern era. These poems have five or seven character lines, with a caesura before the last three characters of each line. They are divided into the original gushi (old poems) and jintishi, a stricter form developed in the Tang dynasty with rules governing tone patterns and the structure of the content. The greatest writers of gushi and jintishi are often held to be Li Bai and Du Fu respectively. The Tang Dynasty was a period of great radiance in literary creation and was especially noted for poetry writing, for which it has been dubbed the golden age of poetry, a predominant genre among all literary forms popular with both the rulers and the populace for about 300 years. There had emerged during this period of time a considerable number of brilliant poets and outstanding poetic compositions.

Towards the end of the Tang dynasty, the ci lyric became more popular. Most closely associated with the Song dynasty, ci most often expressed feelings of desire, often in an adopted persona, but the greatest exponents of the form (such as Li Houzhu and Su Shi) used it to address a wide range of topics.

As the ci gradually became more literary and artificial after Song times, the san qu, a freer form, based on new popular songs, developed. The use of san qu songs in drama marked an important step in the development of vernacular literature.

After the Song dynasty, both shi poems and lyrics continued to be composed until the end of end of the imperial period, and to a lesser extent to this day. However, for a number of reasons, these works have always been less highly regarded than those of the Tang dynasty in particular. Firstly, Chinese literary culture remained in awe of its predecessors: in a self-fulfilling prophecy, writers and readers both expected that new works would not bear comparison with the earlier masters. Secondly, the most common response of these later poets to the tradition which they had inherited was to produce work which was ever more refined and allusive; the resulting poems tend to seem precious or just obscure to modern readers. Thirdly, the increase in population, expansion of literacy, wider dissemination of works through printing and more complete archiving vastly increased the volume of work to consider and made it difficult to identify and properly evaluate those good pieces which were produced. Finally, this period saw the rise of vernacular literature, particularly drama and novels, which increasingly became the main means of cultural expression.

Classical Texts

China has a wealth of classical literature, dating from the Eastern Shou Dynasty (256-770 BCE) and including the Classics, whose compilation is attributed to Confucius. Among the most important classics in Chinese literature is the *book of changes*, a manual of divination based on eight trigrams attributed to the mythical emperor Fu Xi. The *I Ching* is still used by adherents of folk religion. The *Classic of Poetry* is made up of 305 poems divided into 160 folk songs; 74 minor festal songs, traditionally sung at court festivities; 31 major festal songs, sung at more solemn court ceremonies; and 40 hymns and eulogies, sung at sacrifices to gods and ancestral spirits of the royal house. The *Classic of History* is a collection of documents and speeches alleged to have been written by rulers and officials of the early Zhou period and before. It contains the best examples of early Chinese prose. The "Record of Rites"), a restoration of the original *Classic of Rites*, lost in the 3rd century BC, describes ancient rites and court ceremonies. The *Spring and Autumn Annals*is a historical record of the principality of Lu, Confucius' native state, from 722 to

479 B.C.. It is a log of concise entries probably compiled by Confucius himself. The *Analects of Confucius* is a book of pithy sayings attributed to Confucius and recorded by his disciples. There were also important Daoist classics that were written in later periods, such as the *Huainanzi* written by Liu An in the 2nd century BC, during the Han Dynasty. The *Huainanzi* was also one of the earliest Chinese texts to cover topics of Chinese geography and topography.

In the realm of martial classics, the *Art of War* by Sun Tzu in the 6th century BC marks the first milestone in the tradition of Chinese military treatises written in following ages, such as the *Wujing Zongyao* 1044 AD and the *Huolongjing* written before 1375 when Liu Ji died, preface in 1412 AD. Furthermore, the *Art of War* is perhaps the first to outline guidelines for effective international diplomacy. The other two works, the *Wujing Zongyao* and *Huolongjing*, are invaluable written works for the understanding of the gradual development of early Chinese gunpowder warfare.

Historical Texts

The Chinese wrote consistent and accurate records at court after the year 841 BC, with the beginning of the Gonghe regency of the Western Zhou Dynasty. The earliest known narrative history of China was the *Zuo Zhuan*, which was compiled no later than 389 BC, and attributed to the blind 5th century BC historian Zuo Qiuming. The *Classic of History* is thought to have been compiled as far back as the 6th century BC, and was certainly compiled by 300 BC, the latest date for the writing of the Guodian Chu Slips unearthed in a Hubei tomb in 1993. The *Classic of History* included early information on geography in the chapter of the *Yu Gong*. There was also the *Bamboo Annals* found in 281 AD in the tomb of the King of Wei, who was interred in 296 BC. However, unlike the *Zuo Zhuan*, the authenticity of the early date of the *Bamboo Annals* is doubtful. Another early text was the political strategy book of the *Zhan Guo Ce*, compiled between the 3rd and 1st centuries BC, with partial amounts of the text found amongst the 2nd century BC tomb site at Mawangdui. The oldest extant dictionary in China is the *Erya*, dated to the 3rd century BC, anonymously written but with later commentary by the historian Guo Pu (276–324). Other early dictionaries include the *Fangyan* by Yang Xiong (53 BC – 18 AD) and the *Shuowen Jiezi* by Xu Shen (58–147 AD). One of the largest was the *Kangxi Dictionary* compiled by 1716 under the auspices of the Kangxi Emperor (r. 1661-1722); it provides definitions for over 47,000 characters.

Although court records and other independent records existed beforehand, the definitive work in early Chinese historical writing was the *Shiji* (S/S), written by the Han Dynasty court historian Sima Qian (145 BC-90 BC). This groundbreaking text laid the foundation for Chinese historiography and the many official Chinese historical texts compiled for each dynasty thereafter. Han Dynasty is often compared to the Greek Herodotus in scope and method, as he covered Chinese history from the mythical Xia Dynasty up until the contemporary reign of Emperor Wu of Han, while pertaining an objective and non-biased standpoint (which is often difficult for the official dynastic histories who used historical works to justify the reign of the current dynasty). His influence was far and wide and impacted the written works of many Chinese historians, including the works of Ban

Gu and Ban Zhao in the 1st and 2nd centuries, or even Sima Guang in the 11th century with his enormous compilation of the *Zizhi Tongjian* presented to Emperor Shenzong of Song in 1084 AD. The overall scope of the historiographical tradition in China is termed the Twenty-Four Histories, created for each successive Chinese dynasty up until the Ming Dynasty (1368-1644), as China's last dynasty, the Qing Dynasty (1644-1911), is not included.

There were also large encyclopedias produced in China throughout the ages. The *Yiwen Leiju* encyclopedia was completed by Ouyang Xun in 624 during the Tang Dynasty, with aid from scholars Linghu Defen and Chen Shuda. In the Song Dynasty alone, the compilation of the Four Great Books of Song (10th century - 11th century) begun by Li Fang and finalized by Cefu Yuangui represented a massive undertaking of written material covering a wide range of different subjects. This included the *Extensive Records of the Taiping Era* (978), the *Imperial Readings of the Taiping Era* (983), the *Finest Blossoms in the Garden of Literature* (986), and the *Prime Tortoise of the Record Bureau* (1013). Although these Song Dynasty Chinese encyclopedias featured millions of written Chinese characters each, their aggregate size paled in comparison to the later *Yongle Encyclopedia* (1408) of the Ming Dynasty, which had a total of 50 million Chinese characters. Yet even this size was trumped with later Qing Dynasty encyclopedias, such as the printed *Gujin Tushu Jicheng* (1726). This Qing encyclopedic compilation features over 100 million written Chinese characters in over 800,000 pages, printed in 60 different copies using copper-metal Chinese movable type printing. Other great encyclopedic writers and content include the polymath scientist Shen Kuo (1031–1095) and his *Dream Pool Essays,* the agronomist and inventor Wang Zhen (fl. 1290–1333) and his *Nongshu,* and the minor scholar-official Song Yingxing (1587–1666) and his *Tiangong Kaiwu.*

8

Ancient Egyptian literature

Ancient Egyptian literature is characterized by a wide diversity of types and subject matter; it dates from the Old Kingdom (c. 2755-2255 BC) into the Greco-Roman period (after 332 BC). Such literary devices as simile, metaphor, alliteration, and punning are found.

Ancient Egypt was the source of great works written on papyrus or on the walls of temples, tombs, pyramids, obelisks, portraits and monuments. These works of art succeeded for many centuries. Over time many changes took place; many governments and civilizations, vanished and others appeared, but the ideals of the ancient Egyptian literature persisted even in our age. Besides, ancient Egyptian literature formed central elements in folkloric works of many nations. This shows how elevated ancient Egyptians moral and literary perceptions were, even before divine religions were revealed or even before the world knew great literary masterpieces.

Ancient Egyptian literature rose and grew in the bosom of religious beliefs, but it quickly evolved to deal with man's ordinary day-to-day life. Literary works occupied a distinguished position in the ancient Egyptian thought and civilization. The ancient

Egyptians viewed literature as a source of spiritual nourishment and a unique way to elevate style of expression. Refined literary style was a source of pride for the writer and appreciation and enjoyment for the reader.

Ancient Egyptian literature tackled almost all aspects of life. Literary works were classified by subjects into various "genres" such as novels, short stories, poetry, folkloric tales, proverbs, wise-sayings, moral teachings, philosophical meditations and literary messages. The latter were divided into title, introduction, body and conclusion.

Besides, ancient Egyptians wrote plays, dramatic poetry, songs, religious hymns and love poetry, in addition to description of nature, panegyrical poems to glorify their kings and their glorious battles, and songs for workers and farmers and others to be sung in parties.

Range of Literary Forms

The religious literature of ancient Egypt includes hymns to the gods, mythological and magical texts, and an extensive collection of mortuary texts. The range of secular literature includes stories; instructive literature, known as wisdom texts; poems; biographical and historical texts; and scientific treatises, including mathematical and medical texts. Notable also are the many legal, administrative, and economic texts and private documents such as letters, although not actually literature. The individual authors of several compositions dating from the Old Kingdom and the Middle Kingdom (2134-1668 BC) were revered in later periods. They came from the educated class of upper-level government officials, and their audience was largely educated people like themselves. Indeed, many literary compositions of the Middle Kingdom were composed as political propaganda, to teach the students who learned to read and write by copying them to be loyal to the ruling dynasty. Many of these same wisdom texts were still copied by New Kingdom (1570-1070 BC) schoolchildren more than 500 years later, along with more contemporary texts designed to undermine the glamour of the new military profession. Some of the stories include elements of mythology and may owe much to an oral storytelling tradition.

Old Kingdom

The oldest literature preserved, the Pyramid Texts, are mortuary texts carved inside the pyramids of kings and queens of the later part of the Old Kingdom; they were designed to ensure the dead ruler's rightful place in the afterlife. These texts incorporate mythology, hymns to the gods, and daily offering rituals. Many autobiographical inscriptions from private tombs recount the deceased's participation in historical events. Although no stories or wisdom texts are preserved from the Old Kingdom, some Middle Kingdom manuscripts may be copies of Old Kingdom originals; an example is The Instruction of the Vizier Ptahhotep, composed of maxims illustrating basic virtues (such as moderation, truthfulness, and kindness) that should govern human relations and describing the ideal person as a just administrator

First Intermediate Period

Following the breakdown of the Old Kingdom, the Pyramid Texts were appropriated by private individuals; supplemented with new incantations, these texts were painted on coffins, from which the name Coffin Texts is derived. Private individuals also continued to have their tombs inscribed with autobiographical texts, which often recounted their exploits during this time of political unrest. To this First Intermediate period are attributed various laments over the chaotic state of affairs. One of these, The Dialogue of a Man with his Ba (soul), is a debate on suicide; another, the earliest example of the songs sung by harpists at funerary banquets, advises Eat, drink, and be merry, before it's too late!

Middle Kingdom

In addition to Coffin Texts, Middle Kingdom religious literature comprises numerous hymns to the king and various deities including a long hymn to the Nile and ritual texts. Private autobiographies containing historical information continued to be inscribed, and rulers began setting up stelae (stone slabs) on which their important deeds were recorded. From both the First Intermediate period and the Middle Kingdom come instructional texts, each written in the name of a reigning king, telling his son and successor how various specific historic events influenced the kingship and how the son should profit by the father's mistakes.

The Satire on Trades stresses the bad aspects of all possible occupations in contrast to the easy life of the scribe. Among the stories composed during the Middle Kingdom are The Story of Sinuhe, a palace official who fled to Syria at the death of King Amenemhet I and became a rich and important man there; The Tale of the Eloquent Peasant, a man who made such eloquent pleas for the return of his stolen donkeys that he was kept in protective custody for some time so that the officials in charge could enjoy his orations; The Story of the Shipwrecked Sailor, which recounts a fabulous encounter with a giant snake on a lush island; and The Story of King Khufu and the Magicians. The earliest preserved medical and mathematical papyri also date from this period.

New Kingdom

New Kingdom mortuary texts, especially one called the Book of the Dead, were written on papyrus for inclusion in tombs. Among the most famous hymns from the period are those from the reign of Akhenaton dedicated to the sun god as sole deity. King Kamose (reigned about 1576-1570 BC), at the end of the Second Intermediate period (1720-1570 BC), recorded the early stages of driving thc Hyksos out of Egypt (1600 BC).

After the early New Kingdom, the number of such royal historical inscriptions increased greatly, while private autobiographical texts gave way to religious texts. Thutmose III recorded his various wars in Syria both on a freestanding stela (called the Poetical Stela) and on the walls of the temple at El-Karnak. Both records describe how the king calls in his advisers, apprises them of the difficulty of their situation, is advised to try the easy solution, and proceeds to tell them that he is not afraid and will dare the more dangerous route; the king of course succeeds. Late New Kingdom rulers, especially Ramses II and Ramses III, also left extensive records of their military exploits; both poetic accounts and chronicles of the deeds of Ramses II at the Battle of Kadesh against the Hittites have been preserved. The instructive texts, now directed at lower ranks in the bureaucracy, were no longer based on the assumption that right thinking and just action automatically lead to wordly success, but instead counsel contemplation and endurance. Among the many stories that involve mythological characters are The Contendings of Horus and Seth; The Destruction of Mankind, in which human beings are spared from annihilation by getting the goddess Hathor drunk on blood-colored beer; and The Tale of the Two Brothers, a story of a good younger brother betrayed by his suspicious elder brother. The Report of Wenamun recounts the trials and tribulations of an envoy sent to purchase wood in Byblos. Several collections of love poems exist from this period as well.

Late Period

From the subsequent centuries, into the Greco-Roman era, examples from the full range of Egyptian literary forms are known; these include new religious compositions, private and royal historical records, instructions, stories, and scientific treatises such as medical, mathematical, and astronomical papyri. The Instructions of Onchsheshongy, a collection of largely pragmatic maxims, many of which sound like proverbs, and The Instructions of Papyrus Insinger, which portrays the wise person as being moral and pious, contrast sharply with the earlier expressions of belief in rewards in this life. Stories were written in this period about the adventures of various magicians, as was a cycle recounting the exploits of a legendary king, Petubastis. One largely mythological tale consists of a series of animal fables. Contacts with contemporary Greek literature are evident both in the epic cycle and the fables, in Egyptian texts translated into Greek, and in a range of magical texts known in both Greek and Egyptian.

Influence on world literature

In ancient Egyptian literature, there is a story dating back to the Middle Kingdom (2022 BC-1850 BC). This era witnessed a great number of writers and thinkers who left behind a number of works of art reflecting the elevated status of thinking and culture in ancient Egypt. The story is entitled "The Sailor and the Wonder Island". It narrates the story of an ancient Egyptian sailor whose ship was wrecked with all on board drowned. As the only survivor, he lives on an isolated island, finds a treasure, returns home and the mysterious island sinks deep into the sea immediately after his departure.

Scholars of comparative literature maintain that the structure, plot and general theme of the source was inspired by many of the greatest and most famous novelists all over the world. The story had influenced many famous classical and romantic novels invoking adventures in search of valuable treasures and heroes who lived in isolated islands.

Robert Louis Stevenson's "Treasure Island" is a good example. This novel narrates the adventures of the hero "Jim Hawkens" who found a map of a treasure buried in an isolated island. Another example is the French writer "Alexandre Dumas's "Conte De Monte Cristo". This novel tells the story of "Edmound Dante" who suffers much and goes through a series of exciting adventures to find a buried treasure in the isolated island of Monte Cristo. At the end, he gets the treasure and returns home safe. Surprisingly enough, ship the hero's ship was named "Pharaoh".

Critics of comparative literature state that the ancient Egyptian story of "The Sailor and the Wonder Island" had influenced "Hay Ibn Yaqthan", a story written in the 12th century by the Arab Andalusian philosopher "Abo Bakre Ibn Tafayl". "Hay Ibn Yaqthan" a philosophical story of a man who lives since his childhood on an isolated island. Through reasoning, he reaches philosophical conclusions proving the existence of Allah. This story had a wide influence on world philosophers and creative writers after being translated into many languages such as Latin, French, English, German and Dutch.

Divine Comedy versus Message of Forgiveness

Scholars and critics of comparative literature are at logger head on the extent of the influence of the "Message of Forgiveness" written by the great Arabic poet abul-Ala'al- Ma'arri (973-1057 AD) on Dante Aligieri's Divine Comedy". The central theme of both works is the description of heaven and hell in the hereafter.

A number of Impartial scholars believe that this theme has clear roots in ancient Egyptian literature which tackled this theme in many works. It was evident in "The Book of the Dead", "The Book of the Gates", and in the story "Isis, Osiris and the World of Dead ".

Ancient Egyptian writers expressed their imaginative vision of the journey of the soul after leaving the body to the sky until it reaches the court where the deceased's heart is weighed against "Ma'et's feather" that symbolizes justice, truthfulness, rightness and bounty. Then, the deceased is sentenced to eternal paradise or hell.

In heaven, called "Iyarow's fields", the deceased enjoys eternal youth without sickness, senility, or death. He is dressed in magnificent clothes that never wear out or get dirty, eats and drinks the most delicious food, fruits and fresh water. Besides, he enjoys eternal peace of mind, safety, and peace as there is no evil souls, snakes, beasts or insects. In hell, the bad people are thrown, where they undergo eternal punishment in certain lakes full of water like fire flames, voracious crocodiles, snakes, and vipers. Besides, the guardians of these lakes are voracious beasts that inflict all sorts of torture on wicked hell residents.

Cinderella in ancient Egyptian literature

Cinderella's story with the same central themes appears in abundance in the folkloric and literary works of many nations all over world. The most famous writers who tackled the story were the German Grim brothers. Cinderella's story with the same central themes can be traced in some literary works appearing on the ancient Egyptian papyri in different names and styles. The first reference of this story dates back to the era of the fourth Dynasty in the 26th Century BC. Then, a copy of this story, dating back to the Modern Kingdom between 16th and12th centuries BC., was found. This copy contains a detailed description of the humiliation and torture inflicted on Cinderella by her step-mother. Another papyrus dating back to the Sixth Century BC. showed the same story.

Novel

The ancient Egyptians excelled in novel writing. This is reflected in the great number of stories left behind. In some of these stories, a well-traveled hero tells us about his adventures such as the story of the drowned sailor and the dangers he witnessed on the mythical island of snakes.

Another example is "Snohi"; story that became very famous for many centuries. It describes Snohi's escape from Egypt, his stay in Syria for dozens of years, where he won the favor of the king. He become so close to the leader that he allowed him to marry of his elder daughter and gave him a plot of land. When Snohi grows old, he also grows homesick. He appeals to the king for permission to return to Egypt to see, as he says, "the place that his heart is longing to see because the greatest thing in the world for a man is to be buried in the place of his birth". His hope was fulfilled and he honorably comes back to Egypt.

Another example of the marvelous stories is "The Eloquent Farmer". It tells the story of an Egyptian farmer who was robbed and treated unjustly, so he submits eloquent complaint to the Pharaoh saying:

> Look, you are the chief that hold the scales, Do not let it lose balance.
> Your tongue represents that of the scales, Your lips the hub.
> If you shut your eyes to the oppressor, Who else can rebuff.
> It is you that make justice.
> You do all good and destroy all evil.
> You bring satisfaction; as you come, hunger-vanishes,
> You come like a calm sky after a wild storm.
> You give warmth to those stricken with cold.
> Your are like fresh water that quenches thirst.

Proverbs of Ptah Hutep

The oldest text in the ancient literature which expresses, in excellent literary style, the rules of good conduct is "The Proverbs of Ptah Hutep". Ptah Hutep was an ancient Egyptian minister under King Asisi of the Fifth Dynasty (2670 BC) When he felt that he is getting older, he wanted to teach his son wisdom. So, he wrote a papyrus containing his directives and proverbs.

The preface of this 5000 years old- papyrus says that "Here begin the wise sayings said by the prince, sacred father, God's favorite, the true son of the king, ruler of the city; minister Ptah Hutep. He wrote it to educate the ignorant and to teach him styles of wisdom and wise sayings. Glory be to those who follow these teachings and shame be on those who neglect them."

Ptah Hutep addresses his son saying:

> "Do not be arrogant of your knowledge. Consult with all: with the educated as well as the uneducated, as knowledge has no limits and no one can acquire all kinds of learning. If you hear someone, who is older and wiser than you, talking, listen carefully and bow to him. If he says something wrong, do not be angry: people will say "what an ignorant!".

Somewhere else, Ptah Hutep advises his son saying, "If you were a leader of a group of people, treat them well. Do not treat them unjustly; justice is something great."

Concerning table etiquette, Ptah Hutep teaches his son saying, "When you sit to the table of a dignitary, take, when he asks you, from what is immediately before you. Do not look at what is before him. Do not look too much at him. Do not look at him unless he salutes you. Do not talk unless he salutes you. Laugh when he laughs. This will make him delighted and satisfied with you because man does not know the reality of the heart."

Regarding destiny and divine decree and how to be satisfied with the god's judgment, Ptah Hutep tells his son, "Let not a man with no children envy you. Do not step away from him making him sad and grieved. A farther with many children may be worried in spite of his high rank. Similarly, the mother of many children may have less time for rest. God creates man and predestines his share in life".

Urging his son to work and earn his living, he tells him, "Listen son, you can not be rich without exertion. If you work hard, the god will help you gain wealth. But if you keep lethargic and lax, the god will be always ready to inflict his wrath and punishment on you". If not lazy and dull, God will hardly punish you."

As for modesty, Ptah Hutep advises his son saying, "When you rise from mean ranks to higher positions, grow rich after being poor, forget not your past. Do not be proud of your wealth and do not be arrogant but remember you are no better than your mates who had relapsed into poverty."

The Egyptian drama

In addition to novels, proverbs and wise sayings, the ancient Egyptians were the first to write drama. An Egyptian document dating back to king Menes (Narmer); of the 32nd Century BC shows the first dramatic text along man's history on earth. The document, kept at present at the British Museum in London contains dramatic philosophical dialogue between Egypt's ancient deities on the process of creating the world and the cosmic system of things and creatures.

Therefore, historians, called this text a "drama of the start of creation" or "the Memphis drama" named after Memphis; Egypt's capital built by king Menes.

It is astonishing that dialogues between the gods were written in a style typically similar to that used in classical and contemporary drama. More interesting is that the text of this drama contains soliloquies by the reciting priest who plays a role similar to that of the "narrator" who interprets and comments on the events "stage directions". Surprisingly enough, this text contains a number of similar to those used by classical and modern dramatists.

There is another dramatic text, inscribed on the walls of Edfu temple, called by historians "a drama of Horus' victory over his enemies". This text is considered one of the best and most complete dramatic text of the ancient Egyptian era. It is divided into five parts: introduction, three acts, and the end. Events evolve around the conflict between "Horus and his followers" and "Sit and his followers". It ends with the victory of Horus, who represents good, truth, and justice, over "Sit", who represents evil, injustice, and tyranny.

Love Poetry

The ancient Egyptians excelled in writing romantic love poetry. In addition eulogies to Nile River and its merits, there were many love poems that expressed not only vehement poison surging the heart of a lover, but also delicate emotions. Sentiments of love were couched in beautiful similes derived from the aesthetic aspects of Egyptian environment. For example, a lover says to his beloved, "My beloved is like a garden, full of beautiful papyrus blossoms and I am like a wild goose attracted by the taste of love".

Another lover says, "My beloved is there on the other bank. We are separated by the floodwater. On the bankside, there is a crocodile lying in wait. But I am not afraid of it. I will swim through the water until I reach her and be delighted."

In another love song, two lovers exchange most refined expressions of love. The loving woman says, "I will never leave you my darling. My only wish is to stay in your house and at your service. We will always be hand in hand, come and go to gather everywhere. You are my health; my life."

It is to be noted that in many of the love poems in ancient Egypt, the man calls his beloved as "sister" and the woman calls her lover as "brother" in order to show how each one of them highly appreciates the other and rises him.

9

Ancient Sumerian Language

Sumerian literature is the oldest literature in the world. The Sumerians invented the first writing system, beginning with cuneiform logograms, which evolved into a syllabary writing system. The Sumerian language remained in official and literary use in the Akkadian and Babylonian empires, even after the spoken language disappeared from the population; literacy was widespread, and the Sumerian texts that students copied heavily influenced later Babylonian literature.

Sumerian literature has not been handed down to us directly, rather it has been rediscovered through archaeology. Nevertheless, the Akkadians and Babylonians borrowed much from the Sumerian literary heritage, and spread these traditions throughout the Middle East, influencing much of the literature that followed in this region, including the Bible.

Sumerian Language

Sumerian was the language of ancient Sumer, spoken in southern Mesopotamia since at least the 4th millennium BCE (BC). It was gradually replaced by

Akkadian as a spoken language somewhere around the turn of the 3rd and the 2nd millennium BCE (the exact dating being a matter of debate), but continued to be used as a sacred, ceremonial, literary and scientific language in Mesopotamia until the first century CE (AD). Then, it was forgotten until the 19th century, when Assyriologists began deciphering the cuneiform inscriptions and excavated tablets left by these speakers. Sumerian is a language isolate.

The history of written Sumerian can be divided into several periods.

1) Archaic Sumerian — 31st – 26th c. BCE
2) Old or Classical Sumerian – 26th – 23rd c. BCE
3) Neo-Sumerian — 23rd – 21st c. BCE
4) Late Sumerian — 20th – 18th c. BCE
5) Post-Sumerian — after 1700 BCE

Archaic Sumerian is the earliest stage of inscriptions with linguistic content, beginning with the Jemdet Nasr (Uruk III) period from about the 31st to 30th centuries BCE. It succeeds the proto-literate period, which spans abouth the 35th to 30th centuries.

Some versions of the chronology may omit the Late Sumerian phase and regard all texts written after 2000 BCE as Post-Sumerian. The term "Post-Sumerian" is meant to refer to the time when the language was already extinct and only preserved by Babylonians and Assyrians as a liturgical and classical language (for religious, artistic and scholarly purposes). The extinction has been traditionally and dated approximately to the end of the Third Dynasty of Ur, the last predominantly Sumerian state in Mesopotamia, about 2000 BCE. However, this date is very approximate, as many scholars have contended that

Sumerian was already dead or dying as early as around 2100 BCE, by the beginning of the Ur III period, while others believe that Sumerian persisted as a spoken language in a small part of Southern Mesopotamia (Nippur and its surroundings) until as late as 1700 BCE. Whatever the status of spoken Sumerian between 2000 BCE and 1700 BCE, it is from this period that a particularly large amount of literary texts and bilingual Sumerian-Akkadian lexical lists survive, especially from the scribal school of Nippur. This, along with the particularly intensive official and literary use of the language in Akkadian-speaking states during the same time, is the basis for the distinction between a Late Sumerian period and all subsequent time.

Two varieties (dialects or sociolects) of Sumerian are recorded. The standard variety is called *eme-gir*. The other recorded variety is called *eme-sal*. The name is usually translated as "women's language". Eme-sal is used exclusively by female characters in some literary texts (this may be compared to the female languages or language varieties that exist or have existed in some cultures, e.g. among the Chukchis and the Caribs, and to women's use of Prakrit as opposed to men's use of Sanskrit in some of the Indian classics); in addition, it is dominant in certain genres of cult songs etc.. The special features of eme-sal are mostly phonological, but words different from the standard language are also used. Sumerian words adapted into Akkadian were sometimes of the eme-sal variety, so that it may have been the more colloquial variety.

The Sumerian language is the earliest known written language. The "proto-literate" period of Sumerian writing spans ca. 3500 to 3000 BCE. In this period, records are purely logographic, with no linguistic or phonological content. The oldest document of the proto-literate period is the Kish tablet. Falkenstein (1936) lists 939 signs used in the proto-literate period (late Uruk, 34th to 31st centuries)

Records with unambiguously linguistic content, identifiably Sumerian, are those found at Jemdet Nasr, dating to the 31st or 30th century BC. From about 2600 BC, the logographic symbols were generalised using a wedge-shaped stylus to impress the shapes into wet clay. This archaic *cuneiform* ("wedge-shaped") mode of writing co-existed with the pre-cuneiform archaic mode. Deimel (1922) lists 870 signs used in the Early Dynastic IIIa period (26th century). In the same period the large set of logographic signs had been simplified into a logosyllabic script comprising several hundred signs. Rosengarten (1967) lists 468 signs used in Sumerian (pre-Sargonian) Lagash. The pre-Sargonian period of the 26th to 24 centuries BCE is the "Classical Sumerian" stage of the language.

The cuneiform script is adapted to Akkadian writing from the mid 3rd millennium. Our knowledge of Sumerian is based on Akkadian glossaries. During the "Sumerian Renaissance" (Ur III) of the 21st century BC, Sumerian is written in already highly abstract cuneiform glyphs directly succeeded by Old Assyrian cuneiform.

Transcription

Transcription, in the context of cuneiform, is the process in which an epigraphist makes a line art drawing to show the signs on a clay tablet or stone inscription in a graphic form suitable for modern publication. Not all epigraphists are equally reliable, and before a scholar publishes an important treatment of a text, the scholar will often arrange to collate the published transcription against the actual tablet, to see if any signs, especially broken or damaged signs, should be represented differently.

Transliteration is the process in which a Sumerologist decides how to represent the cuneiform signs in Roman script. Depending on the context, a cuneiform sign can be read either as one of several possible logograms, each of which corresponds to a word in the Sumerian spoken language, as a phonetic syllable (V, VC, CV, or CVC), or as a determinative (a marker of semantic category, such as occupation or place). Some Sumerian logograms were written with multiple cuneiform signs. These logograms are called diri-spellings, after the logogram 'diri' which is written with the signs SI and A. The text transliteration of a tablet will show just the logogram, such as the word 'diri', not the separate component signs.

Cuneiform

The key to reading logosyllabic cuneiform came from the Behistun inscription, a trilingual cuneiform inscription written in Old Persian, Elamite and Akkadian.

In 1838, building on the 1802 work of Georg Friedrich Grotefend, Henry Rawlinson (1810–1895) was able to decipher the Old Persian section of the Behistun inscriptions, using his knowledge of modern Persian. When he recovered the rest of the text in 1843, he and others were gradually able to translate the Elamite and Akkadian sections of it, starting with the 37 signs he had deciphered for the Old Persian. Meanwhile, many more cuneiform texts were coming to light from archaeological excavations, mostly in the

Semitic Akkadian language, which were duly deciphered.

By 1850, however, Edward Hincks (1792–1866) came to suspect a non-Semitic origin for cuneiform. Semitic languages are structured according to consonantal forms, whereas cuneiform, when functioning phonetically, was a syllabary, binding consonants to particular vowels. Furthermore, no Semitic words could be found to explain the syllabic values given to particular signs.

In 1855 Rawlinson announced the discovery of non-Semitic inscriptions at the southern Babylonian sites of Nippur, Larsa, and Uruk. Julius Oppert suggested that a non-Semitic, "Turanian" language had preceded Akkadian in Mesopotamia, and that this language had evolved the cuneiform script.

In 1856, Hincks argued that the untranslated language was agglutinative in character. The language was called "Scythic" by some, and, confusingly, "Akkadian" by others. In 1869, Oppert proposed the name "Sumerian", based on the known title "King of Sumer and Akkad", reasoning that if Akkad signified the Semitic portion of the kingdom, Sumer might describe the non-Semitic annex.

Credit for being first to scientifically treat a bilingual Sumerian-Akkadian text belongs to Paul Haupt (1858-1926), who published *Die sumerischen Familiengesetse* (The Sumerian family laws) in 1879.

Ernest de Sarzec (1832-1901) began excavating the Sumerian site of Tello (ancient Ngirsu, capital of the state of Lagash) in 1877, and published the first part of *Découvertes en Chaldée* with transcriptions of Sumerian tablets in 1884. The University of Pennsylvania began excavating Sumerian Nippur in 1888.

The bewildering number and variety of phonetic values that signs could have in Sumerian led to an unfortunate detour in understanding the language – a Paris-based orientalist, Joseph Halévy, argued from 1874 onward that Sumerian was not a natural language, but rather a secret code (a cryptolect), and for over a decade the leading Assyriologists battled over this issue. For a dozen years, starting in 1885, even the great Friedrich Delitzsch accepted Halévy's arguments, not renouncing Halévy until 1897.

François Thureau-Dangin working at the Louvre in Paris also made significant contributions to deciphering Sumerian with publications from 1898 to 1938, such as his 1905 publication of *Les inscriptions de Sumer et d'Akkad*. Charles Fossey at the Collège de France in Paris was another prolific and reliable scholar. His pioneering *Contribution au Dictionnaire sumérien-assyrien*, Paris 1905-1907, now available in whole at Google Books, turns out to provide the foundation for P. Anton Deimel's 1934 *Sumerisch-Akkadisches Glossar*.

In 1908, Stephen Langdon summarised the rapid expansion in knowledge of Sumerian and Akkadian vocabulary in the pages of *Babyloniaca*, a journal edited by Charles Virolleaud, in an article 'Sumerian-Assyrian Vocabularies', which reviewed a valuable new book on rare logograms by Bruno Meissner. Subsequent scholars have found Langdon's work, including his tablet transcriptions, to be not entirely reliable. In 1944, a more careful Sumerologist, Samuel Noah Kramer, provided a detailed and readable summary of the decipherment of Sumerian in his *Sumerian Mythology* accessible on the Internet. Friedrich Delitzsch published a learned Sumerian dictionary and grammar in the form of his *Sumerisches Glossar* and *Grundzüge der sumerischen Grammatik,* both appearing in 1914. Delitzsch's student, Arno Poebel, published a grammar with the same title, *Grundzüge der sumerischen Grammatik,* in 1923, and for 50 years it would be the standard for students studying Sumerian. Poebel's grammar was finally superseded in 1984 on the publication of *The Sumerian Language, An Introduction to its History and Grammatical Structure,* by Marie-Louise Thomsen.

The difficulty in translating Sumerian can be illustrated by a quote from Miguel Civil of the University of Chicago's Oriental Institute, regarding a tablet for making beer:

> "Two previous attempts, by J.D. Prince in 1919 and M. Witzel in 1938, had produced less than satisfactory results. A line that now even a first year Sumerian student will translate *"you are the one who spreads the roasted malt on a large mat (to cool),"* was translated *"thou real producer of the lightning, exalted functionary, mighty one!"* by the first author, and *"stärkest du mit dem Gugbulug(-Tranke) den Gross-Sukkal"* [*"strengthen thou with the Gugbulug (drink) the large Sukkal"*] by the second."
>
> "Two developments during the fifties made possible a better understanding of Sumerian literature. In Chicago, Benno Landsberger was editing the *Materials for the Sumerian Lexicon.* In Philadelphia, where I had been working before 1963, Samuel Noah Kramer was busy making available to scholars as many literary tablets as possible from the collections in Philadelphia, Istanbul, and Jena."

Landsberger worked to publish important bilingual Sumerian-Akkadian lexical tablets from the Old Babylonian period, which have greatly helped our knowledge of Sumerian vocabulary. Kramer and

Thorkild Jacobsen both increased our understanding of Sumerian by publishing and translating Sumerian literary texts.

Prose ad Poetry

Literature is a narrower term than written material, and in the field of cuneiform does not include the several hundred thousand letters and documents of all types. Within the area of literature in Babylon and Assyria, the "scientific" writings, in the widest sense of the term, present the most comprehensive sector, and will deserve a closer look soon in this website. Prayers and incantations are often recorded in their entirety. More frequent1y, however, the beginning the first line is cited and represent the missing title of a work.

Extensive poems, especially many myths and epics which could not be recorded on a single multi-column tablet, were spread over as many as twelve tablets and thus, at least formally, comprised series similar to the larger scientific works. The division into tablets was usually determined in advance. Since the end of a tablet always came at a break in the contents, only in exceptional cases did the partial tablets encompass the same amount of material. Shorter compositions, such as hymns and prayers, were not collected in series with a fixed number of tablets, but were only compiled on larger tablets from case to case.

Literary works other than the royal inscriptions were composed predominantly in a stereotypical language in which the ends of lines and verses usually coincided. Even today, we are in no position to distinguish with certainty between poetic and prose compositions, or to recognize in any reliable way prose sections in verse compositions.

The attempt to analyze poetic rhythm in Sumerian poetic compositions is only in its inception, and we cannot tell whether this will ever meet with any success. We can do somewhat better with the Akkadian, even if the dominant assumption until now-that in Babylonian as in Hebrew poetry, it was always only a question of the number of accented syllables, since there was no basic principle governing the number of unaccented syllables between them - has not always proven to be true. Therefore, in order to recognize an actual rhythm we must first of all come to know the pronunciation and accentuation of individual words in the vernacular much more precisely than is now possible for us regarding the ancient Orient. Even with very careful study of the manner in which words and groups of words were written, we are often unable to get beyond working hypotheses which enable us to understand much, though not all, of the material. In all languages, even if in quite different degrees, words are shortened So that they can fit into the poetic rhythm.

This is done either by omitting vowels or by adding emphasis through a clearer accentuation of open syllables with short vowels. Neither technique is always evident in written texts. On methodological grounds we do well if we reckon as little as possible with altered word forms and shifts in accents in the verses. At the same time, we cannot always determine how often we may do that, so that considerable room is left to our discretion. Thus many are of the opinion that attempts to recognize the poetic rhythm have too little chance of success to be significant. It is my view, however, that those chances are not so negligible and that the study of poetic form can contribute much to our understanding of the nuances of many expressions. Even in other fields of knowledge there is no way around assumptions which are not borne out later, and the correction of initial errors still yields much essential knowledge.

In a great portion of the Babylonian poems of the second millennium one can establish no quantitative meter by counting syllables over alternating verse lengths. According to our terminology, the iambic ('-), trochaic (-'), and amphibrachic (.-') metrical feet alternate with one another in quite variant ways. The triptych predominates in narrative, while verses CompoSed only in diptych lend particular emphasis to pronoUncements. TWO verses generally form a double-verse on the basis of what is usually an antithetical parallelism or, more rarely, a tautological parallelism. Without exception, the thyrmic and syntactical units are concealed by a trochaic conclusion. The strophes compirse four to twelve verses and only rarely more, or by counterstropes only two. The verse structure of much later poetic compositions such as the Gilgamesh Epic and a great number of prayers, sharply departs from the older form, often in the preference for longer verses. In contrast to earlier works, there now appear to be as many as three unaccented syllables - or even none at all - between two accents. In addition, we must reckon with the possiblility that, just as in many of our songs, the strength of the accents varied, especially in the quite popular musical delivery of poetry, and that the accentuation was often quite different from its merely spoken recital.

Inscriptions of Kings

The inscriptions of kings and, less frequently, other functionaries can only be regarded as literature if they offer more than the very brief enumeration of building projects or campaign reports. The great mass of these are shorter or longer building inscriptions which sometimes also record dedications. Such inscriptions are introduced either through the designation of the god or gods for whom the building was built, and include hymnic attributes. They can also open with the self-introduction of the ruler, with brief or more extensive titles and the subsequent mention of the deities. Occasionally, an invocation of the god stands at the beginning.

In the conclusion, blessings are quite often invoked for those who restore the edifice, and curses are called down upon those who neglect it. In more lengthy building inscriptions, the description of the building process itself as a literary form can go beyond the common format of the building report. Generally people were satisfied with an elevated proSe using a somewhat freer word order, and in every case rhythmically metrical language can be found here and there. The inscriptions of the Chaldean kings offer particularly detailed building descriptions, in several cases with historical retrospectives. These inscriptions often replace the usual blessing and curse formulas with prayers to the god to whom the structure is commended.

The second major category of royal inscriptions, the reports of wars and conquests, is found in Babylon in only a minority of inscriptions. In the Sumerian period, for example, these come almost exclusively in the late Early Dynastic period, and particularly fully in the vulture stela of Eannatum of Lagash. Eighty to one hundred years later, Uruinimgina uses this medium to delineate his manifold social reforms instead.

Conversely, the campaign reports in the Sumerian and, more frequently, in the Akkadian inscriptions of the great kings of Akkad from Sargon I to Naram-Sin are again extensive. In the Old Babylonian period only a few kings, among them those of Mari, give brief campaign reports. Hammurabi says in the poetic introduction to his law stela only what he later accomplished for the cities he had conquered; the curse formulas at the conclusion are unusually comprehensive. After 1500 Before Common Era, we find campaign reports from only a few Babylonian kings, who describe particular actions. Normally, one was satisfied with very brief references to victories over enemies, but without supplying any names: the actions of the gods, and of the king on behalf of the gods, were supposed to be given the primary emphasis. A unique text is the grave inscription which Nabonidus dedicated in 548 to his mother, Hadda-hoppe, who died at the age of 103. Here the mother herself speaks at length. From a literary standpoint, the Sumerian sacral and building inscriptions on the statues of the ruler Gudea of Lagash present an exceptional case. In these Gudea speaks of himself as "he," as was customary in Lagash even earlier, and he has adopted many expressions from religious texts. The great building hymn, recorded on two or three multi-column clay cylinders, is unique. It includes many theological reflections as well as a detailed account of the dedication festival following completion of construction of the temple. Little here has been borrowed from the usual building reports.

In Assyria, moreover, there are building inscriptions in which political themes are completely overlooked or resonate only on the periphery. The primary inscriptions of the conquering kings increasingly enlarged and elaborated the depiction of battles and conquests after about 1300, so that the building report often appears as no more than an appendix to the campaign reports. By the time of the NeoAssyrian Empire, the building report was often omitted completely, and several kings even tell of their hunting expeditions. The long inscriptions were most often written on great stone tablets or clay prisms, which could hold up to six, eight, or ten columns and as many as 1,300 lines. If we overlook some kings between 950 and 725 who mainly preferred a very dry style for their reports, the style of these inscriptions was highly polished and in some battle reports could even be gripping. Despite the many conventional formulations, various kings, particularly the Sargonids, revealed elements of a personal style (e.g., sometimes impressive portrayals of nature or technical details by Sennacherib). Frequently the campaigns were not ordered chronologically, but rather according to other criteria, such as geographical considerations or others less easily discernible. In special cases, extremely detailed initial reports of particular campaigns were composed for and dedicated to the god Ashur. These, too, were literarily demanding presentations. Occasionally the governors of larger provinces had inscriptions composed in the style of the royal inscriptions.

The royal inscriptions in other lands of the ancient Orient are to be distinguished from those of Assyria and Babylonia not only by their language, but in many respects by their structure and style as well. That is as true of the Hittite inscriptions as it is of those from Urartu, for the Elamite as well as for the often trilingual inscriptions of the Achaemenaean kings, and for the Phoenician and Aramaic inscription

Myths and Epics

Myths of the gods, which narrate stories of the gods and from which people could extract answers to important questions with respect to their own times, are often much older than the written versions of the myths. However, it is only rarely possible to draw more than speculative conclusions about the preliterary myths from the poetic accounts. Occasionally, remarkably original forms of the myths are briefly narrated in the context of other texts; but the bulk of poetic myths are reflective myths, which transformed the ancient mythic traditions according to certain basic themes and even enriched the earlier myths with new episodes. Most of the creation myths belong to this category. These are concerned not only with the creation of the world, life, and important implements, but also with the ordering of the world following often arduous struggles against the powers of a primeval chaos. Besides these myths there are also somewhat comprehensive poetic myths, which are tied to earlier traditions only in small part or not at all. These can be called "constructed myths," since the entire treatment has been constructed only loosely on the basis of earlier mythic poetry, and has been fleshed out using contemporary mythological schemata. In some cases impressive mythic poems could emerge through this process. It is not accidental, then, that the name of the author often appears in such poetic compositions, whereas the earlier poetic myths considered the author to be unimportant to the essential message and thus were unconcerned to name an author. In fact, anonymity is typical for the greatest portion of literature throughout ancient Mesopotamia.

In addition to those myths in which only gods and demons take part, there are those in which semi-divine heroes, or even humans, play important roles. In such myths, historical reminiscences continue to exist, at least to some degree. Not until after about 1400 did historical events - those of the distant past as well as those only a few years past - become the objects of epics with expressly political intent in Assyria and Babylonia. Small fragments are generally all that remain of these. We possess larger portions from a poem which concerns the events in the last years of the Kassite dynasties and which from a Babylonian perspective depicts and laments the horror ascribed to the Elamites. By contrast, an Assyrian poet of the thirteenth century sings in eight to nine hundred long verses of the great success of Tukulti-Ninurta I in his struggles against Babylonia. He wrings out victory with the help of the gods, Who have been enraged by the crimes of the Babylonians. As in the great majority of the royal inscriptions from Assyria, the language is a dialect of Babylonian colored by Assyrian.

As far as we know, the Sumerians never treated the theme of the creation of the world in a great mythic poem. We do know their ideas from the introductions to dialogues concerning disputes in rank. According to these, the separation of heaven and earth took place at the very beginning. The further course of events involved differentiations. Thus people, who had originally lived as animals, became a special type of creature. Because there were the sick, the crippled, and the helpless elderly, one myth traces these back to a dispute over a contention between Enki and the mother goddess Ninmah.

There are various ideas of creation and theogony among Babylonian myths. The Old Babylonian myth of Atrahasis, which is associated with the name of Nur-

Ayya as the author or scribe, offers the most carefully thought-out presentation. By the later period this myth had been transformed several times and even came to presuppose another myth of theogony. The myth of Atrahasis begins with the words, "When the gods were [simultaneously] humans," in other words, when the types "god" and "human" had not yet been differentiated. At that time, the weaker group of gods, the Igigi, had to perform by themselves all of the works of irrigation and drainage which were necessary for life in Mesopotamia. They finally became tired of the work, went on strike, and threatened the ruling Anunnaki. Immediately before a struggle could break out, a solution was reached: it was agreed that humans should be created to do this work. Enki and the mother goddess then worked together to create the first human from a mixture of clay and the blood of a god, "who possessed the sense to plan." Rites of birth were then established. Twelve hundred years later, however, the humans had become too numerous and restless, and they had even acquired for themselves forbidden wisdom. Therefore, the gods decided to decimate them by pestilence and plagues. Enki (Ea) then advised the humans to withhold prayers and sacrifices from most of the gods, while turning only to one god in particular, so that he would hold the plagues in check.

The god did this, but after twelve hundred years more the same thing recurred, and again a third time, with the same result. At the summons of Enlil, the gods then carne to the decision to exterminate humanity again, this time through the Deluge. The Sumerians already knew the myth of the Deluge, though the sole literary form of this of which we have even limited knowledge first emerged only in the Old

Babylonian period, and was probably influenced by a Babylonian poem.

The creation epic Enuma Elish ("when on high") first appeared in the fourteenth century, and was designed to establish Marduk as king of the gods. A very brief theogony stands at the beginning of this account. Tiamat, the goddess of the seawaters, is the first to rise from the primeval chaos "with her husband Apsu, the god of the groundwater. Thereupon follow further generations of gods, just as in other ancient myths of theogony. Anu, the god of the heavens, appears as the greatgrandson of Tiamat and Apsu, and as the ancestor of other gods. After Anu comes Nudimmud (Ea) with his consort Damkina. Awakened by the younger gods, the old Apsu wants to kill them, but is himself killed by Nudimmud (Ea), who uses magic and erects his own palace upon the groundwaters. There the divine marvel-child Marduk is bom, and by his riotousness he arouses the old Tiamat as well against the young gods.

Tiamat then commissions her "paramour" Kingu to raise an army of all kinds of monsters against the gods. The young gods then tum to some older gods with a plea for help, but when these refuse, they tum to the young Marduk, who agrees, on the condition that they make him king of the gods. This happens and Marduk, using special weapons, kills the dragonlike Tiamat and takes Kingu prisoner. Then Marduk creates the heavens and the earth from the two halves of Tiamat's bodv and, I following this, stars, plants, and other living things. Last of all, Marduk even creates humans from the blood of the rebel god Kingu and, as ever. Tone knows, forces them to work for all time. After founding Babylon and its temple Esagila, the gods hold a victory celebration for themselves and exclaim in laudatory fashion the fifty names of Marduk; the epic gives an explanation for each of these which partially rests on an etymological wordplay. The great struggle between the gods is mitigated here: only three gods are killed, but after their deaths they are integrated into the new order of the world in various ways. This epic in seven tablets became the cult legend recited every year at the New Year festival in Babylon. The Assyrians under Sennacherib substituted Ashur for Marduk in the epic. Berossus later propagated a reshaped version of the epic in his Greek Babyloniaka. Direct influences of the Babylonian creation epic on the biblical account of creation cannot be discerned.

A few references must suffice for myths in this category, which deal with struggles against powers which are at enmity with the created order. Among these, the Sumerians and Babylonians counted the tales of the mythic eagle Anzu. This figure once stole from the gods the tablets of destiny from Enlil, tablets which are indispensable to rule over the world. Ninurta is chosen as the avenger of the gods. Anzu and Ninurta/Zababa meet in combat, and Anzu is killed.

A love story involving a descent to the Underworld, which can be well described and a young couple coming of age is the myth of "Enlil and Ninlil." According to this story, the young Enlil seeks out Ninlil as she bathes, lies with her, and begets the moon god Nanna-Suen. Because Enlil has now become "unclean," for having raped the young goddess, he is then banished from Nippur to the Underworld. Ninlil goes after him in the Great Below and he meets her in disguise three times. Three times they also lay together, and Ninlil thus begets more gods. In the end, both Enlil and Ninlil return to from the Underworld and great praise is sung for both of them.

The Gilgamesh Epic

Sumerian literature is among the earliest known writings. Literature was almost always religious oriented or a historical record of kings. The 'Gilgamesh Epic' is generally regarded as the greatest literature prior to the O.T. Epic poem centered on the heroic tales of a great king.

Several Sumerian tales of the legendary Gilgamesh were combined together into an epic poem more than four thousand years ago. A Semitic Akkadian version was found in the archives of the Hittite capital at Boghazkoy in Anatolia. It was also translated into Hittite and Hurrian, and several Akkadian texts were found in Ashurbanipal's library at Nineveh from the seventh century BC. With the exception of the more historical account already discussed, the twelve tablets of the Gilgamesh cycle will be treated synthesized as they have been by modern translators into the earliest masterpiece of literature.

Gilgamesh is introduced as knowing all things and countries including mysteries and secrets who went on a long journey and had his story engraved on stone. He was endowed with beauty by the sun god Shamash and with strength and courage by the storm god Adad, making him two-thirds god and one-third man. The seven sages laid the foundations, and he built the walls and temples of Uruk for Eanna, the heavenly Anu, and the love goddess Ishtar.

Gilgamesh ruled Uruk so powerfully that his arrogance was resented, for he enjoyed any virgin or wife that he wanted. The gods heard the people's complaints and decide to create his equal to challenge him. So the goddess of creation produces Enkidu, who lives with wild animals. One day a trapper encounters the one who has filled in his pits and torn out his traps. The trapper's father suggests that he get Gilgamesh to give his son a woman to tame Enkidu, and he does. When she sees Enkidu in the hills, she strips herself naked and teaches him her woman's art. Enkidu lies with her for a week.

When Enkidu goes back to the animals, he is weaker; and they run away from him. The woman says that he is wise and has become like a god. Why should he live with animals? She offers to take him to the temples of Anu and Ishtar in Uruk, where he could challenge Gilgamesh. Meanwhile a dream came to Gilgamesh of a star falling from heaven leaving a meteor so heavy he could not lift it, and his mother Ninsun explains that this was a strong friend he would meet. In another dream Gilgamesh found in Uruk an ax he loved like a woman, and Ninsun interprets that this brave man would rescue him.

When Enkidu arrives in Uruk, Gilgamesh is about to exercise his privilege of being the first to sleep with a bride. But Enkidu blocks his way, and they fight like two bulls locked together. Gilgamesh throws Enkidu down, and then in mutual respect for each other's strength they become friends. They decide to confront the monster Humbaba who guards the cedars in the sacred forest. Gilgamesh prays to the sun god Shamash for protection and receives an amulet from his mother. After the counselors of Uruk ask Enkidu to bring their king back safely, they set out on the long journey.

Entering the forest gate, Gilgamesh dreams that a mountain fell on him, but he was saved by a beautiful light. Then Enkidu has an ominous dream of a rainstorm. When Gilgamesh chops down a cedar with the ax, Humbaba hears the sound. Knowing the monster, Enkidu is afraid; but Gilgamesh encourages him. Calling on Shamash, Gilgamesh fells seven cedars, and each time Humbaba roars louder. When the two heroes reach Humbaba, he pleads with Gilgamesh for mercy, offering to serve him. Gilgamesh is moved, but Enkidu convinces him to kill the monster; so they cut off his head.

Gilgamesh cleans himself up and is asked by the divine Ishtar to be her husband, but he scorns her for having been faithless to so many lovers. Enraged Ishtar retreats to heaven and asks her father Anu to create a bull of heaven to torment the earth with a famine. The bull charges Enkidu, and he seizes it by the horns so that Gilgamesh can kill it with his sword. Ishtar curses them, but Enkidu defiantly tears out the bull's right thigh and throws it in her face. Enkidu then dreams that the gods have decided that one of them must die for having killed Humbaba and the bull of heaven. Soon Enkidu gets sick and dies. Gilgamesh mourns for him for seven days until a worm appears in his nose.

In despair at the death of his friend and realizing now that he must die too, Gilgamesh decides to find Utnapishtim, who has lived in Dilmun since before the flood. Coming to a gate guarded by scorpion men, Gilgamesh is allowed to pass where no human has ever gone. Passing through darkness he enters a garden with bushes like gems. The sun god tells him that he will never find eternal life. Gilgamesh comes to a woman of wine who asks him why he is searching for the wind. He explains that he is afraid of death, and she suggests that he eat, drink, dance, and enjoy life. He only asks the way to Utnapishtim, and she tells him that he must take the ferry of Urshanabi across the ocean. Making Gilgamesh cut six score poles so that his hands won't touch the deadly water, Urshanabi agrees to take him.

Finally arriving Gilgamesh asks his question of Utnapishtim, but he declares there is no permanence. When Gilgamesh wonders how he has lived so long, Utnapishtim reveals a secret of the gods, the story of the deluge. Perturbed by the clamor of humans, the gods decided to let loose a flood on them, but Ea warned Utnapishtim to build a large boat and load it with supplies and animals. After the boat was ready, the storm came. The boat weathered the deluge and rested on a mountain. Sending out a dove, it came back, as did a swallow, but then a crow was released and did not return.

Enlil was angry that a human had survived, but Ea suggested that he should punish sin and transgressions, but not with a flood. Utnapishtim, though a mortal, was allowed to live in the distance. Utnapishtim challenges Gilgamesh to stay awake for a week, but instead he falls asleep for that long, which is proved to him by the decaying seven loaves of bread baked each day by Utnapishtim's wife. Utnapishtim does offer Gilgamesh an herb, which eaten, will bring youth back. Gilgamesh dives underwater to get it, but on his way back to Uruk a serpent steals it from him, eats it, and sheds its skin. Gilgamesh returns to Uruk and must realize that he too is not exempt from death.

One can imagine the influence of such an archetypal story. Gilgamesh represents the achievements of mankind who now wonders about death. His arrogance is criticized, and the primordial custom of the dominant male being allowed sexual license seems to be a throwback from our pre-ethical evolution as primates. Dreams are perceived to be symbolic guides and often prophetic. A woman, his mother, seems to be most skilled at interpreting them. Another strong male is needed to challenge a strong male, but female charms are able to tame him. The shift from living in the wild is accomplished by sexual lovemaking, which leads Enkidu to civilization after he is no longer one with the animals.

The invention of the ax enabled humans to use timber for building, but once again a oneness with the spirit of the forest is lost in the process. The love goddess is not treated very sympathetically in this story, perhaps because she has become a goddess of battles in the human strife that now abounds. Enkidu's throwing of a bull's thigh into her face may be an implied criticism of the ancient rites of animal sacrifice. Of course the keeping of animals was a hedge against famine, because they could be slain and eaten in an emergency.

Enkidu is the one to die, perhaps because he was the one who insisted on killing Humbaba and the bull of heaven. The worm coming out of his corpse is a graphic symbol of the grim reality of physical death. Gilgamesh going through a scorpion-guarded gate and passing through darkness before emerging into a paradise symbolizes the spiritual side of death, as he comes out in a kind of astral world where even the plants glow. To really find out the secrets Gilgamesh must be willing to transcend hedonistic temptations.

His passage across the ocean to learn Utnapishtim's story of the flood is suggestive of Atlantis, since an ocean from the landmass of Europe, Asia, and Africa separated it. His account is quite similar to the Hebrew story of Noah. Unable to find immortality, a magical herb is offered as a consolation; but the serpent that seems able to rejuvenate itself by shedding its skin steals this away from humanity. Sleep and Gilgamesh's inability to stay awake is an analog of death, suggesting that life, like waking consciousness, needs a time of rest and renewal in death and rebirth.

The heroic myths of Sumer were woven primarily around the early dynastic kings of Uruk, Enmerkar, Lugalbanda and Gilgamesh (earlier Bilgamesh), who were later divinized. The poetic myths about Enmerkar and his son Lugalbanda focus on conflicts between the kings of Uruk and of central Iran and the city of Aratta. In the Enmerkar myth, Inanna is courted by Enmerkar, king of Aratta, and by the king of Aratta as well. In the end, She chooses Enmerkar, king of Uruk, and Aratta concedes defeat, but the city is not destroyed by Enmerkar.

The sagas about Gilgamesh still had not been compiled into a single Akkadian poem during the Old Babylonian period; yet the extant epics from that time, although they are only preserved incompletely, do show a completely new impres in comparison with the earlier form. After 1400 Before Common Era, there were in Syria-Palestine and in Asia Minor Babylonian, Hittite and Hurrian versions of the Gilgamesh poem. On the basis of the meager remains of these versions, we can conclude that they represent very free imitations of the original Babylonian forms. Then around 1100 Before Common Era, a person listed as Sin-leqe-unnini of Uruk composed the twelvetablet epic of about three thousand verses as the most fully developed form of the material. Nevertheless, the scribes of the first millennium did not hand on this text without alteration in every detail.

The epic begins by praising the 9.5 km. city wall of Uruk, for whose construction Gilgamesh had imposed upon the inhabitants a heavy burden of forced labor. In order to hold this hero in check, the gods created as his counterpart the wild man Enkidu, who grew up among the wild animals but was led to Uruk by a cult prostitute, where he immediately confronted Gilgamesh.

The struggle between these two ended with Gilgamesh and Enkidu declaring their mutual friendship and together planning and undertaking the battle against tluwawa (tiumbaba) in the cedar forest. After a long, difficult trek, and with the help of Shamash, they were victorious. Upon their return, Ishtar offered Gilgamesh her love, which he bluntly rejected with reference to her behavior toward earlier lovers. Ishtar then pleaded with her father Anu that she might have the Bull of Heaven in order to avenge herself.

The Bull plunged many men in Uruk into deep pits with his snorting, but was then killed by the two friends. During the victory celebration Enkidu insulted the goddess so grievously that the gods ordered his death. The premonition of death, final illness, and the actual death of Enkidu are narrated along with the insertion of many dreams, which are presented in detail along with their interpretations, just as in the ex:pedition against tiumbaba. Likewise, there is the dreadful pain of Gilgamesh, who is unable to save his friend.

Now Gilgamesh himself experiences the anxiety of death and sets out to the far west, to learn from Utnapishtin, the hero of the Deluge, how he might escape death. The journey, which ran underground in some stretches, led him to the kind1y pair of scorpion people, the ale-wife Siduri and the ferryman Urshanabi. They are good to Gilgamesh, and Urshanabi brings him across the waters of death despite the ban. These meetings are portrayed in detail, with much repetition.

Utnapishti relates to Gilgamesh the story of the Deluge, after which the gods gave him the gift of life without death. When Gilgamesh fails a test of sleep, Utnapishti advises him to retrieve the herbs of life from the bottom of the sea. Gilgamesh does that and starts back, but along the way he carelessly al1ows a serpent to steal the herbs of life, whereupon the serpent immediately sheds his skin. At this point, all becomes futile; Gilgamesh resignedly returns to Uruk, and on his arrival proudly shows the city walls to Urshanabi, who must ferry him back to mortal humanity in accordance with the ban.

The epic adds as the twelfth and final tablet the translation of the Sumerian poem of"Enkidu and the Underworld," which gives a completely different portrayal of the death of Enkidu from that in Tablet VII. The Gilgamesh Epic has become one of the great works of world literature by virtue of its unique style of composition, by which the greater human concerns (e.g., the friendship between males) are given repeated expression. Members of lowly professions, moreover, such as prostitutes and ale-wives, appear as representatives of a special degree ofhumanity. Over long stretches ofthe epic, the time-bound elements recede almost entirely from view.

A myth about Etana also deals with the search for life, though it is only preserved in incomplete form in some Old Babylonian and later versions. Etana, the first king after the Flood whom the gods set on the throne of Kish, was without a son. At this point, a fablelike story of an eagle and a serpent is inserted. These two become friends and swear themselves to mutual help. Both have young and always care for the offspring of the other. But one day, the eagle takes advantage of the serpent's absence to devour that creature's young, despite the warning by its own offspring about the vengeance of Shamash.

The serpent complains to Shamash about its misfortune and is advised to hide itself in a great carcass in the mountains in order to punish the eagle when it comes to devour. What transpires is this; the serpent rips the eagle's wing off and hurls the bird into a pit, where it begins to starve. The eagle then cries out daily to Shamash, pleading for forgiveness and deliverance. Shamash then commands Etana to go and pull the eagle out and nurse it back to health. Etana does this and then asks Shamash to show him the "plant ofbirth" (so that Etana may have a son). In spite of Etana's prayers, the eagle cannot fulfill his plea but is prepared to carry the king up to heaven on his back, so that he can receive eternal life there. They fly up to the second heaven, but Etana then becomes dizzy, and both crash. This myth proves impressively the ethos of prayer as a determinative power for humans and animals. The myth of Adapa of Eridu shows humorous features. Adapa breaks a wing of the southern storm, who had spoiled his fishing; he is therefore cited for punishment before the god Anu. Ea then advises Adapa not to accept any offer of Anu. Anu, however, who not always lacks in understanding for people, ex:periences compassion for the poor sinner, and instead of the food of death, offers him the food of life. Adapa, however, rejects this and so forfeits for himself life without death.

Constructed Myths

Constructed myths are known primarily from the eighth and seventh centuries. Among these, the myth of the god of pestilence, Erra, assumes a special rank. Composed by Kabt-ilaniMarduk between the end of 765 and the beginning of 763, as is evident from some historical references, these five tablets were claimed by the author to have been revealed by verbal inspiration in a single night.

They were copied in Assyria, although the slant is clearly pro-Babylonian. According to the plot, which was freely invented by the poet, Erra, along with the warring demons created for him by Anu and designated "the seven," is aroused after a long period of rest by his vizier, Ishum. The demons call him to take renewed action against humanity, which has again become restless, and to decimate them and their livestock. Since Marduk is the king of the gods for Babylonia, Erra must first of all move Marduk to relinquish to him his dominion for a time.

As it appears- the text is broken at this point - Marduk withdraws to be with Ea in his groundwater palace; Erra can now instruct other gods (such as Shamash, Sin, and Adad) to withhold their gifts from people as well. Among the humans, "every man is against his brother," even in the family, and many are lost to drought and the heavy fighting.

In Tablet IV; Ishtum shows Erra in detail all that has transpired, and thereby moves him to restraint; in the future, such catastrophes should befall only the enemies of Babylon, such as Assyria and Elam. Marduk's return is never mentioned; the last that is reported of him is his lament over the fate of his city, Babylon. The poem is obviously rich in contemporary features that we can only partly understand, although it contains many literary reminiscences as well. Much in the long discourses of the gods remains obscure to us. The pompous style, which so sharply deviates from the earlier epics, shows that this myth was not composed for presentation at a temple festival.

The political slant of some myths from Assyria is even more obviously massive. On account of his unpopular war of extermination against Babylon, Sennacherib commissioned some theologians with the task of producing a myth which would have as its focal point a divine legal proceeding against Marduk, who would be found guilty. This myth would then be the subject of a cultic presentation. All that survives of this work is fragments of a commentary, and these appear to have interpreted the individual actions for use in the rituals of the New Year festival. The text, composed in Assyrian, has incorrectly been taken as evidence of an actual passion myth. Assyrian commentaries interpret still other, often absurd mythic constructions from that country.

Wisdom Literature

In direct dependence upon the Hebrew word Chochma "wisdom," theologians have coined the term "Wisdom

Literature" as a collective designation for works with predominantly moralistic and didactic purposes, ranging from collections of proverbs and religious stories to the animal fables and dialogues of Babylonia. In many of these texts, humor also comes to the fore as more than simply a brief, relaxing element. Texts of this sort were not compiled into larger works.

For the most part, sayings and jokes are passed on orally everywhere. Many are tied to a particular period and thus are quickly forgotten; others, however, express something that is universally human, and these are often passed from people to people. In Babylonia, the Sumerians were the first to compile larger collections of sayings, which are preserved mostly in transcriptions of the Old Babylonian period. Many of these sayings are difficult to understand, and their interpretation is therefore disputed.

Included among the sayings are animal fables. The themes are manifold and various: they comprise the personal, as well as the social and the religio-cultic realms. More than a few sayings and jokes are richly elaborated and are in alllikelihood only the products of scribal schools. The Babylonians adopted only a portion of the Sumerian collections and passed them on in Akkadian translation. Larger collections of purely Akkadian proverbs are unknown. It is said of an informant: "A scorpion stung a human, what profit did he get from it? An informant brought someone to his death; what advantage did he get?" In a smaller collection of humorous short stories from Assyria, one finds similarities with Arabic short stories. These are often quite well formulated. They frequently contain only a few lines and include many brief fables, as well as human anecdotes which warn against perverse behavior. Sayings are occasionally quoted in letters, and in a few cases there are references to riddles, though we have no collection of riddles.

The dialogic controversy between two partners was one of the most polished genres of Sumerian literature. In it, the respective parties stress the merits of their own arguments while denigrating those of the other.

Since the partners cannot agree, a god is called upon, or in some cases a king, who should conclusively establish who has the advantage. It does not seem to happen that both partners are recognized simultaneously to be right to the same degree. The dialogue partners can be gods or humans, as for example the shepherd represented by Dumuzi and a farmer, or the (scribe)-father and his son, and even the annual seasons summer and winter, the sheep and the barley, the sickle and the plow, and many others. In every case the controversy must concern the order of the world and also be relevant to humanity: that is, it must present more than a trivial issue. Most of the mythic introductions which precede these dialogues point to the same thing: they draw one's attention back to the creation of the world. Occasionally the behavior of one of the partners resolves the controversy, as for example in the dispute between the heron and the turtle, when the turtle devours the heron's nest of eggs; unfortunately, the conclusion to this dialogue has not been preserved. In a departure from the pattern of the fables, the animals in the dialogues of controversy do not represent people.

As already mentioned, the concisely formulated animal fables constitute a portion of the aphoristic literature in which the behavior of animals occupies a very wide space. The few comprehensive compositions in the Akkadian language occur only in the tradition of the dialogues of controversy, as, for example, the dispute between the ox and the horse. Occasionally there are several disputants, such as a fox, wolf, hound, and lion. Plants such as the Euphrates poplar, the dogwood, the tamarisk, and the date palm also serve as important dialogue partners for humans, along with emmer and wheat. In later texts, the dialogues of controversy are more animated and less bound by pattern. Another form of dialogue is represented by the dialogue between two friends concerning divine justice, which was briefly discussed above. This richly elaborated form allows no deity to mediate this ample display of speeches and counter-speeches, showing liberal application of theological erudition. In a thematically related dispute from the Old Babylonian period, the case was different: there the deity himself spoke at the end, promised the sufferer his help, and exhorted him: "Anoint him whose skin is parched; feed the hungry; give drink to the thirsty!" Finally, the dialogue form is satirized in a later conversation between a lord and his slave, in which the lord always says what he wants to do and the slave responds by praising him. The lord then states the opposite, and again receives praise, this time with supporting argumentation. When the lord finally says that he wants to kill the slave, the slave responds quick-wittedly: "My lord will survive me by no more than three days!"

Humorous Stories

The few stories of this type which we know from the Sumerians belong for the most part to the composition É-dub-ba (House ofTablets), which has not yet been published in its entirety. This composition concerns the school of that time. One fragment depicts the daily life of a pupil, both at school and at home, in the form of a conversation, then briefly describes a dismal day in his life during the course of which he is beaten seven times for various reasons. Consequently, the father invites the teacher home for supper and gives him a gift in the bargain; afterwards, the black sheep of the family becomes a model pupil. Some texts which deal with the methods of summoning and examining have come down to us in bilingual form. These instruct not aridly, but often humorously in the form of discourse and counterdiscourse by teacher and pupil.

Another passage presents us with a father's conversation with his son, in which the father repeatedly holds up the son's refractory behavior and his slovenliness, at the same time holding up his own claim to have always been especially careful. A Babylonian story which is completely unique for its time, about 1100, deals with the case of the impoverished Gimil-Ninurta, who out of desperation gives his only possession, a goat, to the mayor of Nippur in the hope of receiving a commensurate gift in return. The mayor, however, contemptuously dismisses the man after giving him a mug of beer.

As Gimil-Ninurta is leaving, he tells the gatekeeper that he will avenge himself three times, and requests as the first item an elegant chariot from the king. With this, he drives forth as the commissioner of the king, demands a private audience with the mayor, and then beats him thoroughly "from the crown of his head to the soles of his feet." Afterward he takes from the mayor the amount in gold for the rental of the chariot. Gimil- Ninurta next disguises himself as a doctor seeking to treat the ill-handled mayor, then beats the offender as before. The mayor and his retainers then take up the pursuit of his tormentor, but he is trapped by Gimil-Ninurta under a bridge and beaten a third time.

The text concludes with the words: "The mayor could only crawl back into the city [again]." Many would certainly have had similar fancies regarding the powerful in that age, and just as today they would have smirked over this story.

Hymns, Prayers, Laments And Incantations

Sharp boundaries can rarely be drawn between the various genres of prayer literature, since so many of the prayers can be classified under a particular genre only with great difficulty. Moreover, careful investigations exist for only a part of the known collections of texts as well as their genres. There are also transitional forms between prayers and incantations. Therefore, the following delineations of the most important genres can have only a provisional character.

As far as our present knowledge goes, the oldest Sumerian hymns are the temple hymns which are attested as early as the middle of the third millennium, focusing on the great temples; a tablet collection which was copied quite often after 2000 contains 545 lines and comprises forty-two of these hymns. Many, often very long hymns to the gods are known after the Ur III period. These describe the descent, the great power, and the place of the deity in the pantheon, as well as his or her significance for humanity; they often end with intercessions for the king.

Narrative pieces are often inserted. The hymns to kings, who are in most cases divinized, are almost entirely written as selflaudatory compositions in the first person singular; the same is true of many hymns written primarily to goddesses. The dominant themes in these are the origin and legitimation of the king, his favor with the gods and his care for their temples, and his care for the poor, the orphans, and the widows, as well as for justice. Along with these one finds the king's physical strength, his exploits in war, and his accomplishments for the economy of the land. This singular genre of hymns ceased after 1650 with the Babylonian kings Hammurabi and Samsu-iluna, who no longer had themselves divinized. The Babylonians translated no royal hymns and passed none on. In addition, some myths contained hymnic prologues. The Sumerians had no specific literary genre of prayer. Very short prayers are found at the end of several ancient Sumerian commemorative inscriptions.

Longer prayers have been inserted into the great building hymn of Gudea of Lagash, as well as a number of myths, a long didactic poem, and as intercessory prayers at the ends of hymns; these follow no established structural schema. The letters to the gods comprise a strange substitute for prayers; in these the petitioner brings his desire before the god in the form of a letter of request. The drafting of such letters was practiced in the schools.

The late Sumerian literature developed new genres after 1500, such as the summary prayers on cylinder seals of the Kassite period and some prayers, generally passed on in bilingual form, which were used in certain rites. The «laments to comfort the heart" are modeled on the Babylonian prayers in particular; these laments are different from all earlier prayers and contain confessions of sin and petitions for redemption from one's sins.

The last genre to be mentioned is that of the Sumerian songs of lament. The quite comprehensive and tiresomely monotonous laments over political catastrophes, such as the destructions of Akkad and Ur, are included. To these must be added primarily rituallaments in the «woman's dialect" Emesal from a later period- including the ersemma-songs, performed in concert with the balang-harp, and laments for the god in the distant underworld, above all, Dumuzi. These were recited down into the Seleucid period. The same elements, with the variation of a member, are very frequently repeated in the litanies of lament in a refrainlike fashion, though they are preserved on tablets only in abbreviated form. Finally, there are some personal laments, such as "A Man and His God," in which the motifs of Job resonate.

Hymns to the gods are preserved for us as early as the Old Babylonian period. Strangely, these are overwhelmingly addressed to goddesses; they repeatedly end in intercession for the king and reveal quite a diversity of forms, along with an unevenness of scope.

Myths are imbedded in some of these hymns. The song of Agushaya is a hymn to Ishtar which depicts the apprehension the gods feel face Ishtar's mighty warrior powers. Ea then creates Saltu/Strife, as a mirror-image of the young gutsy Ishtar so that the Goddess can come to Her senses and appease Her own instincts. Only fragments remain of other hyrnns of this type, and this is a myth of Ishtar in the first person singular.

There is a very long hymn concerning Ishtar of Nippur which probably goes back to the Old Babylonian period. The language of the later hymns, which often comprise two hundred verses and more, is more artistic than that of the Old Babylonian hymns. Some of these are also hymns of repentance. The literary merit and content of the pronouncements found in the great hymn to the sun god Shamash stand out markedly; at the same time, a hymn to Gula in the first person singular which is just as long, is quite meager in content. Finally, some royal prayers from Assyria are to be reckoned among the hymns, and there is a note of self-criticism in these.

Stylistically related to the hymns in many respects are the limited number of psalms of lament and repentance. Among these is one from Tukulti-Ninurta I of Assyria during the last years of his reign, when the revolts against him were by no means able to break his sense of selfrighteousness. The only great hymn of repentance to Ishtar from the Old Babylonian period is unfortunately very badly preserved. The hemerologies often demand the recitation of prayers of repentance of the sigu-genre for certain days in which calamity threatens. As in a great prayer to Nabu, the priest sometimes speaks for the penitent and asks for forgiveness.

A further group of prayers which is richly represented are the prayers of oracular sacrifice of the genre ikribu; these usually include a formulaic conclusion. Finely formulated references to the previous life of the sacrificial animal in its pasture, as well as descriptions of the deep stillness of the night, are found in prayers of this genre from as early as the Old Babylonian period. Petitions for redemption from sin seldom occur in these hymns. Moreover, many personal names are very short prayers of petition or thanksgiving in sentence form; the contents of these vary greatly. We have referred to royal prayers in many inscriptions above.

The so-called individual prayers of lament comprise by far the largest group of prayers. These prayers are often called prayers of incantation because their superscriptions occasionally contain magical formulas and are frequently imbedded in rituals. These begin with shorter or longer sections praising the deity; then follows the lament with the self-introduction, the plea for release from suffering, reconciliation with the guardian deity, and forgiveness for sins.

A generally formulaic promise of thanks forms the conclusion. Some of these prayers are among the most beautiful pieces of prayer literature because of the earnestness of their confession of sin. A prayer begins with the petitioner's complaint that he has not yet been heard; not the slightest echo of magic can be found here. The situation is different with so-called "special prayers" of this genre, which deal with completely distinct forms of suffering and sickness. These often present mixtures of prayer and incantation and are imbedded in extensive magical rituals which have to be carried out by the incantation priest. This priest directs himself primarily to Shamash, Marduk, and Ea, individually or all together. The so-called "cultic medium" prayers apply to the substances which are used in the ritualS. There are many echoes of the individual prayers of lament in the biblical psalms, but the constraints of the genre left the Babylonian poet much less freedom to formulate these.

The psalm of lament "I Will Praise the Lord of Wisdom" holds a special place in the religious literature of the ancient Orient. In this composition of 480 verses, a very long lament is put in the mouth of a high official of the period around 1100, who laments his many illnesses and his loss of social status, which have brought him to the brink of death. In a scene that is presented only slightly more briefly than his suffering, Marduk finally announces the man's deliverance through a messenger in a dream. The praise of Marduk by all who experienced these events provides the final note. Just as in the book of Job, the quantity of suffering heaped on the individual surpasses all that he considers imaginable. The meaning is this: regardless of what form one's suffering may take, everyone should find himself in the poem and find hope in a similarly miraculous solution.

Sumerian and Babylonian Incantations

The incantation literature is quite extensive among the Sumerians as well as the Babylonians. Sumerian incantations have survived in monolingual form mostly in Old Babylonian transcriptions and were later handed on accompanied by Akkadian translations. In many cases, of course, even the Sumerian text is post-Sumerian. The texts of Sumerian demonic exorcisms have been discussed above. In some of them, which were later compiled in the great series Evil udug/utukku's and Bad asag/asakku's, the activities of the demons are portrayed in lively fashion, and we often find long successions of similar pronouncements. Depending on one's purpose, various types of incantations with particular emphases can be distinguished. The post-Sumerian incantations, which were no doubt translated from the Akkadian with some frequency, were not compiled into their own larger tablet series. They have not yet been studied from a literary standpoint. Among these are the incantations directed against spells. By contrast, we still have no evidence for Sumerian incantations against witches.

The number of Akkadian incantations of different sorts is very large, and these were generally compiled, in part with the associated rituals, only in smaller series, as for example those against the Lamashtu, against spells, and against witches. Many of these are found scattered among the collections of medical prescriptions, as well as among rituals against suffering of all kinds. They have not yet been the subject of a literary investigation. Until now, only a few have been found from the Old Assyrian and Old Babylonian periods.

Finally, there are the so-called Abracadabra texts. These are found on small tablets of the Old Babylonian period, and later occur as parts of other incantations. Mostly they consist of what are for us - and no doubt were for most Babylonians as well- senseless combinations of syllables. It has been observed, however, that at least some of them were derived from other languages and subsequently became incomprehensible through the deterioration of texts.

Scientific Literature

The works which can claim to be "scientific," in both the widest sense of the word and their structure, have been treated above in chapter XI and in those parts of chapter XII which have to do with the teachings about the gods and the syncretistic doctrine of identification. Established supplements for school are found in the series, House of Tablets, (Eduba). One finds in this series, for instance, tables of special dialects and technical languages and types of information which are important to us. The writers of scientific works were rarely concerned with a polished literary form, since they were largely bound by a rigid schema.

10

Ancient English Literature

Ancient English literature encompasses literature written in Old English (also called Anglo-Saxon), during the 600-year Anglo-Saxon period of England, from the mid-5th century to the Norman Conquest of 1066. These works include genres such as epic poetry, hagiography, sermons, Bible translations, legal works, chronicles, riddles, and others. In all there are about 400 surviving manuscripts from the period, a significant corpus of both popular interest and specialist research.

Among the most important works of this period is the poem *Beowulf*, which has achieved national epic status in Britain. The *Anglo-Saxon Chronicle* otherwise proves significant to study of the era, preserving a chronology of early English history, while the poem *Cædmon's Hymn* from the 7th century survives as the oldest extant work of literature in English.

Anglo-Saxon literature has gone through different periods of research—in the 19th and early 20th centuries the focus was on the Germanic roots of English, later the literary merits were emphasized, and today the focus is upon paleography and the physical manuscripts themselves more generally: scholars debate such issues as dating, place of origin, authorship, and the connections between Anglo-Saxon culture and the rest of Europe in the Middle Ages.

large number of manuscripts remain from the 600-year Anglo-Saxon period, with most written during the last 300 years (9th–11th century), in both Latin and the vernacular. Old English literature is among the oldest vernacular languages to be written down. Old English began, in written form, as a practical necessity in the aftermath of the Danish invasions—church officials were concerned that because of the drop in Latin literacy no one could read their work. Likewise King Alfred the Great (849–899), wanting to restore English culture, lamented the poor state of Latin education:

> *"So general was [educational] decay in England that there were very few on this side of the Humber who could...translate a letter from Latin into English; and I believe there were not many beyond the Humber"*
>
> (Pastoral Care, introduction).

King Alfred proposed that students be educated in Old English, and those who excelled would go on to learn Latin. In this way many of the texts that have survived are typical teaching and student-oriented texts.

Extant Manuscripts

In total there are about 400 surviving manuscripts containing Old English text, 189 of them considered major. These manuscripts have been highly prized by collectors since the 16th century, both for their historic value and for their aesthetic beauty of uniformly spaced letters and decorative elements.

There are four major manuscripts:

- The *Junius manuscript,* also known as the *Caedmon manuscript,* which is an illustrated poetic anthology.
- The *Exeter Book,* also an anthology, located in the Exeter Cathedral since it was donated there in the 11th century.
- The *Vercelli Book,* a mix of poetry and prose; how it came to be in Vercelli, Italy, no one knows, and is a matter of debate.
- The *Nowell Codex,* also a mixture of poetry and prose. This is the manuscript that contains Beowulf.

Research in the 20th century has focused on dating the manuscripts (19th-century scholars tended to date them older than modern scholarship has found); locating where the manuscripts were created—there were seven major scriptoria from which they originate: Winchester, Exeter, Worcester, Abingdon, Durham, and two Canterbury houses Christ Church and St. Augustine; and identifying the regional dialects used: Northumbrian, Mercian, Kentish, West Saxon (the last being the main dialect).

Not all of the texts can be fairly called literature; some are merely lists of names or aborted pen trials. However those that can present a sizable body of work, listed here in descending order of quantity: sermons and saints' lives (the most numerous), biblical translations; translated Latin works of the early Church Fathers; Anglo-Saxon chronicles and narrative history works; laws, wills and other legal works; practical works on grammar, medicine, geography; lastly, but not least important, poetry.

Nearly all Anglo-Saxon authors are anonymous, with some exceptions.

Old English Poetry

Old English poetry is of two types, the heroic Germanic pre-Christian and the Christian. It has survived for the most part in the four major manuscripts.

The Anglo-Saxons left behind no poetic rules or explicit system; everything we know about the poetry of the period is based on modern analysis. The first widely accepted theory was constructed by Eduard Sievers (1885). He distinguished five distinct alliterative patterns. The theory of John C. Pope (1942), which uses musical notation to track the verse patterns, has been accepted in some quarters;to be hotly debated.

The most popular and well-known understanding of Old English poetry continues to be Sievers' alliterative verse. The system is based upon accent, alliteration, the quantity of vowels, and patterns of syllabic accentuation. It consists of five permutations on a base verse scheme; any one of the five types can be used in any verse. The system was inherited from and exists in one form or another in all of the older Germanic languages. Two poetic figures commonly found in Old English poetry are the kenning, an often formulaic phrase that describes one thing in terms of another (e.g. in Beowulf, the sea is called the *whale's road*) and litotes, a dramatic understatement employed by the author for ironic effect.

Roughly, Old English verse lines are divided in half by a pause; this pause is termed a "caesura." Each half-line has two stressed syllables. The first stressed syllable of the second half-line should alliterate with one or both of the stressed syllables of the first half-line (meaning, of course, that the stressed syllables in the first half-line could alliterate with each other). The second stressed syllable of the second half-line should not alliterate with either of the stressed syllables of the first half.

Poetry represents the smallest amount of the surviving Old English text, but Anglo-Saxon culture had a rich tradition of oral storytelling, of which little has survived in written form.

The Poets

Most Old English poets are anonymous; twelve are known by name from Medieval sources, but only four of those are known by their vernacular works to us today with any certainty: Caedmon, Bede, Alfred, and Cynewulf. Of these, only Caedmon, Bede, and Alfred have known biographies.

Caedmon is the best-known and considered the father of Old English poetry. He lived at the abbey of Whitby in Northumbria in the 7th century. Only a single nine line poem remains, called *Hymn*, which is also the oldest surviving text in English:

> Now let us praise the Guardian of the Kingdom of Heaven the might of the Creator and the thought of his mind, the work of the glorious Father, how He, the eternal Lord established the beginning of every wonder. For the sons of men, He, the Holy Creator first made heaven as a roof, then the Keeper of mankind, the eternal Lord God Almighty afterwards made the middle world the earth, for men.
>
> (Caedmon, *Hymn*, St Petersburg Bede)

Aldhelm, bishop of Sherborne, is known through William of Malmesbury who said he performed secular songs while accompanied by a harp. Much of his Latin prose has survived, but none of his Old English remains.

Cynewulf has proven to be a difficult figure to identify, but recent research suggests he was from the early part of the 9th century to which a number of poems are attributed including *The Fates of the Apostles* and *Elene* (both found in the Vercelli Book), and *Christ II* and *Juliana* (both found in the Exeter Book).

Heroic Poems

The Old English poetry which has received the most attention deals with the Germanic heroic past. The longest (3,182 lines), and most important, is *Beowulf,* which appears in the damaged Nowell Codex. The poem tells the story of the legendary Geatish hero Beowulf who is the title character. The story is set in Scandinavia, in Sweden and Denmark, and the tale likewise probably is of Scandinavian origin. The story is biographical and sets the tone for much of the rest of Old English poetry. It has achieved national epic status, on the same level as the Iliad, and is of interest to historians, anthropologists, literary critics, and students the world over.

Beyond *Beowulf,* other heroic poems exist. Two heroic poems have survived in fragments: *The Fight at Finnsburh,* a retelling of one of the battle scenes in *Beowulf* (although this relation to *Beowulf* is much debated), and *Waldere,* a version of the events of the life of Walter of Aquitaine. Two other poems mention heroic figures: *Widsith* is believed to be very old in parts, dating back to events in the 4th century concerning Eormanric and the Goths, and contains a catalogue of names and places associated with valiant deeds. *Deor* is a lyric, in the style of *Consolation of Philosophy,* applying examples of famous heroes, including Weland and Eormanric, to the narrator's own case.

The *Anglo-Saxon Chronicle* contains various heroic poems inserted throughout. The earliest from 937 is called *The Battle of Brunanburh,* which celebrates the victory of King Athelstan over the Scots and Norse. There are five shorter poems: capture of the Five Boroughs; coronation of King Edgar; death of King Edgar; death of Prince Alfred; and death of King Edward the Confessor.

The 325 line poem *The Battle of Maldon* celebrates Earl Byrhtnoth and his men who fell in battle against the Vikings in 991. It is considered one of the finest, but both the beginning and end are missing and the only manuscript was destroyed in a fire in 1731. A well-known speech is near the end of the poem:

> Thought shall be the harder, the heart the keener, courage the greater, as our strength lessens. Here lies our leader all cut down, the valiant man in the dust; always may he mourn who now thinks to turn away from this warplay. I am old, I will not go away, but I plan to lie down by the side of my lord, by the man so dearly loved.
>
> (*Battle of Maldon*)

Old English heroic poetry was handed down orally from generation to generation. As Christianity began to appear, retellers often recast the tales of Christianity into the older heroic stories.

Elegiac Poetry

Related to the heroic tales are a number of short poems from the Exeter Book which have come to be described as "elegies" or "wisdom poetry". They are lyrical and Boethian in their description of the up and down fortunes of life. Gloomy in mood is *The Ruin,* which tells of the decay of a once glorious city of Roman Britain (cities in Britain fell into decline after the Romans departed in the early 5th c., as the early English continued to live their rural life), and *The Wanderer,* in which an older man talks about an attack that happened in his youth, where his close friends and kin were all killed; memories of the slaughter have remained with him all his life. He questions the wisdom of the impetuous decision to engage a possibly superior fighting force: the wise man engages in warfare to *preserve* civil society, and must not rush into battle but seek out allies when the odds may be against him. This poet finds little glory in bravery for bravery's sake. *The Seafarer* is the story of a somber exile from home on the sea, from which the only hope of redemption is the joy of heaven.

Other wisdom poems include *Wulf and Eadwacer, The Wife's Lament,* and *The Husband's Message.* King Alfred the Great wrote a wisdom poem over the course of his reign based loosely on the neoplatonic philosophy of Boethius called the *Lays of Boethius.*

Classical and Latin Poetry

Several Old English poems are adaptations of late classical philosophical texts. The longest is a 10th century translation of Boethius' *Consolation of Philosophy* contained in the Cotton manuscript. Another is *The Phoenix* in the Exeter Book, an allegorization of the *De ave phoenice* by Lactantius. Other short poems derive from the Latin bestiary tradition. Some examples include *The Panther, The Whale* and *The Partridge.*

Christian Poetry

Saints' Lives

The Vercelli Book and Exeter Book contain four long

narrative poems of saints' lives, or hagiography. In Vercelli are *Andreas* and *Elene* and in Exeter are *Guthlac* and *Juliana*.

Andreas is 1,722 lines long and is the closest of the surviving Old English poems to *Beowulf* in style and tone. It is the story of Saint Andrew and his journey to rescue Saint Matthew from the Mermedonians. *Elene* is the story of Saint Helena (mother of Constantine) and her discovery of the True Cross. The cult of the True Cross was popular in Anglo-Saxon England and this poem was instrumental. *Guthlac* is actually two poems about English Saint Guthlac (7th century). *Juliana* is the story of the virgin martyr Juliana of Nicomedia.

Biblical Paraphrases

The Junius manuscript contains three paraphrases of Old Testament texts. These were re-wordings of Biblical passages in Old English, not exact translations, but paraphrasing, sometimes into beautiful poetry in its own right. The first and longest is of *Genesis*, the second is of *Exodus* and the third is *Daniel*. The fourth and last poem, *Christ and Satan*, which is contained in the second part of the Junius manuscript, does not paraphrase any particular biblical book, but retells a number of episodes from both the Old and New Testament.

The Nowell Codex contains a Biblical poetic paraphrase, which appears right after *Beowulf*, called *Judith*, a retelling of the story of Judith. This is not to be confused with Ælfric's homily *Judith*, which retells the same Biblical story in alliterative prose.

Old English translations of Psalms 51-150 have been preserved, following a prose version of the first 50 Psalms. It is believed there was once a complete psalter based on evidence, but only the first 150 have survived. There are a number of verse translations of the Gloria in Excelsis, the Lord's Prayer, and the Apostles' Creed, as well as a number of hymns and proverbs.

Christian Poems

In addition to Biblical paraphrases are a number of original religious poems, mostly lyrical (non-narrative). The Exeter Book contains a series of poems entitled *Christ*, sectioned into *Christ I*, *Christ II* and *Christ III*. Considered one of the most beautiful of all Old English poems is *Dream of the Rood*, contained in the Vercelli Book. It is a dream vision of Christ on the cross, with the cross personified, speaking thus:

> "I endured much hardship up on that hill. I saw the God of hosts stretched out cruelly. Darkness had covered with clouds the body of the Lord, the bright radiance. A shadow went forth, dark under the heavens. All creation wept, mourned the death of the king. Christ was on the cross."
>
> (*Dream of the Rood*)

The dreamer resolves to trust in the cross, and the dream ends with a vision of heaven. There are a number of religious debate poems. The longest is *Christ and Satan* in the Junius manuscript, it deals with the conflict between Christ and Satan during the forty days in the desert. Another debate poem is *Solomon and Saturn*, surviving in a number of textual fragments, Saturn is portrayed as a magician debating with the wise king Solomon.

Other Poems

Other poetic forms exist in Old English including riddles, short verses, gnomes, and mnemonic poems for remembering long lists of names.The Exeter Book has a collection of ninety-five riddles. Some of them play on obscene interpretations of the object described. The answers are not supplied, a number of them to this day remain a puzzle.

There are short verses found in the margins of manuscripts which offer practical advice There are remedies against the loss of cattle, how to deal with a delayed birth, swarms of bees, etc.. the longest is called *Nine Herbs Charm* and is probably of pagan origin.There are a group of mnemonic poems designed to help memorise lists and sequences of names and to keep objects in order. These poems are named *Menologium, The Fates of the Apostles, The Rune Poem, The Seasons for Fasting,* and the *Instructions for Christians.*

Features of Anglo-Saxon Poetry

Simile and Metaphor

Anglo-Saxon poetry is marked by the comparative rarity of similes. This is a particular feature of Anglo-Saxon verse style, and is a consequence of both its structure and the rapidity with which images are deployed, to be unable to effectively support the expanded simile. As an example of this, the epic Beowulf contains at best five similes, and these are of the short variety. This can be contrasted sharply with the strong and extensive dependence that Anglo-Saxon poetry has upon metaphor, particularly that afforded by the use of kennings. The most prominent example of this in The Wanderer is the reference to battle as a "storm of spears". This reference to battle gives us an opportunity to see how Anglo-Saxons viewed battle: as unpredictable, chaotic, violent, and perhaps even a function of nature. It is with these stylistic and thematic elements in mind, that one should first approach Anglo-Saxon poetry.

Alliteration

Old English poetry traditionally alliterates. Meaning that a sound (usually the initial consonant sound) is repeated throughout a line. For instance in Beowulf the first line *Hwaet! We Gar-Dena || in gear-dagum* "Lo! We... of the Spear Danes in days of yore", the stressed words 'Gar-Dena' and 'gear-dagum' alliterate on the consonant "G".

Caesura

Old English poetry is also commonly marked by the German caesura or pause. In addition to setting pace for the line the caesura also grouped each line into two couplets.

Old English Poetry and Oral tradition

The hypotheses of Milman Parry and Albert Lord on the Homeric Question came to be applied (by Parry and Lord, but also by Francis Magoun) to verse written in Old English. That is, the theory proposes that certain features of at least some of the poetry may be explained by positing Oral-Formulaic Composition. While Anglo-Saxon (Old English) epic poetry may bear some resemblance to Ancient Greek epics such as the *Iliad* and *Odyssey,* the question of if and how Anglo-Saxon poetry was passed down through an oral tradition remains a subject of debate, and the question for any particular poem unlikely to be answered with perfect certainty.

Parry and Lord had already demonstrated the density of metrical formulas in Ancient Greek, and observed that the same phenomenon was apparent in the Old English alliterative line:

> *Hrothgar mathelode helm Scildinga* ("Hrothgar spoke, protector of the Scildings")
>
> *Beowulf mathelode bearn Ecgtheowes* ("Beowulf spoke, son of Ecgtheow")

In addition to verbal formulas, many themes have been shown to appear among the various works of Anglo-Saxon literature. The theory proposes to explain this fact by suggesting that the poetry was composed of formulae and themes from a stock common to the poetic profession, as well as literary passages composed by individual artists in a more modern sense. Larry Benson introduced the concept of "written-formulaic" to describe the status of some Anglo-Saxon poetry which, while demonstrably written, contains evidence of oral influences, including heavy reliance on formulas and themes Frequent oral-formulaic themes in Old English poetry include "Beasts of Battle" and the "Cliff of Death". The former, for example, is characterized by the mention of ravens, eagles, and wolves preceding particularly violent depictions of battle. Among the most thoroughly documented themes is "The Hero on the Beach." D.K. Crowne first proposed this theme, defined by four characteristics:

> A Hero on the Beach.
> Accompanying "Retainers."
> A Flashing Light.
> The Completion or Initiation of a Journey.

One example Crowne cites in his article is that which concludes Beowulf's fight with the monsters during his swimming match with Breca:

> Those sinful creatures had no fill of rejoicing that they consumed me, assembled at feast at the sea bottom; rather, in the morning, wounded by blades they lay up on the shore, put to sleep by swords, so that never after did they hinder sailors in their course on the sea. The light came from the east, the bright beacon of God.
>
> Næs hie ðære fylle gefean hæfdon,
> manfordædlan, þæt hie me þegon,
> symbel ymbsæton sægrunde neah;
> ac on mergenne mecum wunde
> be yðlafe uppe lægon,
> sweordum aswefede, þæt syðþan na
> ymb brontne ford brimliðende
> lade ne letton. Leoht eastan com,
> beorht beacen godes;
>
> Beowulf, lines 562-70a

Crowne drew on examples of the theme's appearance in twelve Anglo-Saxon texts, including one occurrence in Beowulf. It was also observed in other works of Germanic origin, Middle English poetry, and even an Icelandic prose saga. John Richardson held that the schema was so general as to apply to virtually any character at some point in the narrative, and thought it an instance of the "threshhold" feature of Joseph Campbell's Hero's Journey monomyth. J.A. Dane, in an article characterized as "polemics without rigor" claimed that the appearance of the theme in Ancient Greek poetry, a tradition without known connection to the Germanic, invalidated the notion of "an autonomous theme in the baggage of an oral poet."

Old English Prose

The amount of surviving Old English prose is much greater than the amount of poetry. Of the surviving prose, sermons and Latin translations of religious works are the majority. Old English prose first appears in the 9th century, and continues to be recorded through the 12th century as the last generation of scribes, trained as boys in the standardized West Saxon before the Conquest, died as old men.

Christian Prose

The most widely known author of Old English was King Alfred, who translated many books from Latin into Old English. These translations include: Gregory the Great's *The Pastoral Care,* a manual for priests on how to conduct their duties; *The Consolation of Philosophy* by Boethius; and *The Soliloquies* of Saint Augustine. Alfred was also responsible for a translation of the fifty Psalms into Old English. Other important Old English translations completed by associates of Alfred include: *The History of the World* by Orosius, a companion piece for Augustine of Hippo's *The City of God;* the Dialogues of Gregory the Great; and the *Ecclesiastical History of the English People* by Bede.

Ælfric of Eynsham, wrote in the late 10th and early 11th century. He was the greatest and most prolific writer of Anglo-Saxon sermons, which were copied and adapted for use well into the 13th century. He also wrote a number of saints lives, an Old English work on time-reckoning, pastoral letters, translations of the first six books of the Bible, glosses and translations of other parts of the Bible including Proverbs, Wisdom and Ecclesiasticus.

In the same category as Aelfric, and a contemporary, was Wulfstan II, archbishop of York. His sermons were highly stylistic. His best known work is *Sermo Lupi ad Anglos* in which he blames the sins of the British for the Viking invasions. He wrote a number of clerical legal texts *Institutes of Polity* and *Canons of Edgar.*

One of the earliest Old English texts in prose is the *Martyrology,* information about saints and martyrs according to their anniversaries and feasts in the church calendar. It has survived in six fragments. It is believed to date from the 9th century by an anonymous Mercian author. The oldest collection of church sermons are the *Blickling homilies* in the Vercelli Book and dates from the 10th century.

There are a number of saint's lives prose works. Beyond those written by Ælfric are the prose life of Saint Guthlac (Vercelli Book), the life of Saint Margaret and the life of Saint Chad. There are four lives in the Julius manuscript: Seven Sleepers of Ephesus, Saint Mary of Egypt, Saint Eustace and Saint Euphrosyne.

There are many Old English translations of many parts of the Bible. Ælfric made a number of Old Testament translations, which were later used and supplemented by another author for a lavishly illustrated copy of the Old English Hexateuch. There is a translation of the Gospels. The most popular was the *Gospel of Nicodemus,* others included "..the *Gospel of Pseudo-Matthew, Vindicta salvatoris, Vision of Saint Paul* and the *Apocalypse of Thomas*".

One of the largest bodies of Old English text is found in the legal texts collected and saved by the religious houses. These include many kinds of texts: records of donations by nobles; wills; documents of emancipation; lists of books and relics; court cases; guild rules. All of these texts provide valuable insights into the social history of Anglo-Saxon times, but are also of literary value.

Secular Prose

The *Anglo-Saxon Chronicle* was probably started in the time of King Alfred and continued for over 300 years as a historical record of Anglo-Saxon history. A single example of a Classical romance has survived, it is a fragment of the story of *Apollonius of Tyre,* from the 11th century. A monk who was writing in Old English at the same time as Aelfric and Wulfstan was Byrhtferth of Ramsey, whose books *Handboc* and *Manual* were studies of mathematics and rhetoric.

Aelfric wrote two neo-scientific works, *Hexameron* and *Interrogationes Sigewulfi,* dealing with the stories of Creation. He also wrote a grammar and glossary in Old English called *Latin,* later used by students interested in learning Old French because it had been glossed in Old French.

There are many surviving rules and calculations for finding feast days, and tables on calculating the tides and the season of the moon.

In the Nowell Codex is the text of *The Wonders of the East* which includes a remarkable map of the world, and other illustrations. Also contained in Nowell is *Alexander's Letter to Aristotle.* Because this is the same manuscript that contains *Beowulf,* some scholars speculate it may have been a collection of materials on exotic places and creatures.

There are a number of interesting medical works. There is a translation of Apuleius's *Herbarium* with striking illustrations, found together with *Medicina de Quadrupedibus.* A second collection of texts is *Bald's Leechbook,* a 10th century book containing herbal and even some surgical cures. A third collection, known as the *Lacnunga,* includes many charms and incantations.

Anglo-Saxon legal texts are a large and important part of the overall corpus. By the 12th century they had been arranged into two large collections. They include laws of the kings, beginning with those of Aethelbert of Kent, and texts dealing with specific cases and places in the country. An interesting example is *Gerefa* which outlines the duties of a reeve on a large manor estate. There is also a large volume of legal documents related to religious houses.

Historiography

Old English literature did not disappear in 1066 with the Norman Conquest. Many sermons and works continued to be read and used in part or whole up through the 14th century, and were further catalogued and organised. During the Reformation, when monastic libraries were dispersed, the manuscripts were collected by antiquarians and scholars. These included Laurence Nowell, Matthew Parker, Robert Bruce Cotton and Humfrey Wanley. In the 17th century begun a tradition of Old English literature dictionaries and references. The first was William Somner's *Dictionarium Saxonico-Latino-Anglicum* (1659). Lexicographer Joseph Bosworth began a dictionary in the 19th century which was completed by Thomas Northcote Toller in 1898 called *An Anglo-Saxon Dictionary,* which was updated by Alistair Campbell in 1972.

Because Old English was one of the first vernacular languages to be written down, nineteenth century scholars searching for the roots of European "national culture" took special interest in studying Anglo-Saxon literature, and Old English became a regular part of university curriculum. Since WWII there has been increasing interest in the manuscripts themselves—Neil Ker, a paleographer, published the groundbreaking *Catalogue of Manuscripts Containing Anglo-Saxon* in 1957, and by 1980 nearly all Anglo-Saxon manuscript texts were in print. J.R.R. Tolkien is credited with creating a movement to look at Old English as a subject of literary theory in his seminal lecture *Beowulf: The Monsters and the Critics.*

Old English literature has had an influence on modern literature. Some of the best-known translations include William Morris' translation of *Beowulf* and Ezra Pound's translation of *The Seafarer*. The influence of the poetry can be seen in modern poets T. S. Eliot, Ezra Pound and W. H. Auden. Tolkien adapted the subject matter and terminology of heroic poetry for works like *The Hobbit* and *The Lord of the Rings.*

11

Ancient Roman Literature

Ancient Rome was a civilization that grew out of a small agricultural community founded on the Italian Peninsula as early as the 10th century BC. Located along the Mediterranean Sea, it became one of the largest empires in the ancient world.

In its centuries of existence, Roman civilization shifted from a monarchy to an oligarchic republic to an increasingly autocratic empire. It came to dominate South-Western Europe, South-Eastern Europe/Balkans and the Mediterranean region through conquest and assimilation.

Plagued by internal instability and attacked by various migrating peoples, the western part of the empire, including Italy, Hispania, Gaul, Britannia and Africa broke up into independent kingdoms in the 5th century AD.

The Eastern Roman Empire, which was governed from Constantinople, comprising Greece, the Balkans, Asia Minor, Syria and Egypt, survived this crisis. Despite the later loss of Syria and Egypt to the Arab Islamic Empire, the Eastern Roman Empire would live on for another millennium, until its last remains were finally annexed by the emerging Turkish Ottoman

Empire. This eastern, Christian, medieval stage of the Empire is usually referred to as the Byzantine Empire by historians.

Life in ancient Rome revolved around the city of Rome, located on seven hills. The city had a vast number of monumental structures like the Colosseum, the Forum of Trajan and the Pantheon. It had fountains with fresh drinking-water supplied by hundreds of miles of aqueducts, theatres, gymnasiums, bath complexes complete with libraries and shops, marketplaces, and functional sewers. Throughout the territory under the control of ancient Rome, residential architecture ranged from very modest houses to country villas. In the capital city of Rome, there were imperial residences on the elegant Palatine Hill, from which the word *palace* is derived. The low Plebian and middle Equestrian classes lived in the city center, packed into apartments, or Insulae which were almost like modern ghettos. These areas, often built by upper class landlords for the rental incomes collected, were often centred upon collegia or taberna. These people, provided by a free supply of grain, and entertained by gladatorial games, were enrolled as clients of patrons amongst the upper class Patricians, whose assistance they sought and whose interests they upheld.

Language

The native language of the Romans was Latin, an Italic language the grammar of which relies little on word order, conveying meaning through a system of affixes attached to word stems. Its alphabet was based on the Etruscan alphabet, which was in turn based on the Greek alphabet. Although surviving Latin literature consists almost entirely of Classical Latin, an artificial and highly stylized and polished literary language from the 1st century BC, the actual spoken language of the Roman Empire was Vulgar Latin, which significantly differed from Classical Latin in grammar and vocabulary, and eventually in pronunciation.

While Latin remained the main written language of the Roman Empire, Greek came to be the language spoken by the well-educated elite, as most of the literature studied by Romans was written in Greek. In the eastern half of the Roman Empire, which later became the Byzantine Empire, Latin was never able to replace Greek, and after the death of Justinian, Greek became the official language of the Byzantine government. The expansion of the Roman Empire spread Latin throughout Europe, and over time Vulgar Latin evolved and dialectized in different locations, gradually shifting into a number of distinct Romance languages.

Art and Music

Roman painting styles show Greek influences, and surviving examples are primarily frescoes used to adorn the walls and ceilings of country villas, though Roman literature includes mentions of paintings on wood, ivory, and other materials. Several examples of Roman painting have been found at Pompeii, and from these art historians divide the history of Roman painting into four periods. The first style of Roman painting was practiced from the early 2nd century BC to the early- or mid-1st century BC. It was mainly composed of imitations of marble and masonry, though sometimes including depictions of mythological characters. The second style of Roman painting began during the early 1st century BC, and attempted to depict realistically three-dimensional architectural features and landscapes. The third style occurred during the reign of Augustus (27 BC-14 AD), and rejected the realism of the second style in favor of simple ornamentation. A small architectural scene, landscape, or abstract design was placed in the center with a monochrome background. The fourth style, which began in the 1st century AD, depicted scenes from mythology, while retaining architectural details and abstract patterns.

Portrait sculpture during the period utilized youthful and classical proportions, evolving later into a mixture of realism and idealism. During the Antonine and Severan periods, more ornate hair and bearding became prevalent, created with deeper cutting and drilling. Advancements were also made in relief sculptures, usually depicting Roman victories.

Latin literature was from its very inception influenced heavily by Greek authors. Some of the earliest extant works are of historical epics telling the early military history of Rome. As the Republic expanded, authors began to produce poetry, comedy, history, and tragedy.

Roman music was largely based on Greek music, and played an important part in many aspects of Roman life. In the Roman military, musical instruments such as the *tuba* (a long trumpet) or the *cornu* (similar to a French horn) were used to give various commands, while the *bucina* (possibly a trumpet or horn) and the *lituus* (probably an elongated J-shaped instrument), were used in ceremonial capacities. Music was used in the amphitheaters between fights and in the *odea,* and in these settings is known to have featured the *cornu* and the *hydraulis* (a type of water organ). The majority of religious rituals featured musical performances, with *tibiae* (double pipes) at sacrifices, cymbals and Tambourines at orgiastic cults, and rattles and hymns across the spectrum. Some music historians believe that music was used at almost all public ceremonies. Music historians are not certain if Roman musicians made a significant contribution to the theory or practice of music. The graffiti, brothels, paintings, and sculptures found in Pompeii and Herculaneum suggest that the Romans had a very sex-saturated culture.

Scholarly Studies

Interest in studying ancient Rome arose during the Age of Enlightenment in France. Charles Montesquieu wrote a work *Reflections on the Causes of the Grandeur and Declension of the Romans*. The first major work was *The History of the Decline and Fall of the Roman Empire* by Edward Gibbon, which encompassed the period from the end of 2nd century to the fall of the Byzantine Empire in 1453. Like Montesquieu, Gibbon paid high tribute to the virtue of Roman citizens. Barthold Georg Niebuhr was a founder of the examination of ancient Roman history and wrote *The Roman History*, tracing the period until the First Punic war. Niebuhr made an attempt to determine the way the Roman tradition evolved.

According to him, Romans, like other people, had an historical ethos which was preserved mainly in the noble families. During the Napoleonic period a work titled *The History of Romans* by Victor Duruy appeared. It highlighted the Caesarean period popular at the time. *History of Rome, Roman constitutional law* and *Corpus Inscriptionum Latinarum*, all by Theodor

Mommsen, became very important milestones. Later the work *Greatness and Decline of Rome* by Guglielmo Ferrero was published.

Poetry

Ancient thinkers wrote verse about what they observed in nature. They are generally referred to as Presocratic Philosophers. Many aspects of culture were still without distinct form then, during the Archaic Age of Ancient Greece. The origin of drama is mired in legend, but to the best of our information, drama seems to have arisen as part of religious worship and the word tragedy appears to come from the word goat song. The first element in Greek tragedy was the chorus, which danced and sang poetry created by the dramatist at the religious festivals. Actors came later, with the great tragedians. The man credited with creating the epics we know of as the Iliad and Odyssey, (whom we refer to as Homer) was a rhapsode, a person who accompanied his improvised performances with a musical instrument.

Epic poetry came to be distinguished by its distinct (epic) meter. Lyric poetry, developed according to legend, by Terpander, was poetry accompanied by a lyre. Epigrams were composed for funerals. It was an epigrammatist, Mimnermus of Smyrna, who is credited with developing the elegiac meter that was used for love poetry (elegies). The epic is a broadly defined genre of poetry, and one of the major forms of narrative literature. It retells in a continuous narrative the life and works of a heroic or mythological person or group of persons. In the West, the Iliad, Odyssey, and the Nibelungenlied; and in the East, the Mahabharata, Ramayana, and Shahnama are often cited as examples of the epic genre.

Oral Epics

The first epics are associated strongly with preliterate societies and oral poetic traditions. In these traditions, poetry is transmitted to the audience and from performer to performer by purely oral means. World folk epics are those epics which are not just literary masterpieces but also an integral part of the world view of a people. They were originally oral literatures, which were later written down by either single author or several writers.

Studies of living oral epic traditions in the Balkans by Milman Parry and Albert Lord demonstrated the paratactic model used for composing these poems. What they demonstrated was that oral epics tend to be constructed in short episodes, each of equal status, interest and importance. This facilitates memorisation, as the poet is recalling each episode and using them to recreate the entire epic as they perform it. Parry and Lord also showed that the most likely source for written texts of the epics of Homer was dictation from an oral performance.

Epics in Literate Societies

Literate societies have often copied the epic format, and the earliest known European example is Virgil's Aeneid, which follows both the style and subject matter of Homer. Other obvious examples are Tulsidas' Sri Ramacharit Manas, following the style and subject matter of Valmiki's Ramayana,. and the Persian epic Shahnama by Ferdowsi.

Epigrams

An epigram is a short poem with a clever twist at the end or a concise and witty statement. They are among the best examples of the power of poetry to compress insight and wit.

Roman epigrams owe much to their Greek predecessors and contemporaries. Roman epigrams, however, were more often satirical than Greek ones, and at times used obscene language for effect. Latin epigrams could be composed as inscriptions or graffiti, such as this one from Pompeii, which exists in several versions and seems from its inexact meter to have been composed by a less educated person. Its content, of course, makes it clear how popular such poems were:

> Admiror, O paries, te non cecidisse ruinis
> qui tot scriptorum taedia sustineas.
> I'm astonished, wall, that you haven't collapsed into ruins,
> since you're holding up the weary verse of so many poets.

However, in the literary world, epigrams were most often gifts to patrons or entertaining verse to be published, not inscriptions. Many Roman writers seem to have composed epigrams, including Domitius Marsus, whose collection 'Cicuta' (now lost) was named after the poisonous hemlock tree for its biting wit, and Lucan, more famous for his epic Pharsalia. Authors whose epigrams survive include Catullus, who wrote both invectives and love epigrams – his poem 85 is one of the latter.

> Odi et amo. Quare id faciam fortasse requiris.
> Nescio, sed fieri sentio, et excrucior.
> I hate and I love. Perhaps you're asking how I do this?
> I don't know, but I feel it happening, and it's torture.

The master of the Latin epigram, however, is Martial. His technique relies heavily on the satirical poem with a joke in the last line, thus drawing him closer to the modern idea of epigram as a genre. Here he defines his genre against a (probably fictional) critic:

> Disce quod ignoras: Marsi doctique Pedonis
> saepe duplex unum pagina tractat opus.
> Non sunt longa quibus nihil est quod demere possis,
> sed tu, Cosconi, disticha longa facis.

Learn what you don't know: one work of (Domitius) Marsus or learned Pedo often stretches out over a doublesided page. A work isn't long if you can't take anything out of it, but you, Cosconius, write even a couplet too long.

Prose

History, as developed by Herodotus, was a (prose) story about whatever Herodotus set his inquiring mind to. In ancient Rome, satire was a recognized and somewhat defined literary verse genre. It was the only genre the Romans claimed as their own invention. Some early novels fell within the genre of (Menippean) satire.

During the reign of Augustus many commentators proclaimed the arrival of a new Golden Age as Romans returned to traditional values. These values included religion, family, and an appreciation of the Italian countryside and its agrarian roots. Writers and artists from all parts of Italy came to Rome, where generous patronage helped to encourage extraordinary achievements. The Augustan peace and the prosperity that accompanied it brought about the revival of patriotic literature that hailed the triumphs of Rome, its people, and its new leader.

The Golden Age of Roman Drama dates to B.C. 240 when Livius [Livy] Andronicus adapted a Greek comedy and tragedy for performance on a Roman stage. This was not only the beginning of Greek drama in Rome, but of formal Latin literature. This coincides with the end of the first Punic War (264-241) which is relevant because with the Punic War, Romans came into contact with the Greeks of Southern Italy and Sicily. Instead of being concerned entirely with mastering their physical world, the Romans were now becoming a world power. In addition to adapting Greek drama, Livius Andronicus also translated the Odyssey into Latin.

Livy

Livy, who was born in the city of Padua in 59 BC, wrote a history of Rome that spanned the period from mythic times to his own day. An artist more than a scholar, Livy was a marvelous storyteller. His stirring accounts of Rome's early struggle for freedom inspired painters, poets, and political leaders through the centuries, even though only a quarter of his enormous work has survived.

Titus Livius (around 59 BC - 17 AD), known as Livy in English, wrote a monumental history of Rome, Ab Urbe Condita, from its founding (traditionally dated to 753 BC). Livy was a native of Padua on the Po River in northern Italy.

Life and Works

The book's title, Ab Urbe Condita ("From the Founding of the City"), makes Livy's ambition clear, but not his method. He wrote in a mixture of annual chronology and narrative - often having to interrupt a story to announce the elections of new consuls at Rome as this was the way that the Romans kept track of the years. A lack of historical data prior to the sacking of Rome in 386 BC by the Gauls made Livy's task more difficult.

Livy wrote the majority of his works during the reign of Caesar Augustus, in fact, he was hired by Augustus to write the stories and was part of the Augustan Literary Circle. However, he is often identified with an attachment to the Roman Republic and a desire for its restoration. Since the later books discussing the end of the Republic and the rise of Augustus did not survive, this is a moot point.

Certainly Livy questioned some of the values of the new regime but it is likely that his position was more complex than a simple 'republic/empire' preference.

Livy's work was originally composed of 142 books, of which only 35 are extant; these are 1-10, and 21-45 (with major lacunae in 40-45). A fragmentary palimpsest of the 91st book was discovered in the Vatican Library in 1772, containing about a thousand words, and several papyrus fragments of previously unknown material, much smaller, have been found in Egypt since 1900, most recently about forty words from book 11, unearthed in the 1980's.

Some idea of the contents of the remaining books can be gleaned from a thin epitome, the Periochae, and an epitome of books 37-40 and 48-55 uncovered at Oxyrhynchus.

A number of Roman authors used Livy, including Aurelius Victor, Cassiodorus, Eutropius, Festus, Florus, Granius Licinianus and Orosius. Julius Obsequens used Livy, or a source with access to Livy, to compose his De Prodigiis, an account of supernatural events in Rome, from the consulship of Scipio and Laelius

(A.U.C. 453) to that of Paulus Fabius and Quintus Aelius (A.U.C. 742).

A digression in book 9, sections 17-19, of this book, suggests that the Romans would have beaten Alexander the Great if he lived longer and turned west to attack the Romans, making this the oldest known alternative history.

Gnaeus Naevius

Naevius was the first native Roman dramatist. He had served in the first Punic War and wrote a Bellum Punicum (Punic War). He was interested in the Trojan cycle. He also wrote plays on Roman themes and is thus the inventor of the fabula praetexta - Roman historical play. He also wrote comedies (fabulae palliatae). Naevius was imprisoned for being outspoken, wrote two plays while confined, apologized, was released, did it again, and went into exile in Utica where he died.

Gnaeus Naevius, was a Latin epic poet and dramatist. There is great uncertainty in regard to his life. From the expression of Gellius characterizing his epitaph as written in a vein of Campanian arrogance it has been inferred that he was born in one of the Latin communities settled in Campania. But the phrase Campanian arrogance seems to have been used proverbially for gasconade; and, as there was a plebeian gens Naevia in Rome, it is quite as probable that he was by birth a Roman citizen. He served either in the Roman army or among the socii in the first Punic War, and thus must have reached manhood before 241.

His career as a dramatic author began with the exhibition of a drama in or about the year 235, and continued for thirty years. Towards the close he incurred the hostility of some of the nobility, especially, it is said, of the Metelli, by the attacks which he made upon them on the stage, and at their instance he was imprisoned. After writing two plays during his imprisonment, in which he is said to have apologized for his former rudeness, he was liberated through the interference of the tribunes of the commons; but he had shortly afterwards to retire from Rome to Utica. It may have been during his exile, when withdrawn from his active career as a dramatist, that he composed or completed his poem on the first Punic war. Probably his latest composition was the epitaph already referred to, written like the epic in saturnalian verse.

As distinguished from Livius Andronicus, Naevius was a native Italian, not a Greek; he was also an original writer, not a mere adapter or translator. If it was due to Livius that the forms of Latin literature were, from the first, moulded on those of Greek literature, it was due to Naevius that much of its spirit and substance was of native growth.

Like Livius, Naevius professed to adapt Greek tragedies and comedies to the Roman stage. Among the titles of his tragedies are Aegisthus, Lycurgus, Andromache or Hector Proficiscens, Equus Trojanus, the last named being performed at the opening of Pompey's theatre. The national cast of his genius and temper was shown by his deviating from his Greek originals, and producing at least two specimens of the fabula praetexta (national drama) one founded on the childhood of Romulus and Remus (Lupus or Alimonium Romuli et Remi), the other called Clastidium, which celebrated the victory of Marcus Claudius Marcellus over the Celts.

But it was as a writer of comedy that he was most famous, most productive and most original. While he is never ranked as a writer of tragedy with Ennius, Pacuvius or Accius, he is placed in the canon of the grammarian Volcacius Sedigitus third (immediately after Caecilius and Plautus) in the rank of Roman comic authors. He is there characterized as ardent and impetuous in character and style.

He is also appealed to, with Plautus and Ennius, as a master of his art in one of the prologues of Terence. His comedy, like that of Plautus, seems to have been rather a free adaptation of his originals than a rude copy of them, as those of Livius probably were, or an artistic copy like those of Terence. The titles of most of them, like those of Plautus, and unlike those of Caecilius and Terence, are Latin, not Greek.

He drew from the writers of the old political comedy of Athens, as well as from the new comedy of manners, and he attempted to make the stage at Rome, as it had been at Athens, an arer, a of political and personal warfare. A strong spirit of partisanship is recognized in more than one of the fragments; and this spirit is thoroughly popular and adverse to the senatorial ascendancy which became more and more confirmed with the progress of the second Punic war.

Besides his attack on the Metelli and other nembers of the aristocracy, the great Scipio is the object of a censorious criticism on account of a youthful escapade attributed to him. Among the few lines still remaining from his lost comedies, we seem to recognize the idiomatic force and rapidity of movement characteristic of the style of Plautus. There is also found that love of alliteration which is a marked feature in all the older Latin poets down even

In one considerable comic fragment attributed to himthe description of a coquettethere is great truth and shrewdness of observation. But we find no trace of the exuberant comic power and geniality of his great contemporary.

He was not only the oldest native dramatist, but the first author of an epic poem (Bellum Punicum) which, by combining the representation of actual contemporary history, with a mythical background, may be said to have created the Roman type of epic poetry. The poem was one continuous work, but was divided into seven books by a grammarian of a later age.

The earlier part of it treated of the mythical adventures of Aeneas in Sicily, Carthage and Italy, and borrowed from the interview of Zeus and Thetis in the first book of the Iliad the idea of the interview of Jupiter and Venus; which Virgil has made one of the cardinal passages in the Aeneid.

The later part treated of the events of the first Punic war in the style of a metrical chronicle. An important influence in Roman literature and belief, which had its origin in Sicily, first appeared in this poem the recognition of the mythical connection of Aeneas and his Trojans with the foundation of Rome. The few, remaining fragments produce the impression of vivid and rapid narrative, to which the flow of the native Saturnian verse, in contradistinction to the weighty and complex structure of the hexameter, was naturally adapted.

The impression we get of the man is that, whether or not he actually enjoyed the full rights of Roman citizenship, he was a vigorous representative of the bold combative spirit of the ancient Roman commons.

He was one of those who made the Latin language into a great organ of literature.

The phrases still quoted from him have nothing of an antiquated sound, while they have a genuinely idiomatic ring. As a dramatist he worked more in the spirit of Plautus than of Ennius, Pacuvius, Accius or Terence; but the great Umbrian humorist is separated from his older contemporary, not only by his breadth of comic power, but by his general attitude of moral and political indifference.

The power of Naevius was the more genuine Italian gift the power of satiric criticism which was employed in making men ridiculous, not, like that of Plautus, in extracting amusement from the humours, follies and eccentricities of life.

Although our means of forming a fair estimate of Naevius are scanty, all that we do know of him leads to the conclusion that he was far from being the least among the makers of Roman literature, and that with the loss of his writings there was lost a vein of national feeling and genius which rarely reappears.

Mime

We don't know when mime first came to Rome, but by 211, the Romans were watching mimic actors. Mimes were normal parts of the Floralia (an annual festival from 173) which was first celebrated in 238. The word mime is from the Greek mimeisthai (to imitate). Romans often called mimic actors planipes (with bare feet). The bare feet let the mimic actors, male and female, move around better than actors wearing tragedy's cothurnus (buskin) or comedy's soccus (slipper).

In ancient Greece and ancient Rome, a mime is a farcical drama characterized by mimicry and ludicrous representations of characters, or the script for such a performance. In 204 Cato brought Ennius to Rome, where he he worked as a teacher and writer. He wrote poems called Saturae and an epic, the Annales. Ennius replaced the dactylic hexameter of Greek epic with the Saturnian Latin meter. He wrote comedies, and fabulae praetextae, and most of all, tragedy.

Plautus was an Umbrian. At Rome he acted as a clown in Atellan farces. His name Maccius may come from this occupation. Plautus may also be a stage name and a variation on the word planipes. Plautus worked in the theater in some capacity and may hace been a stage hand or carpenter. Duckworth provides a rough chronology of his comedies: *Asinaria, Mercator, Miles Gloriosus around 205 B.C., Cistellaria, before 201. Stichus (200 B.C.) Aulularia and Curculio before 191. Pseudolus (191) and then Bacchides, followed by Casina in 185 or 184.*

An Insubrian Gaul, Caecilius Statius was a friend of Ennius and according to Volcacius Sedigitus, was the best of the Roman comic poets. Caecilius stuck close to Greek originals, but was not a literal translator. Horace praised Caecilius for his gravitas. Varro praised him plot construction. Although an argument from silence, Caecilius may have introduced the idea of avoiding contamination—meaning following only one Greek original.

Marcus Pacuvius

Pacuvius was the nephew of Ennius. We know of thirteen of his tragedies. His ancient reputation was "learned." Cicero considered Pacuvius the greates tragic poet of Rome.

Marcus Pacuvius (c. 220-130 BC) was the greatest of the tragic poets of ancient Rome prior to Accius. He was the nephew and pupil of Ennius, by whom Roman tragedy was first raised to a position of influence and dignity. In the interval between the death of Ennius and the advent of Accius, the youngest and most productive of the tragic poets, Pacuvius alone maintained the continuity of the serious drama, and perpetuated the character first imparted to it by Ennius.

Like Ennius he probably belonged to an Oscan stock, and was born at Brundisium, which had become a Roman colony in 244. Hence he never attained to that perfect idiomatic purity of style, which was the special glory of the early writers of comedy, Naevius and Plautus.

Pacuvius obtained distinction also as a painter; and Pliny the Elder mentions a work of his in the temple of Hercules in the Forum Boarium. He was less productive as a poet than either Ennius or Accius; and we hear of only about twelve of his plays, founded on Greek subjects (among them the Antiope, Teucer, Armorum Judicium, Dulorestes, Chryses, Niptra, &c., most of them on subjects connected with the Trojan cycle), and one praetexta (Paulus) written in connexion with the victory of Lucius Aemilius Paulus at the battle of Pydna, as the Clastidium of Naevius and the Ambracia of Ennius were written in commemoration of great military successes.

He continued to write tragedies till the age of eighty, when he exhibited a play in the same year as Accius, who was then thirty years of age. He retired to Tarentum for the last years of his life, and a story is told by Aulus Gellius of his being visited there by

Accius on his way to Asia, who read his Atreus to him.

The story is probably, like that of the visit of the young Terence to the veteran Caecilius, due to the invention of later grammarians; but it is invented in accordance with the traditionary criticism of the distinction between the two poets, the older being characterized rather by cultivated accomplishment (doctus), the younger by vigour and animation.

Pacuvius's epitaph, said to have been composed by himself, is quoted by Aulus Gellius, with a tribute of admiration to its "modesty, simplicity and fine serious spirit": *Adulescens, tam etsi properas, to hoc saxum rogat Ut sese aspicias, deinde quod scriptum 'st legas Hic Bunt poetae Pacuvi Marci sita Ossa. Hoc volebam nescius ne esses. Vale.*

Cicero, who frequently quotes from him with great admiration, appears to rank him first among the Roman tragic poets, as Ennius among the epic, and Caecilius among the comic poets. The fragments of Pacuvius quoted by Cicero in illustration or enforcement of his own ethical teaching appeal, by the fortitude, dignity, and magnanimity of the sentiment expressed in them, to what was noblest in the Roman temperament.

They are inspired also by a fervid and steadfast glow of spirit and reveal a gentleness and humanity of sentiment blended with the severe gravity of the original Roman character. So far too as the Romans were capable of taking interest in speculative questions, the tragic poets contributed to stimulate curiosity on such subjects, and they anticipated Lucretius in using the conclusions of speculative philosophy as well as of common sense to assail some of the prevailing forms of superstition.

Among the passages quoted from Pacuvius are several which indicate a taste both for physical and ethical speculation, and others which expose the pretensions of religious imposture. These poets aided also in developing that capacity which the Roman language subsequently displayed of being an organ of oratory, history and moral disquisition.

The literary language of Rome was in process of formation during the 2nd century B.C., and it was in the latter part of this century that the series of great Roman orators, with whose spirit Roman tragedy has a strong affinity, begins. But the new creative effort in language was accompanied by considerable crudeness of execution, and the novel word-formations and varieties of inflexion introduced by Pacuvius exposed him to the ridicule of the satirist Lucilius, and, long afterwards, to that of his imitator Persius.

But, notwithstanding the attempt to introduce an alien element into the Roman language, which proved incompatible with its natural genius, and his own failure to attain the idiomatic purity of Naevius, Plautus or Terence, the fragments of his dramas are sufficient to prove the service which he rendered to the formation of the literary language of Rome as well as to the culture and character of his contemporaries.

Lucius Accius

Lucius Accius, a Roman tragic poet, the son of a freedman, was born at Pisaurum in Umbria, in 170 BC. The year of his death is unknown, but he must have lived to a great age, since Cicero speaks of having conversed with him on literary matters.

He was a prolific writer and enjoyed a very high reputation. The titles and considerable fragments (about 700 lines) of some fifty plays have been preserved. Most of these were free translations from the Greek, his favorite subjects being the legends of the Trojan war and the house of Pelops. The national history, however, furnished the theme of the Brutus and Decius—the expulsion of the Tarquins and the self-sacrifice of Publius Decius Mus the younger. The fragments are written in vigorous language and show a lively power of description.

Accius wrote other works of a literary character: Didascalicon and Pragmaticon libri, treatises in verse on the history of Greek and Roman poetry, and dramatic art in particular; Parerga and Praxidica (perhaps identical) on agriculture; and an Annales. He also introduced innovations in orthography and grammar. A saying attributed to Accius was oderint dum metuant ("let them hate, as long as they fear"), later a famous motto of Caligula.

12

Ancient African Literature

African literature refers to the literature of and for the African peoples. As George Joseph notes on the first page of his chapter on African literature in Understanding Contemporary Africa, while the European perception of literature generally refers to written letters, the African concept includes oral literature. As George Joseph continues, while European views of literature often stressed a separation of art and content, African awareness is inclusive: "Literature" can also imply an artistic use of words for the sake of art alone. Without denying the important role of aesthetics in Africa, we should keep in mind that, traditionally, Africans do not radically separate art from teaching. Rather than write or sing for beauty in itself, African writers, taking their cue from oral literature, use beauty to help communicate important truths and information to society. Indeed, an object is considered beautiful because of the truths it reveals and the communities it helps to build.

Beginnings of African Literature

The first African literature is circa 2300-2100, when ancient Egyptians begin using burial texts to accompany their dead. These include the first written accounts of creation—the *Memphite Declaration of Deities*. Not only that, but 'papyrus', from which we originate our word for paper, was invented by the Egyptians, and writing flourished. In contrast, Sub-Saharan Africa feature a vibrant and varied oral culture.

To take into account written literary culture without considering literary culture is definitely a mistake, because they two interplay heavily with each other. African oral arts are "art's for life's sake" (Mukere) not European "art's for art's sake", and so may be considered foreign and strange by European readers.

However, they provide useful knowledge, historical knowledge, ethical wisdom, and creative stimuli in a direct fashion. Oral culture takes many forms: proverbs and riddles, epic narratives, oration and personal testimony, praise poetry and songs, chants and rituals, stories, legends and folk tales. This is present in the many proverbs told in *Things Fall Apart*, and the rich cultural emphasis of that book also is typically African.

The earliest written Sub-Saharan Literature (1520) is heavily influenced by Islamic literature. The earliest example of this is the anonymous history of the city-state of Kilwa Kisiwani. The first African history, *History of the Sudan*, is written by Abd al-Rahman al-Sadi in Arabic style. Traveling performers, called griots, kept the oral tradition alive, especially the legends of the Empire of Mali. In 1728 the earliest written Swahili work, *Utendi wa Tambuka* borrows heavily from Muslim tradition. However, there are little to no Islamic presence in *Things Fall Apart*.

Oral Traditions

The storyteller speaks, time collapses, and the members of the audience are in the presence of history. It is a time of masks. Reality, the present, is here, but with explosive emotional images giving it a context. This is the storyteller's art: to mask the past, making it mysterious, seemingly inaccessible. But it is inaccessible only to one's present intellect; it is always available to one's heart and soul, one's emotions. The storyteller combines the audience's present waking state and its past condition of semiconsciousness, and so the audience walks again in history, joining its forebears.

And history, always more than an academic subject, becomes for the audience a collapsing of time. History becomes the audience's memory and a means of reliving of an indeterminate and deeply obscure past. Storytelling is alive, ever in transition, never hardened in time. Stories are not meant to be temporally frozen; they are always responding to contemporary realities, but in a timeless fashion. Storytelling is therefore not a memorized art.

The necessity for this continual transformation of the story has to do with the regular fusing of fantasy and images of the real, contemporary world. Performers take images from the present and wed them to the past, and in that way the past regularly shapes an audience's experience of the present. Storytellers reveal connections between humans—within the world, within a society, within a family—emphasizing an interdependence and the disaster that occurs when obligations to one's fellows are forsaken. The artist makes the linkages, the storyteller forges the bonds, tying past and present, joining humans to their gods, to their leaders, to their families, to those they love, to their deepest fears and hopes, and to the essential core of their societies and beliefs.

Period of Colonization

With the period of Colonization, African oral traditions and written works came under a serious outside threat. Europeans, justifying themselves with the Christian ethics, tried to destroy the "pagan" and "primitive" culture of the Africans, to make them more pliable slaves. However, African Literature survived this concerted attack. In 1789, *The Interesting Narrative of the Life of Olaudah Equiano, or Gustava Vassa* was the first slave narrative to be published. Kidnapped from Nigeria, this Ibo man wrote his autobiography in Great Britain in English, and like Achebe used his narrative as a platform to attack the injustices of slavery and cultural destruction. Back in Africa, Swahili poetry threw off the dominating influence of Islam and reverted back to native Bantu forms. One exemplar of this was *Utendi wa Inkishafi (Soul's Awakening)*, a poem detailing the vanity of earthly life. The Europeans, by bringing journalism and government schools to Africa, helped further the development of literature.

Local newspapers abounded, and often they featured sections of local African poetry and short stories. While originally these fell close to the European form, slowly they broke away and became more and more African in nature. One of these writers was Oliver Schreiner, whose novel *Story of an African Farm* (1883) is considered the first African classic analysis of racial and sexual issues. Other notable writers, such as Samuel Mqhayi and Thomas Mofolo begin portraying Africans as complex and human characters. Achebe was highly influenced by these writers in their human portrayal of both sides of colonization.

Emerging from Paris in the 1920s and 1930s, the negritude movement established itself as one of the premiere literary movements of its time. It was a French-speaking African search for identity, which ofcourse took them back to their roots in Africa. Africa was made into a metaphorical antipode to Europe, a golden age utopia, and was often represented allegorically as a woman. In a 1967 interview, Cesaire explained: "We lived in an atmosphere of rejection, and we developed an inferiority complex." The desire to establish an identity begins with "a concrete consciousness of what we are...that we are black... and have a history... [that] there have been beautiful and important black civilizations...that its values were values that could still make an important contribution to the world." Léopold Sédar Senghor, one of the prime thinkers of this movement, eventually became president of the country of Senegal, creating a tradition of African writers becoming active political figures. Achebe was doubtless familiar with the negritude movement, although he preferred to less surrealistic and more realistic writing.

In 1948, African literature came to the forefront of the world stage with Alan Paton's publishing of *Cry the Beloved Country*. However, this book was a somewhat paternalistic and sentimental portrayal of Africa. Another African writer, Fraz Fanon, also a psychiatrist, becomes famous in 1967 through a powerful analysis of racism from the African viewpoint—*Black Skin, White Masks*. Camara Laye explored the deep psychological ramification of being

African in his masterpiece, *The Dark Child,* and African satire is popularized by Mongo Beti and Ferdinand Oyono. Respected African literary critic Kofi Awoonor systematically collects and translates into English much of African oral culture and art forms, preserving native African culture.

Chinua Achebe then presents this native African culture in his stunning work, *Things Fall Apart.* This is probably the most read work of African Literature ever written, and provides a level of deep cultural detail rarely found in European literature. Achebe's psychological insight combined with his stark realism make his novel a classic.

13

Ancient Arabic Literature

Arabic literature is the writing produced, both prose and poetry, by writers of the Arabic language. The Arabic word used for literature is *adab* which is derived from a word meaning "to invite someone for a meal," has the additional meaning of etiquette, and implies politeness, culture and enrichment.

Arabic literature emerged in the 6th century with only fragments of the written language appearing before then. It was the Qur'an in the 7th century which would have the greatest lasting effect on Arabic culture and its literature. Arabic literature flourished during the Islamic Golden Age and continues to the present day.

Pre-Islamic Poetry

The pre-Islamic poetry is commonly referred to in Arabic as Jahili poetry, literally "the poetry of the period of ignorance". The first major poet in the pre-Islamic era is Imru' al-Qais the last king of the kingdom of Kenda. Although most of the poetry of that era was not preserved, what remains is well regarded as the finest of Arabic poetry to date. In addition to the eloquence and artistic value, pre-

Islamic poetry constitutes as a major source for classical Arabic language both in grammar and vocabulary, and as a reliable historical record of the political and cultural life of the time.

Poetry held an important position in pre-Islamic society with the poet or *sha'ir* filling the role of historian, soothsayer and propagandist. Words in praise of the tribe (*qit'ah*) and lampoons denigrating other tribes (*hija'*) seem to have been some of the most popular forms of early poetry. The *sha'ir* represented an individual tribe's prestige and importance in the Arabian peninsula, and mock battles in poetry or *zajal* would stand in lieu of real wars. 'Ukaz, a market town not far from Mecca, would play host to a regular poetry festival where the craft of the *sha'irs* would be exhibited.

Alongside the *sha'ir*, and often as his poetic apprentice, was the *rawi* or reciter. The job of the rawi was to learn the poems by heart and to recite them with explanations and probably often with embellishments. This tradition allowed the transmission of these poetic works and the practice was later adopted by the *huffaz* for their memorisation of the Qur'an. At some periods there have been unbroken chains of illustrious poets, each one training a *rawi* as a bard to promote his verse, and then to take over from them and continue the poetic tradition. For example, Tufayl trained 'Awas ibn Hajar, 'Awas trained Zuhayr ibn Abî Sûlmâ, Zuhayr trained his son Ka'b bin Zuhayr, Ka'b trained al-Hutay'ah, al-Hutay'ah trained Jamil Buthaynah and Jamil trained Kuthayyir 'Azzah.

Among the most famous poets of the pre-Islamic era are Imru' al-Qais, al-Nabighah al-Dhubyani,

Tarafah ibn al 'Abd, and Zuhayr ibn Abî Sûlmâ. Other poets, such as Ta'abbata Sharran, al-Shanfara, 'Urwah ibn al-Ward, were known as *su'luk* or vagabond poets, much of whose works consisted of attacks on the rigidity of tribal life and praise of solitude. Some of these attacks on the values of the clan and of the tribe were meant to be ironic, teasing the listeners only in order finally to endorse all that the members of the audience held most dear about their communal values and way of life. While such poets were identified closely with their own tribes, others, such as al-A'sha, were known for their wanderings in search of work from whoever needed poetry.

The very best of these early poems were collected in the 8th century as the *Mu'allaqat* meaning "the hung poems" (because they were hung on or in the Kaaba) and the *Mufaddaliyat* meaning al-Mufaddal's examination or anthology. The Mu'allaqat also aimed to be the definitive source of the era's output with only a single example of the work of each of the so-called "seven renowned ones", although different versions differ in which "renowned ones" they chose. The *Mufaddaliyat* on the other hand contains rather a random collection.

There are several characteristics that distinguish pre-Islamic poetry from the poetry of later times. One of these characteristics is that in pre-Islamic poetry more attention was given to the eloquence and the wording of the verse than to the poem as whole. This resulted in poems characterized by strong vocabulary and short ideas but with loosely connected verses. A second characteristic is the romantic or nostalgic prelude with which pre-Islamic poems would often start. In these preludes, a thematic unit called *nasib*, the poet would remember his beloved and her deserted home and its ruins. This concept in Arabic poetry is referred to as "'DHBHA– 9DI– 'D#7D'D" ("standing at the ruins") because the poet would often starts his poem by saying that he stood at the ruins of his beloved, a kind of *ubi sunt*. This characteristic was later dropped from the Arabic poem and some Arab poets, such as Abu Nuwas, became a target of mockery of pre-Islamic poetry.

The Qur'an and Islam

The Qur'an had a significant influence on the Arab language. The language used in the Qur'an is called classical Arabic and while modern Arabic is very similar, the classical is still the style to be admired. Not only is the Qur'an the first work of any significant length written in the language it also has a far more complicated structure than the earlier literary works with its 114 suras (chapters) which contain 6,236 ayat (verses). It contains injunctions, narratives, homilies, parables, direct addresses from God, instructions and even comments on itself on how it will be received and understood. It is also, paradoxically, admired for its layers of metaphor as well as its clarity, a feature it mentions itself in sura 16:103.

Although it contains elements of both prose and poetry, and therefore is closest to *Saj* or rhymed prose, the Qur'an is regarded as entirely apart from these classifications. The text is believed to be divine revelation and is seen by some Muslims as being eternal or 'uncreated'. This leads to the doctrine of *i'jaz* or inimitability of the Qur'an which implies that nobody can copy the work's style and no one should try.

Aside from the Qur'an the *hadith* or tradition of what Muhammed is supposed to have said and done are important literature. The entire body of these acts and words are called *sunnah* or way and the ones regarded as *sahih* or genuine of them are collected into hadith. Some of the most significant collections of hadith include those by Muslim ibn al-Hajjaj and Muhammad ibn Isma'il al-Bukhari.

The other important genre of work in Qur'anic study is the *tafsir* or commentaries Arab writings relating to religion also includes many sermons and devotional pieces as well as the sayings of Ali which were collected in the 10th century as *Nahj al-Balaghah* or *The Peak of Eloquence.*

Islamic Scholarship

The research into the life and times of Muhammad, and determining the genuine parts of the sunnah, was an important early reason for scholarship in or about the Arabic language. It was also the reason for the collecting of pre-Islamic poetry; as some of these poets were close to the prophet—Labid actually meeting Muhammed and converting to Islam—and their writings illuminated the times when these event occurred. Muhammad also inspired the first Arabic biographies, known as *al-sirah al-nabawiyyah*; the earliest was by Wahb ibn Munabbih, but Muhammad ibn Ishaq wrote the best known. Whilst covering the life of the prophet they also told of the battles and events of early Islam and have numerous digressions on older biblical traditions.

Some of the earliest work studying the Arabic language was started in the name of Islam. Tradition has it that the caliph Ali, after reading a Qur'an with errors in it, asked Abu al-Aswad al-Du'ali to write a work codifying Arabic grammar. Khalil ibn Ahmad would later write *Kitab al-Ayn,* the first dictionary of Arabic, along with works on prosody and music, and his Persian pupil Sibawayh would produce the most respected work of Arabic grammar known simply as *al-Kitab* or *The Book.*

Other caliphs exerted their influence on Arabic with 'Abd al-Malik making it the official language for administration of the new empire, and al-Ma'mun setting up the *Bayt al-Hikma* or House of Wisdom in Baghdad for research and translations. Basrah and Kufah were two other important seats of learning in the early Arab world, between which there was a strong rivalry.

The institutions set up mainly to investigate more fully the Islamic religion were invaluable in studying many other subjects. Caliph Hisham ibn Abd al-Malik was instrumental in enriching the literature by instructing scholars to translate works into Arabic. The first was probably Aristotle's correspondence with Alexander the Great translated by Salm Abu al-'Ala'. From the east, and in a very different literary genre, the Persian scholar Abdullah Ibn al-Muqaffa translated the animal fables of the *Panchatantra.* These translations would keep alive scholarship and learning, particularly that of ancient Greece, during the dark ages in Europe and the works would often be first re-introduced to Europe from the Arabic versions. Quran was revealed to Hazrat Muhammad through the angel Gabriel.

Poetry Under Islam

These early poems were to some extent considered a

threat to the newly emerging faith of Islam and if not actually suppressed, fell into disuse for some years. The *sha'ir* and their pronouncements were too closely associated with the religion practiced before Islam, and the role of the poet was singled out for criticism in the Qur'an. They also praised subjects of dubious merit such as wine, women and gambling, which clashed with the new ideology. Satirical poems attacking an idea or leader were less censured. While some poets were early converts, poetry about or in praise of Islam took some time to develop.

It was the early poems' importance to Islamic scholarship, though, which would lead to their preservation. Not only did the poems illuminate life in the early years of Islam and its antecedents but they would also prove the basis for the study of linguistics of which the Qur'an was regarded as the pinnacle.

Many of the pre-Islamic forms of verse were retained and improved upon. *Naqa'id* or flytings, where two poets exchange creative insults, were popular with al-Farazdaq and Jarir swapping a great deal of invective. The tradition continued in a slightly modified form as *zajal,* in which two groups 'joust' in verse, and remains a common style in Lebanon.

Court Poets

Ghaylan ibn 'Uqbah, nicknamed Dhu al-Rummah, is usually regarded as the last of the Bedouin poets. His works had continued the themes and style of the pre-Islamic poets particularly eulogising the harsh but simple desert life, traditionally recited round a campfire. Although such themes continued and were returned to by many modern, urban poets, this poetic life was giving way to court poets. The more settled, comfortable and luxurious life in Ummayyad courts led to a greater emphasis on the *ghazal* or love poem. Chief amongst this new breed of poet was Abu Nuwas. Not only did Abu Nuwas spoof the traditional poetic form of the qasida and write many poems in praise of wine, his main occupation was the writing of ever more ribald *ghazal* many of them openly homosexual.

While Nuwas produced risqué but beautiful poems, many of which pushed to the limit what was acceptable under Islam, others produced more religiously themed poetry. It is said that Nuwas struck a bargain with his contemporary Abu al-Alahijah: Abu Nuwas would concentrate on wine and love poems whilst al-Alahijah would write homilies. These homilies expressed views on religion, sin and the afterlife, but occasionally strayed into unorthodox territory. While the work of al-Alahijah was acceptable, others such as the poet Salih ibn 'Abd al-Quddus were executed for heresy. Waddah al-Yaman, now the national poet of Yemen, was also executed for his verse, but this was probably due to his over-familiarity with the wife of the caliph Al-Walid I.

Court poets were joined with court singers who simply performed works included Ibrahim al-Mawsili, his son Ishaq al-Mawsili and Ibrahim ibn al-Mahdi son of caliph al-Mahdi. Many stories about these early singers were retold in the *Kitab al-Aghani* or *Book of Songs* by Abu al-Faraj al-Isfahani.

The Sufi tradition also produced poetry closely linked to religion. Sufism is a mystical interpretation of Islam and it emphasised the allegorical nature of language and writing. Many of the works of Sufi poets appear to be simple *ghazal* or *khamriyyah*. Under the guise of the love or wine poem they would contemplate the mortal flesh and attempt to achieve transcendence. Rabia al-Adawiyya, Abd Yazid al-Bistami and Mansur al-Hallaj are some of the most significant Sufi poets, but their poetry and doctrine were considered dangerous, and al-Hallaj was eventually crucified for heresy.

The caliph himself could take on the role of court poet with Al-Walid II a notable example, but he was widely disliked for his immorality and was deposed after only a year.

An important doctrine of Arabic poetry from the start was its complexity, but during the period of court poetry this became an art form in itself known as *badi'* (Arabic (/J9—). There were features such as metaphor, pun, juxtaposing opposites and tricky theological allusions. Bashar ibn Burd was instrumental in developing these complexities which later poets felt they had to surpass. Although not all writers enjoyed the baroque style, with argumentative letters on the matter being sent by Ibn Burd and Ibn Miskawayh, the poetic brinkmanship of *badi* led to a certain formality in poetic art, with only the greatest poets' words shining through the complex structures and wordplay. This can make Arabic poetry even more difficult to translate than poetry from other languages, with much of a poet's skill often lost in translation.

Arabic poetry declined after the 13th century along with much of the literature due to the rise of Persian and Turkish literature. It flowered for a little longer in Al-Andalus (Islamic Spain) but ended with the expulsion of the Arabs in 1492. The corpus suffered large-scale destruction by fire in 1499 when Cardinal Jimenez de Cisneros made a public *auto de fé* in Granada, burning 1,025,000 Arabic volumes.

Romantic Poetry

A famous example of Arabic poetry on romance is *Layla and Majnun*, dating back to the Umayyad era in the 7th century. It is a tragic story of undying love much like the later *Romeo and Juliet*, which was itself said to have been inspired by a Latin version of *Layla and Majnun* to an extent.

Another medieval Arabic love story was *Hadith Bayad wa Riyad* (*The Story of Bayad and Riyad*), a 13th-century Arabic love story written in Al-Andalus. The main characters of the tale are Bayad, a merchant's son and a foreigner from Damascus, and Riyad, a well educated girl in the court of an unnamed Hajib of Al-Andalus (vizier or minister) which is referred to as the lady. The *Hadith Bayad wa Riyad* manuscript is believed to be the only illustrated manuscript known to have survived from more than eight centuries of Muslim and Arab presence in Spain.

There were several elements of courtly love which were developed in Arabic poetry, namely the notions of "love for love's sake" and "exaltation of the beloved lady" which have been traced back to Arabic literature of the 9th and 10th centuries. The notion of the "ennobling power" of love was developed in the early 11th century by the Persian psychologist and philosopher, Ibn Sina (known as "Avicenna" in English), in his Arabic treatise *Risala fi'l-Ishq* (*Treatise on Love*). The final element of courtly love, the concept of "love as desire never to be fulfilled", was also at times implicit in Arabic poetry.

The 10th century *Encyclopedia of the Brethren of Purity* features a fictional anecdote of a "prince who strays from his palace during his wedding feast and, drunk, spends the night in a cemetery, confusing a corpse with his bride. The story is used as a gnostic parable of the soul's pre-existence and return from its terrestrial sojourn".

Many of the tales in the *One Thousand and One Nights* are also love stories or involve romantic love as a central theme, including the frame story of Scheherazade, and many of the stories she narrates, such as "Aladdin", "Ali Baba", "The Ebony Horse" and "The Three Apples".

Satirical Poetry

The genre of Arabic satirical poetry was known as *hija*. Satire was introduced into Arabic prose literature by the Afro-Arab author Al-Jahiz in the 9th century. While dealing with serious topics in what are now known as anthropology, sociology and psychology, he introduced a satirical approach, "based on the premise that, however serious the subject under review, it could be made more interesting and thus achieve greater effect, if only one leavened the lump of solemnity by the insertion of a few amusing anecdotes or by the throwing out of some witty or paradoxical observations. He was well aware that, in treating of new themes in his prose works, he would have to employ a vocabulary of a nature more familiar in *hija*, satirical poetry."

For example, in one of his zoological works, he satirized the preference for longer human penis size, writing: "If the length of the penis were a sign of honor, then the mule would belong to the (honorable tribe of) Quraysh". Another satirical story based on this preference was an *Arabian Nights* tale called "Ali with the Large Member".

In the 10th century, the writer Tha'alibi recorded satirical poetry written by the poets As-Salami and Abu Dulaf, with As-Salami praising Abu Dulaf's wide breadth of knowledge and then mocking his ability in all these subjects, and with Abu Dulaf responding back and satirizing As-Salami in return.

An example of Arabic political satire included another 10th century poet Jarir satirizing Farazdaq as "a transgressor of the Sharia" and later Arabic poets in turn using the term "Farazdaq-like" as a form of political satire.

Non-fiction Literature

Compilations and Manuals

In the late 9th century Ibn al-Nadim, a Baghdadi bookseller, compiled a crucial work in the study of Arabic literature. *Kitab al-Fihrist* is a catalogue of all books available for sale in Baghdad and it gives a fascinating overview of the state of the literature at that time.

One of the most common forms of literature during the Abbasid period was the compilation. These were collections of facts, ideas, instructive stories and poems on a single topic and covers subjects as diverse as house and garden, women, gate-crashers, blind people, envy, animals and misers. These last three compilations were written by al-Jahiz the acknowledged master of the form. These collections were important for any *nadim,* a companion to a ruler or noble whose role was often involved regaling the ruler with stories and information to entertain or advise.

A type of work closely allied to the collection was the manual in which writers like ibn Qutaybah offered instruction in subjects like etiquette, how to rule, how to be a bureaucrat and even how to write. Ibn Qutaybah also wrote one of the earliest histories of the Arabs, drawing together biblical stories, Arabic folk tales and more historical events.

The subject of sex was frequently investigated in Arabic literature. The *ghazal* or love poem had a long history being at times tender and chaste and at other times rather explicit. In the Sufi tradition the love poem would take on a wider, mystical and religious importance. Sex manuals were also written such as *The Perfumed Garden, lawq al-$ammah* or *The Dove's Neckring* by ibn Hazm and *Nuzhat al-albab fi-ma la yujad fi kitab* or *Delight of Hearts Concerning What will Never Be Found in a Book* by Ahmad al-Tifashi. Countering such works are one like *Rawdat al-muhibbin wa-nuzhat al-mushtaqin* or *Meadow of Lovers and Diversion of the Infatuated* by ibn Qayyim al-Jawziyyah who advises on how to separate love and lust and avoid sin.

Biography, History, and Geography

Aside from the early biographies of Muhammad, the first major biographer to weigh character rather than just producing a hymn of praise was the Persian scholar al-Baladhuri with his *Kitab ansab al-ashraf* or *Book of the Genealogies of the Noble,* a collection of biographies. Another important biographical dictionary was begun by ibn Khallikan and expanded by al-Safadi and one of the first significant autobiographies was *Kitab al-I'tibar* which told of Usamah ibn Munqidh and his experiences in fighting in the Crusades. This time period saw the emergence of the genre of *tabaqat.*

Ibn Khurdadhbih, apparently an official in the postal service wrote one of the first travel books and the form remained a popular one in Arabic literature with books by ibn Hawqal, ibn Fadlan, al-Istakhri, al-Muqaddasi, al-Idrisi and most famously the travels of ibn Battutah. These give a fascinating view of the many cultures of the wider Islamic world and also offer Muslim perspectives on the non-Muslim peoples on the edges of the empire. They also indicated just how great a trading power the Muslim peoples had become. These were often sprawling accounts that included details of both geography and history.

Some writers concentrated solely on history like al-Ya'qubi and al-Tabari, whilst others focused on a small portion of history such as ibn al-Azraq, with a history of Mecca, and ibn Abi Tahir Tayfur, writing a history of Baghdad. The historian regarded as the greatest of all Arabic historians though is ibn Khaldun whose history *Muqaddimah* focuses on society and is a founding text in sociology and economics.

Diaries

In the medieval Near East, Arabic diaries were first being written from before the 10th century, though the medieval diary which most resembles the modern diary was that of Ibn Banna in the 11th century. His diary was the earliest to be arranged in order of date (*ta'rikh* in Arabic), very much like modern diaries.

Fiction Literature

In the Arab world, there was a great distinction between *al-fusha* (quality language) and *al-ammiyyah* (language of the common people). Not many writers would write works in this *al-ammiyyah* or common language and it was felt that literature had to be improving, educational and with purpose rather than just entertainment. This did not stop the common role of the *hakawati* or story-teller who would retell the entertaining parts of more educational works or one of the many Arabic fables or folk-tales, which were often not written down in many cases. Nevertheless, some of the earliest novels, including the first philosophical novels, were written by Arabic authors.

Epic Literature

The most famous example of Arabic fiction is the *One Thousand and One Nights* (*Arabian Nights*), easily the best known of all Arabic literature and which still affects many of the ideas non-Arabs have about Arabic culture. Although regarded as primarily Arabic it was in fact developed from a Persian work and the stories in turn may have their roots in India. A good example of the lack of popular Arabic prose fiction is that the stories of Aladdin and Ali Baba, usually regarded as part of the *Tales from One Thousand and One Nights,* were not actually part of the *Tales.* They were first included in French translation of the *Tales* by Antoine Galland who heard them being told by a traditional storyteller and only existed in incomplete Arabic manuscripts before that. The other great character from Arabic literature Sinbad is from the *Tales.*

The *One Thousand and One Nights* is usually placed in the genre of Arabic epic literature along with several other works. They are usually, like the *Tales,* collections of short stories or episodes strung together into a long tale. The extant versions were mostly written down relatively late on, after the 14th century, although many were undoubtedly collected earlier and many of the original stories are probably pre-Islamic. Types of stories in these collections include animal fables, proverbs, stories of *jihad* or propagation of the faith, humorous tales, moral tales, tales about the wily con-man Ali Zaybaq and tales about the prankster Juha.

Dante Alighieri's *Divine Comedy,* considered the greatest epic of Italian literature, derived many features of and episodes about the hereafter directly or indirectly from Arabic works on Islamic eschatology: the *Hadith* and the *Kitab al-Miraj* concerning Muhammad's ascension to Heaven, and the spiritual writings of Ibn Arabi.

Maqama

Maqama not only straddles the divide between prose and poetry, being instead a form of rhymed prose, it is also part way between fiction and non-fiction. Over a series of short narratives, which are fictionalised versions of real life situations, different ideas are contemplated. A good example of this is a maqama on musk, which purports to compare the feature of different perfumes but is in fact a work of political satire comparing several competing rulers.

Maqama also makes use of the doctrine of *badi* or deliberately adding complexity to display the writer's dexterity with language. Al-Hamadhani is regarded as the originator of the maqama and his work was taken up by Abu Muhammad al-Qasim al-Hariri with one of al-Hariri's maqama a study of al-Hamadhani own work. Maqama was an incredibly popular form of Arabic literature, being one of the few forms which continued to be written during the decline of Arabic in the 17th and 18th century.

Romantic Literature

A famous example of romantic Arabic poetry is *Layla and Majnun,* dating back to the Umayyad era in the 7th century. It is a tragic story of undying love much like the later *Romeo and Juliet,* which was itself said to have been inspired by a Latin version of *Layla and Majnun* to an extent.

Layla and Majnun is considered part of the Virgin Love genre, so-called because the couple never marry or consummate their relationship, that is prominent in Arabic literature, though the literary motif is found throughout the world. Other famous Virgin Love stories include "Qays and Lubna", "Kuthair and Azza", "Marwa and Al Majnoun Al Faransi" and "Antara and Abla".

The 10th century *Encyclopedia of the Brethren of Purity* features a fictional anecdote of a "prince who strays from his palace during his wedding feast and, drunk, spends the night in a cemetery, confusing a corpse with his bride. The story is used as a gnostic parable of the soul's pre-existence and return from its terrestrial sojourn".

Another medieval Arabic love story was *Hadith Bayad wa Riyad* (*The Story of Bayad and Riyad*), a 13th-century Arabic love story written in Al-Andalus. The main characters of the tale are Bayad, a merchant's son and a foreigner from Damascus, and Riyad, a well educated girl in the court of an unnamed Hajib (vizier or minister) of Al-Andalus which is referred to as the lady. The *Hadith Bayad wa Riyad* manuscript is believed to be the only illustrated manuscript known to have survived from more than eight centuries of Muslim and Arab presence in Spain.

Many of the tales in the *One Thousand and One Nights* are also love stories or involve romantic love as a central theme. This includes the frame story of Scheherazade herself, and many of the stories she narrates, including "Aladdin", "The Ebony Horse", "The Three Apples", "Tale of Tàj al-Mulúk and the Princess Dunyà: The Lover and the Loved", "Adi bin Zayd and the Princess Hind", "Di'ibil al-Khuza'i With the Lady and Muslim bin al-Walid", "The Three Unfortunate Lovers", and others.

There were several elements of courtly love which were developed in Arabic literature, namely the notions of "love for love's sake" and "exaltation of the beloved lady" which have been traced back to Arabic literature of the 9th and 10th centuries. The notion of the "ennobling power" of love was developed in the early 11th century by the Persian psychologist and philosopher, Ibn Sina (known as "Avicenna" in Europe), in his Arabic treatise *Risala fi'l-Ishq* (*Treatise on Love*). The final element of courtly love, the concept of "love as desire never to be fulfilled", was also at times implicit in Arabic poetry.

Murder Mystery

The earliest known example of a whodunit murder mystery was "The Three Apples", one of the tales narrated by Scheherazade in the *One Thousand and One Nights* (*Arabian Nights*). In this tale, a fisherman discovers a heavy locked chest along the Tigris river and he sells it to the Abbasid Caliph, Harun al-Rashid, who then has the chest broken open only to find inside it the dead body of a young woman who was cut into pieces. Harun orders his vizier, Ja'far ibn Yahya, to solve the crime and find the murdererer within three days, or be executed if he fails his assignment.

Satire and Comedy

In Arabic poetry, the genre of satirical poetry was known as *hija*. Satire was introduced into prose literature by the Afro-Arab author Al-Jahiz in the 9th century. While dealing with serious topics in what are now known as anthropology, sociology and psychology, he introduced a satirical approach, "based on the premise that, however serious the subject under review, it could be made more interesting and thus achieve greater effect, if only one leavened the lump of solemnity by the insertion of a few amusing anecdotes or by the throwing out of some witty or paradoxical observations. He was well aware that, in treating of new themes in his prose works, he would have to employ a vocabulary of a nature more familiar in *hija*, satirical poetry."

For example, in one of his zoological works, he satirized the preference for longer human penis size, writing: "If the length of the penis were a sign of honor, then the mule would belong to the (honorable tribe of) Quraysh". Another satirical story based on this preference was an *Arabian Nights* tale called "Ali with the Large Member".

In the 10th century, the writer Tha'alibi recorded satirical poetry written by the poets As-Salami and Abu Dulaf, with As-Salami praising Abu Dulaf's wide breadth of knowledge and then mocking his ability in all these subjects, and with Abu Dulaf responding back and satirizing As-Salami in return.

An example of Arabic political satire included another 10th century poet Jarir satirizing Farazdaq as "a transgressor of the Sharia" and later Arabic poets in turn using the term "Farazdaq-like" as a form of political satire.

The terms "comedy" and "satire" became synonymous after Aristotle's *Poetics* was translated into Arabic in the medieval Islamic world, where it was elaborated upon by Arabic writers and Islamic philosophers, such as Abu Bischr, his pupil Al-Farabi, Avicenna, and Averroes. Due to cultural differences, they disassociated comedy from Greek dramatic representation and instead identified it with Arabic poetic themes and forms, such as *hija* (satirical poetry). They viewed comedy as simply the "art of reprehension", and made no reference to light and cheerful events, or troublous beginnings and happy endings, associated with classical Greek comedy. After the Latin translations of the 12th century, the term "comedy" thus gained a new semantic meaning in Medieval literature.

Theatre

While puppet theatre and passion plays were popular in the medieval Islamic world, live theatre and drama has only been a visible part of Arabic literature in the modern era. There may have been a much longer theatrical tradition but it was probably not regarded as legitimate literature and mostly went unrecorded. There is an ancient tradition of public performance amongst Shi'i Muslims of a play depicting the life and death of al-Husayn at the battle of Karbala in 680 CE. There are also several plays composed by Shams al-din Muhammad ibn Daniyal in the 13th century when he mentions that older plays are getting stale and offers his new works as fresh material.

The most popular forms of theater in the medieval Islamic world were puppet theatre (which included hand puppets, shadow plays and marionette productions) and live passion plays known as *ta'ziya*, where actors re-enact episodes from Muslim history. In particular, Shia Islamic plays revolved around the *shaheed* (martyrdom) of Ali's sons Hasan ibn Ali and Husayn ibn Ali. Live secular plays were known as *akhraja*, recorded in medieval *adab* literature, though they were less common than puppetry and *ta'ziya* theater.

The Moors had a noticeable influence on the works of George Peele and William Shakespeare. Some of their works featured Moorish characters, such as Peele's *The Battle of Alcazar* and Shakespeare's *The Merchant of Venice, Titus Andronicus* and *Othello*, which featured a Moorish Othello as its title character. These works are said to have been inspired by several Moorish delegations from Morocco to Elizabethan England at the beginning of the 17th century.

Philosophical Novels

The Arab Islamic philosophers, Ibn Tufail (Abubacer) and Ibn al-Nafis, were pioneers of the philosophical novel as they wrote the earliest novels dealing with philosophical fiction. Ibn Tufail wrote the first Arabic novel *Philosophus Autodidactus* as a response to al-Ghazali's *The Incoherence of the Philosophers*. This was followed by Ibn al-Nafis who wrote a fictional narrative *Theologus Autodidactus* as a response to Ibn Tufail's *Philosophus Autodidactus*. Both of these narratives had protagonists (Hayy in *Philosophus Autodidactus* and Kamil in *Theologus Autodidactus*) who were autodidactic individuals spontaneously generated in a cave and living in seclusion on a desert island, both being the earliest examples of a desert island story. However, while Hayy lives alone on the desert island for most of the story in *Philosophus Autodidactus* (until he meets a castaway named Absal), the story of Kamil extends beyond the desert island setting in *Theologus Autodidactus* (when castaways take him back to civilization with them), developing into the earliest known coming of age plot and eventually becoming the first example of a science fiction novel.

Ibn al-Nafis described his book *Theologus Autodidactus* as a defense of "the system of Islam and the Muslims' doctrines on the missions of Prophets, the religious laws, the resurrection of the body, and the transitoriness of the world." He presents rational arguments for bodily resurrection and the immortality of the human soul, using both demonstrative reasoning and material from the hadith corpus to prove his case. Later Islamic scholars viewed this work as a response to the metaphysical claim of Avicenna and Ibn Tufail that bodily resurrection cannot be proven through reason, a view that was earlier criticized by al-Ghazali.

Ibn al-Nafis' work was later translated into Latin and English as *Theologus Autodidactus* in the early 20th century. A Latin translation of Ibn Tufail's work, entitled *Philosophus Autodidactus,* first appeared in 1671, prepared by Edward Pococke the Younger. The first English translation by Simon Ockley was published in 1708, and German and Dutch translations were also published at the time. These translations later inspired Daniel Defoe to write *Robinson Crusoe,* which also featured a desert island narrative and was regarded as the first novel in English.

Philosophus Autodidactus also inspired Robert Boyle, an acquaintance of Pococke, to write his own philosophical novel set on an island, *The Aspiring Naturalist,* in the late 17th century.

The story also anticipated Rousseau's *Émile* in some ways, and is also similar to the later story of Mowgli in Rudyard Kipling's *The Jungle Book* as well the character of Tarzan, in that a baby is abandoned in a deserted tropical island where he is taken care of and fed by a mother wolf. Other European writers influenced by *Philosophus Autodidactus* include John Locke, Gottfried Leibniz, Melchisédech Thévenot, John Wallis, Christiaan Huygens, George Keith, Robert Barclay, the Quakers, and Samuel Hartlib.

Science Fiction

Al-Risalah al-Kamiliyyah fil Siera al-Nabawiyyah (*The Treatise of Kamil on the Prophet's Biography*), known in English as *Theologus Autodidactus*, written by the Arabian polymath Ibn al-Nafis (1213–1288), is the earliest known science fiction novel. While also being an early desert island story and coming of age story, the novel deals with various science fiction elements such as spontaneous generation, futurology, apocalyptic themes, the end of the world and doomsday, resurrection and the afterlife.

Rather than giving supernatural or mythological explanations for these events, Ibn al-Nafis attempted to explain these plot elements using his own extensive scientific knowledge in anatomy, biology, physiology, astronomy, cosmology and geology. His main purpose behind this science fiction work was to explain Islamic religious teachings in terms of science and philosophy. For example, it was through this novel that Ibn al-Nafis introduces his scientific theory of metabolism, and he makes references to his own scientific discovery of the pulmonary circulation in order to explain bodily resurrection.

The novel was later translated into English as *Theologus Autodidactus* in the early 20th century. A number of stories within the *One Thousand and One Nights* (*Arabian Nights*) also feature science fiction elements. One example is "The Adventures of Bulukiya", where the protagonist Bulukiya's quest for the herb of immortality leads him to explore the seas, journey to the Garden of Eden and to Jahannam, and travel across the cosmos to different worlds much larger than his own world, anticipating elements of galactic science fiction; along the way, he encounters societies of jinns, mermaids, talking serpents, talking trees, and other forms of life.

In another *Arabian Nights* tale, the protagonist Abdullah the Fisherman gains the ability to breathe underwater and discovers an underwater submarine society that is portrayed as an inverted reflection of society on land, in that the underwater society follows a form of primitive communism where concepts like money and clothing do not exist. Other *Arabian Nights* tales deal with lost ancient technologies, advanced ancient civilizations that went astray, and catastrophes which overwhelmed them.

"The City of Brass" features a group of travellers on an archaeological expedition across the Sahara to find an ancient lost city and attempt to recover a brass vessel that Solomon once used to trap a jinn, and, along the way, encounter a mummified queen, petrified inhabitants, life-like humanoid robots and automata, seductive marionettes dancing without strings, and a brass horseman robot who directs the party towards the ancient city. "The Ebony Horse" features a robot in the form of a flying mechanical horse controlled using keys that could fly into outer space and towards the Sun, while the "Third Qalandar's Tale" also features a robot in the form of an uncanny boatman.

"The City of Brass" and "The Ebony Horse" can be considered early examples of proto-science fiction. Other examples of early Arabic proto-science fiction include Al-Farabi's *Opinions of the residents of a splendid city* about a utopian society, Al-Qazwini's futuristic tale of *Awaj bin Anfaq* about a man who travelled to Earth from a distant planet, and elements such as the flying carpet.

Bibliography

Amber Haque (2004), "Psychology from Islamic Perspective: Contributions of Early Muslim Scholars and Challenges to Contemporary Muslim Psychologists", *Journal of Religion and Health* 43 (4): 357-377.

Clay, Albert T. (2003). *Atrahasis: An Ancient Hebrew Deluge Story*. Book Tree. p. 34.

Eccles, Sir John Carew (1989). *Evolution of the Brain: Creation of the Self*. Routledge. p. 118.

Geraldine McCaughrean, Rosamund Fowler (1999), *One Thousand and One Arabian Nights*, Oxford University Press, pp. 247–51.

Grimbly, Shona (2000). *Encyclopedia of the Ancient World*. Taylor & Francis. p. 216.

Hamori, Andras (1971), "An Allegory from the Arabian Nights: The City of Brass", *Bulletin of the School of Oriental and African Studies*. Cambridge University Press. 34 (1): 9–19.

Hamori, Andras (1971), "An Allegory from the Arabian Nights: The City of Brass", *Bulletin of the School of Oriental and African Studies* (Cambridge University Press) 34 (1): 9–19.

Irwin, Robert (2003), *The Arabian Nights: A Companion*, Tauris Parke Paperbacks, p. 209.

Irwin, Robert (2003), *The Arabian Nights: A Companion*, Tauris Parke Paperbacks, p. 213.

James Thurber, "The Wizard of Chitenango", p 64 *Fantasists on Fantasy* edited by Robert H. Boyer and Kenneth J. Zahorski.

Jones, Mark (2006). *Criminals of the Bible: Twenty-Five Case Studies of Biblical Crimes and Outlaws.* FaithWalk Publishing. p. 6.

Nahyan A. G. Fancy (2006), "Pulmonary Transit and Bodily Resurrection: The Interaction of Medicine, Philosophy and Religion in the Works of Ibn al-Naf+s (d. 1288)", p. 95-101, *Electronic Theses and Dissertations*, University of Notre Dame.

Pinault, David (1992), *Story-Telling Techniques in the Arabian Nights*, Brill Publishers, pp. 148–9 & 217-9.

Pinault, David (1992), *Story-Telling Techniques in the Arabian Nights*, Brill Publishers.

Richardson, Matthew (2001), *The Halstead Treasury of Ancient Science Fiction*, Rushcutters Bay, New South Wales: Halstead Press, September 2002,

Toomer G. J. (1996), *Eastern Wisedome and Learning: The Study of Arabic in Seventeenth-Century England*, p. 222, Oxford University Press.

Index